As a son of a mufti in Mecca, Saudi Arabia, I have to say that there is no other western book that looks into fundamentals of Islam with complete precision and understanding better than *In the Shadow of the Qur'an*. Dr. Ed Hoskins has the mind of Christ and is aided by the love of the Holy Spirit in dissecting essential aspects of fundamental Islam that can be seen throughout the book. This is also evident, as Dr. Ed explains throughout the book, through the twelve main distinct persons (from Adam to Jesus) and periods (in Islam). This book will help you not only to understand Islam and its movements, but to act on 1 Corinthians 13:5 toward neighboring Muslims to be true ambassadors of Christ and His kingdom.

I highly recommend this book to be a cornerstone in the study of the fundamentals of Islam and related Islamic movements. If you are wondering about the past, current, future political and religious changes in the Middle East, this book will enlighten your path to comprehend such historical changes. When I first met Dr. Ed, I was astonished by the love he has for Muslims and the in-depth knowledge and understanding of Islam—as if Dr. Ed himself grew up in Mecca. If you are a Christian in the West, I hope the experience of rejection Sayyid Qutb found when he lived among Christians would move your heart. I, too, have experienced similar rejections. Sayyid Qutb could've followed Jesus with Christians being hospitable and welcoming toward those who seek the everlasting kingdom.

—Dr. Ahmed Joktan, MD, MBA
author, *From Mecca to Christ*

This is a must-read book for those who want to gain a better understanding of Islam and how to communicate the gospel of our Lord Jesus Christ to them. As a former Muslim who came to faith through the ministry of Dr. Hoskins, a professor of cross-cultural studies, and a pastor who has been ministering among Muslims for thirty years, I highly recommend *In the Shadow of the Qur'an* to those who have the love of Christ for Muslims. It is clear, culturally sensitive, and true to the Bible. It is essential to comprehend the influence of Sayyid Qutb's teaching on Muslims' minds to grasp what is happening in the Middle East. His teachings have had a vast and deep influence from Shiite to Sunni spectrum of Islamic movements in the twentieth and twenty-first centuries. Dr. Hoskins helps the reader to gain such understanding. I am going to make this book required reading for my students.

—Dr. Sohrab Ramtin
pastor, Iranian Christian Church of San Diego
Professor of Cross-Cultural Studies, Southern California Seminary

I first met Dr. Ed Hoskins in the mountains of Lebanon forty years ago in the middle of the Lebanese Civil War. At that time, I witnessed his desire for Muslims to know Christ personally through building bridges of Biblical truth. Dr. Ed's current book, *In the Shadow of the Qur'an*, accurately reflects that desire and is unique and fascinating in its approach. The many stories, questions, and individual examples make it winsome and readable.

I believe this valuable book will be a worthwhile and stimulating read for Muslims as well as for Christians. I encourage my own friends, colleagues, and neighbors, to get it and savor it!

—Jean (John) G. Bouchebel, LHD
founder and president, Witness as Ministry, Inc.

IN THE SHADOW OF THE

QUR'AN

PROPHETS, MESSENGERS, TRUTH & LIES

Edward J Hoskins, MD, PhD

Deep River BOOKS

Cover design by Joe Bailen, Contajus Designs

ISBN—13: 9781632695741
Library of Congress Control Number: 2022905558

Printed in the USA
2022—First Edition

30 29 28 27 26 25 24 23 22   10 9 8 7 6 5 4 3 2 1

TABLE OF CONTENTS

ACKNOWLEDGMENTS

I want to start by thanking a friend and teacher, Dr. Nabeel Jabbour, who first introduced me to Sayyid Qutb more than twenty-five years ago through his studies on Islamic fundamentalism.[1] I am also grateful to Drs. Dudley Woodberry and Don McCurry for their kind encouragement, guidance, comments, and questions at this project's conception as well as throughout the process. Also, a big thanks goes to Jim Petersen for providing the foreword to the book.

I am also grateful to Adel Salahi for his monumental work in 2011 of translating Sayyid Qutb's work *Fi Zilal al-Qur'an (In the Shade of the Qur'an)* into English.[2]

I am also indebted to the many Christian friends who gave their precious time to accompany me on each mosque visit. These folks included the entire pastoral staff at Covenant Evangelical Presbyterian Church in West Lafayette, Indiana: Pastors David Henderson, Rob Eyman, Tom Johnson, Brently Jordan, and Andrew Patton. They also included a young student, Andrew G., as well as other Covenant church members: David N., Harlan Day, Kevin Kaufman, John Heller, Mark Bell, and Mark Cumberworth. A longtime friend, Allen B., also helped in this capacity. Just knowing you were there as support to back me up and to pray gave me courage to continue.

Two other long-term friends arranged for me to stay at their homes and interview their own Muslim friends, Phil and Ruth Ann Saksa, and

Bud V—thanks for your kindness and hospitality. Two other friends at Covenant Church also had me interview their Muslim friends, Adedayo Adeyanju and Linda G.—thanks for caring!

I am grateful to the dear friends who agreed to read and endorse the final product—thanks to each of you. Another set of thanks go to the entire staff of Deep River Books for all their work—may God bless you for your faith.

None of this would have been possible if not for the many Muslim friends and acquaintances, both new and old, at each of the mosques I visited throughout Indiana, Illinois, and Michigan, as well as Muslim friends I have known for many years. Every mosque, with one exception, welcomed me and was happy to help with the project. Thanks to each of you from the bottom of my heart.

I am also thankful to my family who were always willing to read my writing efforts and give comments, as well as to put up with my "geekiness" and "grand obsession."

Most important, I am grateful to my Lord and Savior Jesus Christ, who gave his life on the cross for me—thank you, not just for the "facts" of what you did for me, but also for the beauty of the facts, the glory of the gospel, you who are the very image of God.

—Soli Deo Gloria
Dr. Ed Hoskins
West Lafayette, Indiana
February 2021

FOREWORD

by Jim Petersen

Once in a while you come across a book that you find priceless. That is because the author has done significant research on a subject that is of importance to you. This is that kind of book. I first met Dr. Ed Hoskins in the '80s in Beirut, Lebanon. He was involved in medicine but was also busy doing what this book is about—lovingly helping Muslims get to know Jesus Christ. But what I didn't realize about Ed at that time was that he is also a brilliant scholar with a seemingly infinite capacity for research and analysis.

Years passed and then one day he sent me a draft of a book he was writing titled *A Muslim's Mind*. It was about the Hadith, the book of Muslim traditions. When I saw the sources he used and the extent to which he had studied them, I was amazed. To this day I continue to use that book as a primary reference on Islam.

Now he has done it again, and much more. Actually, what you have in your hands is the result of a lifetime of learning—an account of years of experience and study. For most of Ed's life, he has focused on one question: What do we need to understand and know how to do in order to draw Muslims toward Jesus Christ?

To answer that question for himself, Ed learned Arabic, studied the Qur'an, the Hadith, and the writings of the primary religious leaders within Islam. He has also conversed with scores of Muslims about what they think and believe. He has synthesized all of this within the pages of this book.

One fourth of the population of the world is Muslim—1.8 billion people. God is at work among them today in ways we have never seen before in the history of Islam. There are many signs of that. Many Muslim communities that have been stable for centuries are currently being disrupted by politics and conflict. Many are dislocated or are refugees. This is a hard way to live, but it gives the people who live under such circumstances more space and freedom to ask questions and to think for themselves concerning their relationship with God. Many are turning to Christ—something that has not happened in the history of Islam until the last few decades.

God, in His love, is reaching out to Muslims today. It may be that He is putting it on your heart to participate with Him in this. If He is, you'll need to prepare. That is where this book comes in. Most everything you will need to know is in your hands right now. Ed puts the Bible alongside the Qur'an to show the similarities and differences in the two accounts. He calls the differences the *shadows*. He took that term from the writings of Sayyid Qutb, a prominent Muslim intellectual who wrote "In the Shade of the Qur'an." This part of the book will help you understand Muslim theology and equip you for discussion. Ed finishes the book with many practical suggestions on how to proceed friend-to-friend with the people you are involved with. One thing is clear, but not mentioned: he loves his Muslim friends and respects them.

—Jim Petersen
Author of *Church without Walls: Moving beyond Traditional Boundaries*
and *The Insider: Bringing the Kingdom of God into Your Everyday World*
(Living the Questions), (coauthored with Mike Shamy)

INTRODUCTION

Looking for inspirations of faith, the Qur'an takes the hand of each human soul and guides it throughout the universe. Together they watch light and darkness, along with the sun, moon, and stars. They also see growing vegetation, both cultivated and wild, with falling rain and flowing waters.—Sayyid Qutb[1]

He will be the sure foundation for your times, a rich store of salvation and wisdom and knowledge; the fear of the LORD is the key to this treasure. (Isa. 33:6)

During one visit I made to a mosque, a Pakistani physician showed great concern for my choice of research topic. "Why did you pick Sayyid Qutb - pronounced |SAY-yid KUU-tib|? Also, the reference that you made about his seminal work, *Fi Zilal al Qur'an* (In the Shade of the Quran), is an academic point to ponder, but our mosque, our congregation, and pretty much all the mosques or Muslim congregations at least here in Indiana do not derive guidance from his academic work to the best of my understanding."

He was jittery. However, he had no argument with any of the general information points about Islam from Sayyid Qutb. Even so, he felt, "If you interview Muslims and they agree with these major Qur'an points, then non-Muslims in the United States will assume that we Muslims agree with Sayyid Qutb's views, when we truly don't!" Why was he so nervous?

The Inner Tension Muslims Face Today

In their 2016 book, *The State of Social Progress of Islamic Societies,* Ahmed Renima, Habib Tillouine, and Richard J. Estes write, "Many scholars believe that, even today, Muslims are awaiting the rebirth of its Golden Age and, through it, the resurgence of Islam as one of the world's renewed cultural and religious influences."[2]

What was the Golden Age of Islam? Most scholars believe it was the flourishing of cultural, intellectual, scientific, economic, and architectural achievements by Muslims throughout the Middle East, African, and Asian world. It lasted for nearly five hundred years, from the eighth through thirteenth centuries, and ended with the Mongol invasion and fall of the Abbasid caliphate in Baghdad. The Golden Age of Islam largely coincided with the Western world's Dark Ages. The tension Muslims face today comes when they compare the past glories of the Golden Age of Islam with their ignominy in the twentieth and twenty-first centuries, largely dominated by non-Muslims through British, French, Dutch, Russian, and now American colonialism. This added fuel to the modern Islamic Awakening.

The Fulcrum Shaping the Entire Muslim World Today:

The Islamic Awakening

Over the last thousand years, periodic calls for a renewed commitment to the fundamental principles of Islam have risen and given birth to Islamic revivals. Six hundred years ago the Arab historian Ibn Khaldun speculated that the tension of Islamic revivals could be due to the austere life of desert living versus the easier life in towns.[3] Some of the most well-known ancient movements came out of the Berber Almoravid and Almohavid dynasties (eleventh and twelfth centuries), the Indian

Naqshbandi Ahmad Sirhindi (late sixteenth century), and the Indian Ahl-Hadith (nineteenth century). Also among these movements were those attributed to the preachers Ibn Taymiyyah (fourteenth century), Shah Wallullah and Muhammad Ibn al-Wahhab (both of the eighteenth century), and Jamal al-Din Afghani (nineteenth century).

What spawned the modern Islamic Awakening? During the middle half of the twentieth century this was actually stimulated by the nonreligious causes of Pan-Arab nationalism and socialism led by the Egyptian President Gamal Abdel Nasir. Its major contender was a religious arm which grew out of Hassan al-Banna's Muslim Brotherhood (*Ikhwan al-Muslimun*) which al-Banna founded in 1928.

John Esposito writes that the Arab-Israeli Six-Day War of 1967 was the turning point. The combined Arab forces of Pan-Arab nationalism (Egypt, Jordan, and Syria) suffered a disastrous defeat and the loss of Jerusalem, the third holiest city of Islam. That wasn't all they lost: the West Bank, the Golan Heights, Gaza, and the Sinai Peninsula were also surrendered. This event is still known in Arab literature as "the catastrophe." Thus, Pan-Arab nationalism and socialism proved to be a dismal failure. In contrast, six years later in 1973, a new Egyptian president, Anwar Sadat, led Egyptian armed forces under the banner of Islam. Even though the Arabs ultimately lost that war too, they did have a number of relative successes. This caused many Muslims to consider that war a moral victory.[4]

That same year (1973) also saw the advent of the Arab oil embargo, with the resultant quadrupling of the price of oil. Enter the petrodollar. This helped to finance the rising Islamic religious fervor of groups like the Muslim Brotherhood and the teachings of their martyred ideologue, Sayyid Qutb.

During this time period Saudi Arabia openly supported and promulgated Sayyid Qutb's writings. Then 1979 brought another watershed. In that year, four major events occurred to fuel a resurgence in Islam. First was the Iranian Revolution in February, with the advent of Ayatollah Khomeini and a resurgence of Shiite Islam. Second, only a month later, the Egyptian–Israeli peace treaty was signed by Egyptian president Anwar Sadat and Israeli prime minister Menachem Begin. That treaty horrified the rest of the Muslim world and practically assured Sadat's assassination two years later. Third, November of 1979 saw the two-week seizure of the Grand Mosque in Mecca with the proclamation of the new *Mahdi* (expected Muslim deliverer) Muhammad Abdullah al-Qahtani. His armed supporters called for the overthrow of the House of Saud, Saudi Arabia's controlling dynasty. The proclaimed *Mahdi* was killed during the fighting, and sixty-eight of the attacking survivors were beheaded. Fourth and finally, in December of that year the Soviet Union invaded Afghanistan; that incursion lasted ten years. All over the world, Muslim recruits volunteered for *jihad* to fight against Russia on the side of Afghanistan.

Enter Sayyid Qutb: A Key Idealogue and Stimulator of the Islamic Awakening

Each of these modern cases just cited were based on the teachings of Sayyid Qutb. In his epic work *Milestones*, Qutb wrote, "The foremost duty of Islam in this world is to depose *jahiliyyah* (any non-Islamic thinking) from the leadership of man, and to take the leadership into its own hands and enforce the particular way of life which is its permanent feature."[5] In their book *The Contemporary Islamic Revival: A Critical Survey and Bibliography,* Yvonne Haddad, Kathleen Moore, and David Sawan described Qutb's *Milestones* as "the Islamic revolutionary text of this century," as well as a justification for the execution of the author: Its ideas are radically dividing the world into Muslim and un-Islamic, with "the latter deserving obliteration."[6]

Even more radically, Qutb was possibly the first Muslim in modern times to suggest that another Muslim might not actually be a real Muslim if he exhibited *jahiliyyah* thinking and actions. In other words, any non-Islamic action was *jahiliyyah* and must be eradicated.[7] Both of these were applied to Sadat, and as a result the Muslim Brotherhood concluded that "Sadat must die." Dr. Frankenstein's monster was turning on its maker.

Saudi Arabia first felt the sting of Qutb's radical thinking with the seizure of the Grand Mosque in 1979. Then there was a petrochemical company bombing in 1988 in Jubail, Saudi Arabia and a car bombing in Riyadh in 1995. Next, in June of 1996, was the Al-Khobar Towers apartment complex bombing in northern Saudi Arabia. After the 1990s and the US Twin Towers attack on September 11, 2001, terrorist attacks against Saudi Arabia escalated (Muslims against Muslims, but following Qutb's teachings): two incidents in 2002, eleven incidents in 2003, and more than thirty incidents in 2004.

After that, Saudi Arabia tightened its ship. The current Crown Prince Muhammad bin Salman (known as MBS) has taken a much harder line on homegrown terrorists. Other freedoms have also been restricted, in addition to the murder of Saudi dissident and *Washington Post* columnist Jamal Ahmad Khashoggi in 2018. Incidentally, in 2015 Saudi Arabia banned Sayyid Qutb's writings. Egypt followed suit.

It is essential to remember that not all Muslims hold to Qutb's extremist views. Yusuf al-Qaradawi is a respected Egyptian Islamic theologian who currently lives in Qatar. He is ninety-three years old and regularly broadcasts on Al-Jazeera with an audience of 40 to 60 million people worldwide. In his book *Islamic Awakening*, he addresses the dangers of religious extremism:

> Islam recommends moderation and balance in everything. in belief, worship, conduct, and legislation. . . . Islamic texts call upon Muslims to exercise moderation and to reject and oppose all kinds of extremism.[8]

Who Was Sayyid Qutb?

Sayyid Qutb was the first of five children born into a family in Musha, Upper Egypt in 1906. Although the village was relatively poor, Qutb's father was one of the most well-to-do and saw that all five of his children were educated—including the daughters. His father was also religious and raised his children accordingly.[9]

By the time he was ten years old Qutb was a *hafiz*—that is, he had memorized the entire Qur'an. He turned this accomplishment to lucrative account, using the Qur'an and books of the Hadith to place spells and curses on others for a fee. When he was in his teens his father sent him to Cairo for higher education, choosing a modern school rather than the religious Al-Azhar University. There he fell in love with poetry and classical religious literature, and studied to be a teacher. At the age of twenty-seven he graduated with a certificate in Arabic language and literature. He became a published poet and novelist but remained a moderate Muslim. Throughout this time Egypt was going through the throes of British colonialism—and its accompanying tension between modernity, with the trappings of secular European culture, versus religious tradition. The Second World War took place and was followed by the rise of Arab nationalism.

Because of his writing and speaking abilities Qutb rose through the ranks of the Ministry of Education. He also became more involved in politics. In the late 1940s, the Ministry of Education wanted to expose him to the educational system of the United States. In 1948 they sent him to study at North Colorado Teachers College in Greeley (now the University of Northern Colorado).

An important note here is that the above Ministry of Education move was the official position. However, James Toth, in his work on the life of Sayyid Qutb, gives more details. Toth notes that by 1948 Sayyid Qutb had already angered the Egyptian government by his writings and a warrant for his arrest was issued. It took the intervention of a sympathetic Egyptian prime minister to arrange Qutb's travel to the United States to get him "out of harm's way."[10] Just before he sailed for America, Qutb gave his brother the completed text for one of his most famous books, *Social Justice in Islam*,[11] which was published in 1949 while he was abroad. The book was acclaimed as a major landmark by Islamic groups and intellectuals throughout the Arab world.[12]

He completed a master's degree in education at North Colorado Teachers College in 1952 and returned to Egypt. His ocean travel and time in the United States was a disappointing experience for him. He described it later as a time of moral and sexual temptation. This included a "half-naked British woman who tried to seduce him" while onboard ship coming to the United States. While in America he witnessed "brutal boxing matches and bad haircuts." At a church social in Greeley he describes "the seductive atmosphere of unmarried men and women dancing closely together." He later wrote about what he saw firsthand of the American culture as "shallow, materialistic, and shameful."[13]

Qutb had the opportunity to stay and work on a PhD but chose to return to Egypt because of his negative experience in the West. He had come to America in 1948 as a moderate Muslim; he had been a teacher, author, and poet, and later an editor. He returned to Egypt a committed radical Muslim and joined the Muslim Brotherhood in 1953.

Because of his eloquence and writing abilities he rapidly rose to the top leadership in the Muslim Brotherhood and became its recognized ideologue. His political writing increased. This was during the regime of Gamal Abdul Nasir. Qutb's views and writings angered President Nasir, who had him arrested. He spent most of the next ten years in prison and was hanged in 1966 because of his subversive writings. He was, and is today, known as a *shaheed* (Islamic martyr). While in prison, he wrote what he later considered his magnum opus, a complete commentary on the Qur'an, *In the Shade of the Qur'an*, the work he was most proud of. It is also the work of immediate interest to us.

Sayyid Qutb's Controversial Nature

Of Qutb's other published books, arguably the most famous and inflammatory was political—*Milestones* (also known as *Signposts along the Road*). This was also written while in prison and was published in

1964. *Milestones* is still used worldwide as part of the training manual for radical fundamentalist Islamic groups, including Al-Qaeda.

In my experience, most moderate Muslims want to publicly distance themselves from Sayyid Qutb. He is controversial to non-Muslims as well. John Calvert, in his excellent and well-researched biography of Sayyid Qutb, calls Qutb "one of the most significant figures of radical Islamism."[14] Calvert also noted, "Qutb, gripped by the design of the universe, was driven by the belief that he was defending God's absolute truth against the apparent barbarism of the modern world. . . . Scholars, journalists and other observers generally credit Sayyid Qutb with formulating the theoretical bases of Islamism in the post-colonial Sunni Muslim world." Calvert further adds that "one cannot deny Qutb's contribution to the contemporary tide of global *jihad*."[15]

Toth adds, even more plainly, that Qutb was "the architect of the mind-set that inspired the September 11, 2001 hijackers."[16] In a March 23, 2003 *New York Times Magazine* article, Paul Berman called Sayyid Qutb "the philosopher of Islamic terror."[16] Of interest is the portrait on the magazine's cover, showing Qutb wearing the toothbrush mustache of Adolph Hitler. In addition, there was the US governmental document *The 9-11 Commission Report,* which came out in 2003.[17] The manuscript devotes a full paragraph on page fifty-one to Sayyid Qutb's intellectual contribution to the attacks.

Following Qutb's death, his brother Muhammad Qutb, also a teacher, moved to Saudi Arabia—and two of his noted pupils were Osama bin Laden and Ayman al-Zawahiri. Both bin Laden and al-Zawahiri acknowledged that they were deeply influenced by the writings of Sayyid Qutb.

More than one Muslim in the United States has asked why I use Sayyid Qutb as a teacher for the Qur'an, including the Indiana imam's question highlighted at the beginning of the Introduction. But as a Christian scholar it was essential to examine the accuracy and relevance of what Sayyid Qutb taught about Islam. To do this, the author personally interviewed many respected and knowledgeable Muslims, mostly imams (mosque prayer leaders), using a list of nineteen major Qur'anic themes gleaned from Qutb's *tafsir,* his eighteen-volume monumental commentary on the Qur'an. To do this, more than 6,700 miles were driven to visit thirty-two mosques in Indiana, Michigan, and Illinois over a period of slightly more than a year.

At this point it is important to note that all of the Muslims interviewed (seventy to date) reside here in the United States, speak excellent English, and are well educated. The majority were either official imams or had led group Islamic prayers (90%) and were already familiar with Qutb (82%). One imam was trained at Al-Azhar University in Egypt and patterned his local US Islamic school after that training. Even though the overwhelming majority of those interviewed (99%) agreed with what Sayyid Qutb wrote about the basic tenets of Islam, fewer, in my opinion, would support his radical Islamic views, at least publicly.

Another Reason Sayyid Qutb Was Chosen for This Project

A book was kindly given me by an imam of a northern Indiana mosque. The book is titled *An Introduction to the Sciences of the Qur'aan,* by a respected Muslim scholar.[18] The imam affirmed this as the textbook they currently use in teaching their own students in the local Islamic school. On page 338 of chapter 15 of this book, "The Interpretation of the Qur'aan—*Tafsir,*" it says, "To claim that [Qutb's] *tafsir* (*In the Shade of the Qur'an*) is the most popular *tafsir* of modern times would not be an exaggeration. The *tafsir* is very simple to read." Other Muslims I have interviewed have said the same thing. A Libyan friend who teaches the Qur'an at his mosque told my son, when they discussed my project, that the choice to use Sayyid Qutb to understand what Muslims believe was a good one.

Toth's previously mentioned book further states:

> *In the Shade of the Qur'an* remains Qutb's magnum opus . . . his most impressive intellectual undertaking and one carried out

under the brutal conditions of the Liman Tura prison. It is what Olivier Carré called an 'icon-text,' which is to say it appears at the very top of the canon of commentaries and interpretations studied by faithful and learned Islamists from the Philippines to Morocco, from Africa to Europe, and on to the Muslim diaspora in both North and South America.[19]

Is Qutb's work *In the Shade of the Qur'an—Fi Zilal al-Qur'an* unique, or is it just one of many *tafsirs*? Dr. Badmas Lanre Yusuf, in his PhD work, had this to say, "As a *mufassir*, Sayyid Qutb adopted a novel approach which had never been followed by any *mufassir* before him."[20] Dr. Badmas went on to enumerate six principles Qutb followed: "high literary style" conveying "precise and accurate" Qur'an meanings; using "relevant material drawn from some books of *tafsir*;" avoiding any Jewish material which other *tafsirs* often made use of; keeping away from "doctrinal polemics" between various Islamic legal schools; giving "comprehensive commentary on every Qur'anic passage"; and finally, evidencing "good intention coupled with sincerity of faith and clear understanding of the Glorious Qur'an."[21] Waxing poetic, Dr. Yusuf describes Sayyid Qutb's *tafsir*: "*Fi Zilal* is like a sea with a lot of pearls in it."[22] He further notes the already accomplished widespread translation of this *tafsir* into other languages including French, Turkish, Urdu, Malay/Indonesian, and finally into English, covering most of the Muslim world.[23]

Is this approach—using Qutb's *In the Shade of the Qur'an*—risky? Absolutely! The very name Sayyid Qutb strikes fear in the hearts of most non-Muslims as well as many moderate Muslims. But this attitude does not apply to every Muslim. When I spoke with one Palestinian Muslim friend about this project he responded with pleasure, "If Sayyid Qutb wrote it, then I believe it!" He is not alone. The real issue then is to evaluate *In the Shade of the Qur'an* based on its own merits, accuracy, and fidelity, and not on the emotionalism surrounding the controversial person who produced it. For me, the bottom line has been that using *In the Shade of the Qur'an* has provided the work of a well-known, popular, and broadly respected Muslim scholar with which to better understand and appreciate the Qur'an. It also gave me a natural opportunity to get next to Muslims with the hope of Christ. Further, it assisted in clarifying the misconceptions and misunderstandings—and they are many—of both Christians and Muslims.

A Twenty-Four-Month Odyssey

Just over two years ago my goal was to read through the entire eighteen volumes of *In the Shade of the Qur'an*, completing every page and every word while making notes. In that experience, no evidence was found of Sayyid Qutb advocating political unrest or governmental overthrows. There were no examples of gratuitous violence. There was, however, ample evidence of a sincere man who wanted to truly understand and comprehensively relate the teachings of the Qur'an in a simple, modern, personal, entertaining, and well-written form. It was definitely not dry. Having previously studied Islam for the past forty years, including reading the Qur'an multiple times, I learned new things about Islam and the Qur'an. New stories were experienced in a refreshing way. Old topics were seen in new picture frames. I witnessed the beauty of what many of my dear Muslim friends experience.

A Brief Note on Sayyid Qutb Quotes

In order to avoid the confusing tangle of existing national and international copyright laws and their topics of "fair use" and "intellectual property" agreements, I chose not to quote Qutb directly. However, since the book focuses on Qutb, they were referenced and summarized extensively more than two hundred times. In each instance my goal was to meticulously maintain the content and meaning behind

Qutb's ideas and words. Any errors in transmission are mine, for which I take full responsibility.

Qutb's *Tafsir* Compared to Other Respected Qur'an Commentaries

For the sake of accuracy the author also read through, and made notes, of the entire Qur'an commentaries of *Ibn Kathir*[24] and the two *Jalalains* (*Jalal al-din al-Mahali* and *Jalal al-din al-Suyuti*),[25] two of the most respected *mufassirs* (interpreters of the Qur'an) in Sunni Islam. Gratefully, no contradictions were noted. The only difference evident was that Qutb's view of *jahiliyyah* (pre-Islamic) thinking was more rigid. In other words, Qutb believed *jahiliyyah* was not limited to a "time of ignorance" that came before Islam. Rather, it dealt with any non-Islamic thinking or action at any time in history, including the modern day. Other than that, they were the same.

Four Main Strands Found in Qutb's *Tafsir*

Throughout Qutb's entire work four interwoven rope strands were apparent. First, there were nineteen major Islamic themes—such as the "Oneness" of God (*Tawhid*), the Danger of Attributing Partners to God, and the Day of Judgment (plus sixteen others). This "List of Nineteen" is not exhaustive nor is it comprehensive—Islam is broader and more extensive than that. But those are the major nineteen points that stood out to me. Those are the nineteen I evaluated with Muslims when interviewing them. That list is included in its entirety in Appendix I of this book. These nineteen themes provide a good overview to non-Muslims of what Muslims believe informationally about their faith.

A second strand was the many stories unique only to the Qur'an. Each one highlights major beliefs and teachings within Islam. Half of these stories originated out of Meccan (early) *surahs* of the Qur'an before Muhammad and his followers left for Medina in the *hijra* (flight or pilgrimage in AD 622). The other half came from Medina (later) after the *hijra*. Many of these stories are included in each chapter that follows. Each of these stories give new insights and appreciation for the Islam of our Muslim friends and the Qur'an's time-associated events.

The third, and most significant strand, came from twelve stories common to both the Qur'an and the Bible. What became glaringly evident from these shared stories were the differences—the shadows that caused new ideas to become apparent. Yes, contrasting shadows can enhance truth, but they can also hide it! Everything learned here supported my own high view of God's Word, the Bible. These twelve stories, from Adam through Jesus, thematically determine the content of each chapter.

Finally, for the fourth rope strand, *In the Shade of the Qur'an* brings to light nine major objections Islam has to Christianity and Judaism. By and large, these are the same concerns Muslims have presented over the last decades and centuries. Whenever Qutb wrote about Islam, his thoughts were organized and well-researched. This same careful organization and documentation, however, was lacking in his references to Christianity and Judaism. Each of these provided opportunities for clarification and, if possible, setting the record straight. These include such comments as "Jesus didn't die on the cross"; "Jesus never said that he was God"; "Christians believe in three Gods"; and "The Bible is not a trustworthy document—it has been changed." These comments stimulated me to investigate the historical documents and facts of each case. In each chapter a brief overview of one of these topics is included as "A New Perspective on Christianity." A complete document on these nine sets of apologetic answers is available from the author upon request, at secondstar53@gmail.com.

The Interview Process

It was not enough to research and completely review Sayyid Qutb's *In the Shade of the Qur'an*. It was also essential to know if what I had learned accurately reflected Islam and the Qur'an. Thus I set out to interview a hundred Muslims regarding Qutb's "List of Nineteen Major Qur'anic Themes." Before publishing the book and out of respect for my Muslim friends, I wanted to make absolutely certain I was not misrepresenting Islam or the Qur'an in any way. It was also my desire that these interviews might provide natural opportunities to present Muslim friends and acquaintances with the hope of Christ. A copy of the one-page interview sheet is found in Appendix II; interview findings are presented in Appendix III.

Seventy of the projected hundred interviews and my thirty-second mosque visit were completed before the process terminated, in the wake of the worldwide coronavirus pandemic. Gratifyingly, there was nearly ninety-nine percent agreement with Qutb's "List of Nineteen Major Qur'anic Themes," and a verdict that *In the Shade of the Qur'an* accurately reflects Islam. I am confident that Qutb's work can assist others in better understanding Islam and their Muslim friends. It helped me; I believe it can help you too.

Recap: Where This Book Is Heading

With few exceptions, Muslims today live in tension between two extremes. On one hand, they live with the memory of a long-past glorious Golden Age of Islam. On the other hand, Muslims live in a modern world largely dominated by non-Muslims. They long to return to the glory days of Islam. This tension feeds into the modern Islamic Awakening. Possibly the most visible and popular writer and idealogue for Islam and the Islamic Awakening was the Egyptian Sayyid Qutb. His writings and pupils directly led to Islamic extremist groups such as Al-Qaeda, Taliban, ISIS, and modern terrorist attacks worldwide.

Qutb was also a modern interpreter of the Qur'an, and his Qur'an commentary is arguably the most popular one used by Muslims throughout the world today. Since the Qur'an is the key to understanding Islam and the geopolitics of today's world, it is essential for Christians and other non-Muslims to have more than a kindergarten understanding of the Qur'an. This book helps provide that understanding. It is the result of a complete review and evaluation of *In the Shade of the Qur'an*. Focusing on stories and their contexts, this book gives Christians and other non-Muslims new insights into the Qur'an, as well as practical ideas on how to relate to Muslims and share truth with them.

This introduction ends with a recent story from an Indiana mosque interview with a delightful imam, and shows how the process worked, as well as how the person of our Lord was represented.

A Scientist of the Mind and a Doctor of the Heart

I was raised among the Taliban fighters in Afghanistan as a child; all I knew was radical Islam. By the time I was ten I memorized the entire Qur'an and became a *hafiz*. At that time there were two possible schools for me to attend—the *madrasa*, the ultra-religious one which my family all preferred, and the *maktaba*, the nonreligious institution my teachers wanted me to attend. My teachers recommended this because of increased opportunities in careers such as medicine and engineering. My family said, "If he goes to the government *maktaba* he will become a *kafir* (unbeliever)." My teachers won and I attended the *maktaba*. There I saw and learned about a broader and more tolerant Islam. Later, when I returned home, my family said that instead of becoming a *kafir*, I was now a better Muslim than they were, and I had better character. I learned many languages such as Persian, Uzbek, Turkish, Arabic, and English. I am now finishing a PhD in anthropology in the United States.

When I met him at the mosque, this *hafiz* was the imam. He wore his *hajji* cap (he had completed the *Hajj*) and was delivering the *khutbah* (sermon at the Friday prayers). During his talk he stressed that a modern Muslim must become "a scientist of the mind and a doctor of the heart." After the *khutbah* we met in his office. He explained his background and views more completely. My accompanying Christian friend David was able to share how Jesus became personal to him. We left this dear man with my business card and an invitation to visit my home in West Lafayette.

As you progress through the book, be prepared to ask questions and think outside the box. It is my prayer that you will view the Qur'an and Islam, as well as the Bible and Christianity, through new picture frames. Hopefully, like me, it will make you more knowledgeable, full-bodied, and compassionate as you consider Islam, the Qur'an, and Muslims. As you close the book's cover for the last time, I hope you will agree that both the Qur'an and the Bible focus as much on story as they do on informational content.

CHAPTER 1

ADAM AND THE ORIGIN OF SIN

In Islam there is no "original sin" as described by Christians. No payment for sins is necessary except what every person pays because of their own sins.—Sayyid Qutb [1]

Therefore, just as sin entered the world through one man, and death through sin, and in this way death came to all men, because all sinned. (Rom. 5:12)

"Did You Do This?"

My wife listened to a Muslim friend venting about her three-year-old daughter. "I heard a crash in our living room and rushed in to find my daughter standing beside a shattered glass vase. I asked her, 'Did you do this?' My daughter shook her head in denial. I knew she had broken it. I never taught my daughter to lie! How could that have happened?" My wife wisely chose not to mention a topic they had recently discussed: original sin. Our Muslim friends don't share this Christian belief.

In Islam, every child is born morally neutral, a clean slate. As Christians, we see it differently. Christians believe that all children need to be taught to tell the truth. In contrast, children don't need to learn how to lie. It comes naturally.

As our quest begins, remember that each chapter is organized around a rope consisting of four interwoven strands discovered during my examination of Sayyid Qutb's *In the Shade of the Qur'an*. The first and most important one elucidates the lives of twelve characters shared by both the Qur'an and Bible, starting with Adam and ending with Jesus. In fact, these twelve stories are so important that they form the central unifying theme and title for each chapter. The second strand consists of nineteen major Islamic themes from the Qur'an (see Appendix I). This strand summarizes what Muslims believe about their religion. The third strand is formed from the many stories unique only to the Qur'an, which highlight and give context to the Qur'an. The fourth and final strand comes from nine statements made by Sayyid Qutb about Christianity and Judaism, which I believe to be less than accurate. Keep this four-stranded pattern in mind. It gives our rope strength and meaning. And now—start your engines!

Charlotte Brontë published her novel *Jane Eyre* in 1847. A century and a half later (1996), Franco Zeffirelli adapted it to the screen. In Zeffirelli's film, Jane instructs her pupil Adele in art: "Remember, the shadows are just as important as the light." That phrase haunts me every time I read of the prophets shared by both the Qur'an and Bible. Let's see why!

Twenty-eight prophets are mentioned by name in the Qur'an. Twenty-five of these are also common to the Bible. About a third of the twenty-five have only a passing reference in the Qur'an. The others have more detail: Adam, Cain and Abel, Noah, Abraham (with Lot, Ishmael, and Isaac), Joseph, Moses, Job, Jonah, David (and Solomon), Zechariah (and his son John the Baptist), Mary (the mother of Jesus), and finally Jesus the Messiah. We will cover each of these stories in the pages to come. Of those with more detail, how are they similar? How do they differ? Is there a pattern hidden in the shadows?

Our quest begins with the story of Adam and the origin of sin.

Adam: Setting the Stage

Adam, the first man, was created by God approximately four thousand years before the time of Christ. God placed him and his wife Eve (also created by God) in the garden of Eden. No one knows exactly where the garden of Eden is located today. Some scholars hypothesize it to be where the Tigris and Euphrates rivers empty into the waters of the Persian (Arab) Gulf in southern Mesopotamia (today's southern Iraq/ Armenia). Let's look at how these stories appear in both the Qur'an and Bible.

Adam in the Qur'an

In the Qur'an, the story of Adam appears primarily in two places: Surah 2 (al-Baqara—the Cow) and Surah 7 (al-Araf—the Heights).

Qur'an 2:30–39

[30]And when thy Lord said unto the angels: Lo! I am about to place a viceroy in the earth, they said: Wilt thou place therein one who will do harm therein and will shed blood, while we, we hymn Thy praise and sanctify Thee? He said: Surely I know that which ye know not. [31]And He taught Adam all the names, then showed them to the angels, saying: Inform Me of the names of these, if ye are truthful. (Surah 2.30–31)

In verses 32–33, the angels responded that they did not know the answer. God then told Adam to give the answer and he did. God replied that He knew the secrets of heaven and earth.

[34]And when We said unto the angels: Prostrate yourselves before Adam, they fell prostrate, all save Iblis (Satan). He demurred through pride, and so became a disbeliever. [35]And We said: O Adam! Dwell thou and thy wife in the Garden, and eat ye freely (of the fruits) thereof where ye will; but come not nigh this

tree lest ye become wrong-doers. ³⁶But Satan caused them to deflect therefrom and expelled them from the (happy) state in which they were; and We said: Fall down, one of you a foe unto the other! There shall be for you on earth a habitation and provision for a time. (Surah 2:34–36)

Then in verses 37–39 God encouraged Adam. After this He made Adam and Eve exit the garden. God then promised judgment on all those who reject God's signs.

Qur'an 7:11–25

In verses 11–15 of this surah God commanded the angels to bow down to Adam. Only Satan refused. God asked why he would not bow. Satan answered that he was better than Adam because he (Satan) was created out of fire while Adam was made from clay. God then expelled Satan from the garden.

¹⁶He said: Now, because Thou hast sent me astray, verily I shall lurk in ambush for them on Thy Right Path. ¹⁷Then I shall come upon them from before them and from behind them and from their right hands and from their left hands, and Thou wilt not find most of them beholden (unto Thee). (Surah 7:16–17)

In verses 18–21 God promised hell for all who followed Satan. God then told Adam and his wife to enjoy every blessing of the garden except "this tree" which would lead to their harm. Satan began whispering thoughts of their shame saying that God only wanted to prevent them from becoming like the angels and living forever.

Thus did he lead them on with guile. And when they tasted of the tree their shame was manifest to them and they began to hide (by heaping) on themselves some of the leaves of the

Garden. And their Lord called them, (saying): Did I not forbid
you from that tree and tell you: Lo! Satan is an open enemy to
you? (Surah 7:22)

In verses 23–25 Adam and Eve asked for God's mercy and
forgiveness. God still sent them out of the garden down to earth
where they would experience enmity, life, and death, and then be
taken away.

Adam in the Bible

Adam appears mainly in the first three chapters of the book of
Genesis. In the first chapter we see God creating mankind in His own
image, male and female. He then gave humans responsibility over all
living things on earth. God told them to "be fruitful and increase
in number; fill the earth" (Gen. 1:28). In chapter 2 we are provided
more details of their origin. God gave them the responsibility to
multiply and make the earth fruitful. God only forbid them to eat
from the Tree of the Knowledge of Good and Evil. Disobedience
would result in death. In chapter 3 is the advent of Satan in the form
of a serpent. The serpent tempted Eve to taste the forbidden fruit.
She did, then caused Adam to join in her disobedience. As a result,
God cast them out of the garden of Eden. In verses 14–15 we see the
first reference to God's plan of ultimate rescue from their sin as God
addresses the serpent:

> [14]So the Lord God said to the serpent, "Because you have done
> this, "Cursed are you above all livestock and all wild animals!
> You will crawl on your belly and you will eat dust all the
> days of your life, [15]and I will put enmity between you and the
> woman, and between your seed and her seed; he shall bruise
> you on the head, and you shall bruise him on the heel."

We also see the consequences of sin.

[22]"Then the LORD God said, "Behold, the man has become like one of Us, knowing good and evil; and now, he might stretch out his hand, and take also from the tree of life, and eat, and live forever"—[23]therefore the Lord God sent him out from the garden of Eden, to cultivate the ground from which he was taken. [24]So He drove the man out; and at the east of the garden of Eden He stationed the cherubim and the flaming sword which turned every direction to guard the way to the tree of life." (Gen. 3:22–24)

The Shadow When the Qur'an Is Compared to the Bible

So, what do the shadows reveal in the two accounts?

1. In the Qur'an, before creating mankind, God describes His plan to the angels. They question God about the wisdom of His doing this. God responds, "I know what ye know not." In the Bible there is no mention of God discussing His plan with the angels.

2. In the Qur'an there is no mention of man having been created in the image of God. This is central to the Bible's view of the high station of mankind, as well as to the seriousness of sin as well as their fall due to rebellion.

3. In the Qur'an God teaches Adam the names of all the creatures. In the Bible, Adam is the one who names all the creatures, not God. In the ancient world, giving and receiving names were acts of authority and submission. Adam naming the creatures illustrates the significance and worth of mankind. It highlights their unique place in creation as having been formed in the image of God.

4. In the Qur'an Adam's wife is left unnamed. In the Bible she is called "Eve" because "she is the mother of all the living." There

is no evidence in the Qur'an of Eve having been tempted first by Satan.

5. In the Qur'an God commands the angels to bow down to Adam. Satan refuses to bow down out of pride. There is no evidence in the Bible of this verbal exchange between God, the angels, and Satan. According to the Bible angels are to worship and obey God, not to argue with Him.

6. In the Qur'an, because of disobedience and pride, God casts Satan out of the garden. As a result, Satan promises perpetual enmity to Adam and all mankind.

7. In the Qur'an there is no specific name for the forbidden tree or its fruit, nor details about humanity's rebellion. In the Bible the tree is identified as the "Tree of the Knowledge of Good and Evil."

8. In the Qur'an, mankind's sin is only a "slip" that Satan foists on humans by deceit. This sin is easily rectified by repentance. Forgiveness is freely given by God simply by mankind's asking for it.

9. In the Qur'an there is no mention of the Bible's promise (Gen. 3:15) of a coming "seed" who would "crush Satan's head" but have his own "heel bruised by Satan."

10. There is also no cursing of the ground by God in the Qur'an as a consequence of people's sin.

Summarizing the differences of Adam's story, in the Bible there is no interchange of God with the angels where they question the wisdom of God's choice and creation of mankind. Of greater importance, in the Qur'an there is no evidence of people being created in the image of God, no naming of the animals by Adam, no temptation of Eve as a start to the fall of mankind, no promise of a "coming one" who would crush Satan's head and be bruised by Satan on his own heel, and no mention of humanity's rebellion/sin resulting in a curse on all creation. In short, in Islam there is no "original sin" and no promise of a savior who would come to rectify creation's curse.

For our second rope strand, let's examine two of the key Sayyid Qutb Nineteen Qur'anic themes that are relevant to the story of Adam.

Sayyid Qutb Themes

This first chapter highlighting the story of Adam relates most closely to two of our Qur'anic themes from Sayyid Qutb, numbers 3 and 8, dealing with the nature of mankind and humanity's ever-present battle with Satan.

3. Nature of Mankind (a unique creature created by God, placed in heaven to eat of its fruit—all except the forbidden tree—given a measure of choice by God, man is weak and has two main weaknesses—his love of survival and his desire to possess) and God's Covenant with Mankind (God allowed people to choose either to obey Him or lean toward Satan [also created by God] mankind's perpetual enemy—God did this to test mankind in their role to build human life on earth).

8. Ever-Present Battle between Satan and Believers, Faith, and Submission and the Danger of *Jahiliyyah* Thinking (anything that is not consistent with Islam)

Qutb notes that mankind started with Adam and Eve, the first human beings on earth. Satan started at the same time and God permitted him to tempt humans, and all their offspring, to stray from God. All humans are given a choice: they can choose to follow their agreement with God and follow Him, or they can choose to lean toward Satan and follow him.[2] Qutb continues that the gap between mankind and earth is great.

Even the basic atoms that make up earth and man are far separate. Man's feet may be placed on earth, but his heart and soul are able to fly to heaven.[3] Qutb also writes that by making this new call (Islam) to people, the oneness of God's divine faith becomes clear. God makes the same agreement with all His servants, which causes them to believe only in God, to obey His messengers, and make no difference between them.[4]

Associated Qur'an Story

The next strand in our rope comes from a Qur'an story illustrating the sin which all people since Adam have struggled with. This story emphasizes the sin of pride and that we would be wise to always take our values from God and not from people!

The Frowning—from Surah 80 (al-Abasa)

This surah was revealed early in Islam. It has forty-two verses and takes its name from an incident related in the first two verses:

> [1]He frowned and turned away [2]because the blind man came unto him. (Surah 80:1–2)

The prophet of Islam was busy with a few Qurayshi dignitaries explaining the message of Islam to them. Suddenly a poor blind man, Abdullah Ibn Um-Makhtum, interrupted him. The blind man repeatedly asked the prophet of Islam to teach him some verses from the Qur'an. Displeased, Muhammad frowned at the blind man and turned away. Later, the prophet of Islam received a rebuke from God that appeared in this surah in verses 8–11:

> [8]But as for him who cometh unto thee with earnest purpose [9]and hath fear, [10]from him thou art distracted. [11]Nay, but verily it is an admonishment,

Qutb notes that this is the only place in the Qur'an where Muhammad was addressed by *"Kal-la!"* (in verse 11 translated as "Nay!"). Qutb also notes that *Kal-la* is a term of reproof in addition to an order to stop. The principle involved here, he says, is that all mankind should take its standards and values from God and not from anything worldly.

Qutb further notes that after this incident, whenever Muhammad met Ibn Um-Makhtum he greeted him warmly, telling him that he was the man through "whom my Lord corrected me." Later Muhammad appointed this man to be deputy governor of Medina when he himself needed to be away.[5]

A New Perspective on Christianity: The Bible Has Been Changed

Our fourth and final strand for this chapter is the apologetic topic, dealing with the reliability of the Christian Bible. Qutb wrote that both Jews and Christians distorted their scriptures[6] and that the original version of the Scriptures no longer existed.[7] He also wrote that all copies of the Torah revealed by God to Moses were burned by the Babylonians when they enslaved the Jews and that the New Testament was not written down for more than a century after Christ lived.[8] A summary of Qutb's conclusion was that the Old and New Testaments are unreliable and cannot establish certainty on any matter,[9] and that the only reliable source left for us is the Qur'an.[10]

The following is a brief overview of the topic: Ancient documents, like the Bible, originated before the printing press. An *autograph*, the original piece of writing, from this time period was first written by hand in ink. The writing material was usually on papyrus (from split and pressed reeds) or parchment (stretched, scraped, and dried animal skin).

Fortunately, ancient historical documents can be evaluated by applying the principles of *historiography*. Historiography is the study of the writing of historical events. It is an examination of the methods historians use in the development of history as a branch of knowledge. Historians use three primary tests to determine the reliability of a historical document. First is the bibliographic test: whether the written historical record was transmitted accurately down through the ages starting with the original autograph and progressing from copy to successive copy. The second historiographical test is the external evidence test; this looks for outside corroborative evidence such as extrabiblical sources and archaeological finds that support the autograph. The final test is the internal evidence test: Is the book consistent within its own contents? Are there internal contradictions in the material such as incorrect geographical locations or anachronistic mistakes? The Bible passes all three tests with flying colors. Considering modern scientific dating of manuscripts, as well as archaeological finds such as those contained in the Dead Sea Scrolls of 1947, it is safe to say that no other ancient historical manuscript even approaches the reliability demonstrated by the Bible.

"Ed, Just Tell Your Story!"

This first chapter ends with an encounter where Adam was the stimulus. My Christian friend Phil and I neared the end of our visit with an imam in arguably the densest Muslim population in America. The outside temperature was more than ninety degrees Fahrenheit and there was no air conditioning.

Our host asked me, "You and I both know that God created Adam and Jesus from dust. How can you, as a Christian, actually believe that Jesus was divine?"

I was tired after a long day and perspiring. "I think I'm going to let my friend Phil answer that question."

Phil responded, "No Ed, I think our friend wants to hear your answer."

Silently I prayed a Nehemiah prayer, "Lord, help." A quietness entered my soul, almost as if I could hear God's gentle Spirit, "Ed, just tell your story."

I did. I also quoted two Bible verses in Arabic from John 14:27: "Peace I leave with you; my peace I give you. I do not give to you as the world gives. Do not let your hearts be troubled and do not be afraid." The second verse was from 1 Peter 3:18: "For Christ also suffered once for sins, the righteous for the unrighteous, to bring you to God. He was put to death in the body but made alive in the Spirit." I ended by telling him, "God raised me from the dead to bring this message to you so that you can have new life in Christ because of what He did for you on the cross." Phil added that in his own life he had also encountered the risen Christ. Our Muslim friend then stood up, left the room to prepare a watermelon, and served it to us.

Summary Questions for Reflection

1. God is a spirit, and any reference to man's being formed in the "image of God" necessarily implies "spiritual image." What could be the implications of believing or not believing that people are formed in the spiritual image of God?

2. What do you think is the importance, if any, of seeing the true seriousness of sin? Is Satan only interested in making us "slip" or "stumble?" How do you think God views sin? How could our answers determine our view of God's approach to a remedy for sin?

3. Most Muslims have been taught all their lives that the Christian Bible has been changed. What are the implications if that assumption is not true? If we truly believe that God is all-powerful, isn't He powerful enough to preserve His own Word intact?

4. Serious Bible scholars for many years have investigated textual criticism of the Bible. What results might come from Muslim scholars who have done the same with the Qur'an?

CHAPTER 2

CAIN AND ABEL AND THE CONSEQUENCES OF SIN

Feeling sorry for past failure and then deciding to try harder next time is not the end of the road. What matters is the subsequent corrective action. It either gives value to the sorrowful feeling or else makes the whole experience worthless. —Sayyid Qutb[1]

Do not be deceived: God cannot be mocked. A man reaps what he sows. The one who sows to please his sinful nature, from that nature will reap destruction; the one who sows to please the Spirit, from the Spirit will reap eternal life. (Gal. 6:7 8)

Five Stories Down

I stared five stories down into an empty pit. I was not alone. Hundreds of pin-drop-silent people joined me. It was February 2005; I was in New York City attending a medical conference. I stood at Ground Zero, the site of the 9/11 World Trade Center destruction. Every person with me had their own questions. I could imagine what they were because they're some of the same questions I've heard from others:

"Why do Muslims hate us? What did we ever do to make them do this to us?" Unfortunately, many in the non-Western world believe, "what goes around comes around"!

There were others among us who looked different—a vanload of bearded men and covered women who had also come to pay their respects. They had questions of their own. I had heard these before too: "Why do Christians hate us? Why can't they just leave us alone? Are we safe here?" I could give answers to both groups, but most wouldn't understand.

Less than twenty-four hours after those towers came crashing down, most Islamic nations condemned the attack and expressed sadness and revulsion. There were a few notable exceptions that attracted American press. On the West Bank and in East Jerusalem, television crews filmed Palestinians dancing in the streets, passing out sweets, shouting *"Allahu Akbar"* ("Allah is the greatest"), and holding up the "V-for-victory" sign. Saddam Hussein's Iraq issued an official report that "the American cowboys are reaping the fruit of their crimes against humanity." Most Muslims living in the West stayed indoors, fearing retribution. Osama bin Laden denied any involvement in the attack. The resulting US war on terror escalated into the invasions of Afghanistan and Iraq. We are still dealing with the results.

Our exploration into the shadows continues by looking at the story of Cain and Abel and the deadly consequences of sin.

Cain and Abel: Setting the Stage

Cain and Abel were the first two sons of Adam and Eve. They were born outside the garden of Eden, to the east, probably Mesopotamia, in modern-day southern Iraq. Cain was the eldest and became a farmer. His younger brother Abel became a herdsman. There was jealousy and conflict.

Cain and Abel in the Qur'an 5:30–35

27But recite unto them with truth the tale of the two sons of Adam, how they offered each a sacrifice, and it was accepted from the one of them and it was not accepted from the other. (The one) said: I will surely kill thee. (The other) answered: Allah accepteth only from those who ward off (evil). [28]Even if thou stretch out thy hand against me to kill me, I shall not stretch out my hand against thee to kill thee, lo! I fear Allah, the Lord of the Worlds. [29]Lo! I would rather thou shouldst bear the punishment of the sin against me and thine own sin and become one of the owners of the Fire. That is the reward of evil-doers. [30]But (the other's) mind imposed on him the killing of his brother, so he slew him and became one of the losers. [31]Then Allah sent a raven scratching up the ground, to show him how to hide his brother's naked corpse. He said: Woe unto me! Am I not able to be as this raven and so hide my brother's naked corpse? And he became repentant. [32]For that cause We decreed for the Children of Israel that whosoever killeth a human being for other than manslaughter or corruption in the earth, it shall be as if he had killed all mankind, and whoso saveth the life of one, it shall be as if he had saved the life of all mankind. Our messengers came unto them of old with clear proofs (of Allah's Sovereignty), but afterwards lo! Many of them became prodigals in the earth. (Surah 5:27–32)

Cain and Abel in the Bible

In Genesis 4 we see the birth of Cain and Abel, the first sons of Adam and Eve. Cain grew up to be a farmer while Abel was a shepherd. Each one brought an offering of their produce to God as a burnt offering. God accepted Abel's offering but not Cain's. Cain got angry. God told him that sin was "crouching at the door" (v. 6) and that he must master it. Later, Cain killed his brother and God cursed Cain's future efforts. Cain complained about God's harsh verdict and then left God's presence. He moved east of Eden, to the land of Nod.

In the New Testament book of Hebrews (11:4) we see Cain and Abel's sacrifices discussed briefly. Only Abel, who was killed by his brother Cain, was considered righteous.

The Shadow When the Qur'an Is Compared to the Bible

What are the differences in the two accounts?

1. In the Qur'an the two sons of Adam are unnamed. Islamic tradition identifies them as Cabil and Habil. In the Bible they are named Cain and Abel.

2. As in the Bible account, both sons present sacrificial offerings to God, but only one is accepted. In the Qur'an, the type of each son's sacrifice is not mentioned. However, the reason given for why one sacrifice was accepted was because that son was "righteous."

3. In the Bible, Cain was a farmer who brought some of his first crops as his sacrifice. Abel was a shepherd who brought the first and best of his flocks ("fat portions") as his sacrifice. God was pleased with Abel's offering but not with Cain's.

4. In the Qur'an, out of anger for not having had his sacrifice accepted, he announced to his brother that he was going to kill him.

5. The "righteous" son in the Qur'an told his brother he would not try to hurt him back for three reasons. First, the "righteous" son feared Allah. Second, he wanted to place his own sin on his wicked brother. And finally, the unrighteous son would be condemned to hell. In the Bible, the above discussion between the two brothers did not take place.

6. In the Bible, before the murder, God pursued Cain, telling him that "sin is crouching at the door" and "you must master it."

7. In both the Bible and Qur'an, one son murders the other. In the Bible, it is the older son, Cain, who is the murderer.

8. In the Bible after the murder, God pursues Cain (as He did Adam in the garden of Eden). "Where is your brother Abel?" And Cain said, "I do not know. Am I my brother's keeper?" (v. 9). God curses the ground (as He also did with Adam) and condemns Cain to being a vagrant wanderer. Cain whines and blames God as well as others. Out of mercy God provides Cain with a mark of protection. Cain moves eastward. In the Qur'an, the above pursuit by God and resulting interactions did not take place.

9. In the Qur'an the significance of the murderer's crime is explained by the lack of all the people who would have been born to the murdered son.

10. In the Bible, the significance of the murdered son Abel foreshadows a picture of faith and the coming of Jesus. This Jesus would be "the mediator of a new covenant, and to the sprinkled blood, which speaks better than the blood of Abel" (Heb. 12:24).

In summarizing the story of Cain and Abel, in the Qur'an the origin of the conflict was "unrighteousness." The solution is for each person to do right things on their own. In the Qur'an there is no evidence of God pursuing the offender and there is no curse placed on mankind or his work.

In the Bible the conflict's foundation is "sin crouching at the door." The solution comes out of a pursuing God and prefigured by "Jesus, the mediator of a new covenant, and to the sprinkled blood, which speaks better than the blood of Abel."

Now, for the second strand in our chapter's rope, let's examine one of the key "Nineteen Qur'anic themes" of Sayyid Qutb that relates to the story of Cain and Abel.

Sayyid Qutb Themes

This second chapter highlighting the story of Cain and Abel relates most closely to one of our Qur'anic themes from Sayyid Qutb, number 7, dealing with the nature of sin, repentance, forgiveness, testing, and faith in Islam.

> 7. Nature of Sin, Repentance, Forgiveness, Testing, and Faith in Islam (see #3 above)—Because of Satan's enmity and mankind's weakness, humans make mistakes and sin. When mankind realizes this and repents, asking God for forgiveness, God freely forgives the person. God tests the faith of all believers. Faith is the action that demonstrates a person's true repentance. Faith is based on God's oneness and is a light that shines in the human heart and illuminates the soul so that it sees the way leading to God.

Qutb affirms that in Islam there is no inherited or original sin which is spoken about by the Church. There is no atonement needed except for that done by an individual's own actions.[2]

Qutb writes that because of God's grace, the door for repentance and return to God is always open. Following a slip into sin or lapse of memory, man can simply repent and God forgives him. When man performs a good deed, it is substituted in place of a bad deed. God did not make man's sin inherited or one that permanently haunts him. There is no such thing as inherited sin, and no one bears the burden of another person. The Islamic idea is much easier and simpler: Adam simply slipped into sin, but then repented and asked God for forgiveness. God accepted his repentance and forgave him—that put an end to the sin.[3]

According to Sayyid Qutb, in order to be accepted, repentance has a clear rule. True repentance is marked by true regret as well as stopping the bad deeds. It is made complete through doing good deeds and is the proof of genuine repentance.[4]

Qutb also notes that all people are tested to see if their repentance is genuine. Qutb claims people are given tests to prove their truth and sincerity just as gold is tested by fire to separate anything that is not real gold.[5] He also states that God tests the human soul with difficulty and hardship and purges it from anything evil. The powers that remain are made stronger and more solid.[6]

Qutb adds that faith is the building block of all that is good in life. Faith is where all the fruits in life originate. Any branch of the tree that does not come from faith is cut off.[7] According to Qutb, doing what is right is the fruit that comes from faith. When faith settles in the human heart, doing good spontaneously results. Faith is positive and active. When faith penetrates the human conscience, it results in good deeds. This is the Islamic view of faith. It is either dynamic or it is nonexistent and phony. Faith is like a flower that cannot keep its fragrance from naturally spreading.[8]

Associated Qur'an Story

This unique Qur'an story shows the same struggle Cain was faced with: how to control our sinful tendencies and the "sin which is crouching at the door." This story emphasizes that all people suffer from temporary periods of weakness. We also see the importance of hearing all the facts of a case before making a decision.

Hatib and the Hidden Letter   from Surah 60 Al-Mumtahana ("the woman to be examined")

This Medinan surah has thirteen verses and takes its name from an incident depicted in the first verse:

> O ye who believe! Choose not My enemy and your enemy for allies. Do ye give them friendship when they disbelieve in that truth which hath come unto you, driving out the messenger and you because ye believe in Allah, your Lord? If ye have come forth to strive in My way and seeking My good pleasure, (show them not friendship). Do ye show friendship unto them

in secret, when I am Best Aware of what ye hide and what ye proclaim? And whosoever doeth it among you, he verily hath strayed from the right way. (Surah 60:1)

Six years after the *hijra* (AD 628 / 6 AH), Muhammad concluded the Treaty of Hudaybiyyah with the polytheistic Meccan Qurayshis. This treaty allowed safe and free access for Muslims going on annual *Hajj* (pilgrimage) to Mecca. Two years later the Meccans broke the treaty. Muhammad immediately organized his followers to conquer Mecca and took with him a military force of ten thousand fighters. Muhammad wanted to keep this attack private and told his plans to only his few close companions (*Sahaba*).

One of these companions was a *muhajir* (one who left Mecca to go with Muhammad to Medina as a Muslim), Hatib ibn Abi Balta'ah. He was a trusted Muslim companion who had also fought alongside Muhammad at the famed Battle of Badr. Like many of the *muhajir,* when Hatim left Mecca, he also left behind members of his family. Unlike the other *muhajirin,* Hatim did not come from the Quraysh tribe. Hatim was now considered an enemy of Mecca and the other Qurayshis. If retribution was enacted on his remaining family, he had no one left in Mecca to protect them.

In a moment of weakness Hatim tried to "play both sides of the fence." He secretly wrote a letter warning the Meccan Qurayshis of Muhammad's impending attack. The letter was hidden in the hair of a woman. According to Qutb, God warned Muhammad of this treachery and he sent two soldiers to retrieve the letter.

The soldiers caught up with the woman who was fleeing to Mecca on a camel. They asked her for the letter. She said she had no letter. The soldiers said Muhammad told them she did have it and they believed their prophet. The soldiers searched her camel and possessions and failed to find it. They said if she did not surrender the letter, they would strip her to find it. She then undid her hair and gave them the letter, which was taken back to Muhammad.

Muhammad read the letter and called Hatim in for questioning. Hatim assured Muhammad that he was a true Muslim but had only done this to help protect his remaining family in Mecca. Muhammad believed him, especially since he was also a veteran of the Battle of Badr. Umar ibn al-Khattab, another of the *Sahaba*, wanted "to behead the hypocrite." Muhammad didn't agree, saying that God might have forgiven Hatim because of his faithfulness at Badr.

Qutb discusses lessons to be derived from this story. He notes that even the most faithful people can be overcome during moments of weakness. He also highlights the patience of Muhammad in listening to all facts before jumping to any conclusions. Qutb finally reminds us to look at the will of God as events in life unfold.[9]

Now for this chapter's fourth rope strand and another new perspective on Christianity. This one addresses Cain's problem of how to get rid of sin in one's own life. To Muslims it is also one of the most controversial of topics! Once again, we only see an overview of the topic below.

A New Perspective on Christianity: "No one can bear the sins of another person," i.e., "There is no original sin."

Some people would like to harmonize Islam and Christianity. Others want to believe that "All religions teach the same basic things and that all these roads lead to God." However, in the final analysis, it all boils down to how sin is viewed by God and how it is ultimately resolved.

In Islam, according to Qutb, sin is only a "slip," a "lapse of memory," a "forgotten instruction," or a "bad deed." Muslims agree that sin is breaking God's laws. But in Islam it is easy for a person who has slipped into sin to take care of it. An individual simply acknowledges the sin, decides not to do it again, and then comes to God in prayer asking God for forgiveness. God freely forgives the sin. The person now does good deeds, which God then uses to replace the bad deeds and all is forgotten.

According to Christianity sin is much deeper than that. Yes, it is breaking God's laws, but it is actually an assault on and rebellion against the God of the universe. It is a violation of the very holiness of His character. Sin is a permanent cancer that destroys every person and thing, including creation. God's justice demands that all sin be punished and paid for and eradicated. According to the Bible, "the wages of sin is death" (Rom. 3:23). God is a God of justice, but sometimes people don't get punished for what they deserve. That is called mercy—and God is also a God of mercy. So, which prevails? The answer lies in what God in Christ accomplished at the cross with His substitutionary atonement.

In my opinion, Qutb gave a fairly accurate assessment of the Christian belief in Christ's substitutionary atonement. He writes that it (original sin) shows Adam as a sinner and that sin becomes a permanent curse threatening all mankind. The only way for man to be saved is for God to take the form of a man, Christ, who bore the burden of atonement for inherited sin and was allegedly crucified. This meant that forgiveness would be given only to those in communion with Christ who sacrificed himself.[10]

"This Could Be a Man of Peace."

This second chapter about Cain and Abel concludes with an encounter where the remedy for sin was an extreme act of terrorism!

My Christian friend David and I interviewed an older Iranian man who led prayers at a small mosque in Indiana. We discussed the "nature of God and the absolute importance of His 'Oneness.'" We also looked at a point of comparison in the Bible, from Psalm 139. Aloud he slowly and distinctly read the entire psalm, commenting on each verse. He agreed with everything he read, until he came to verse 19: "If only you, God, would slay the wicked! Away from me, you who are bloodthirsty!" He commented, "This does not represent Islam, which doesn't support 'wickedness' or 'hatred' or being 'bloodthirsty.'" He looked up, raised his eyebrows, and elevated his voice about 20 decibels. "Those people who flew airplanes into the two towers to destroy them [the September 11, 2001 attacks], where did they get that? It's not true Islam!" I gave no answer to his rhetorical question.

Near the end of our time together I invited him to ask me any question. He replied, "I want you to honestly tell me why you are really doing all this research?" This occasioned an opportunity to relate my personal story of how I came to know Christ. I ended by telling him, "Now my greatest joy is telling my Muslim friends that they can have new life in Christ because of what he did for them on the cross!"

He served us tea and dates. As we prepared to leave, I invited his family to our home for tea. I left him a signed copy of a previous book I had written as well as a gift of chocolates. We parted warmly. As David and I drove away I thought of what Jesus said when he sent out the twelve in Luke 10:5–6: "When you enter a house, first say, 'Peace to this house.' If someone who promotes peace is there, your peace will rest on them; if not, it will return to you." Jesus instructed them to be on the lookout for a "man of peace." Because of this man's gentle, honest, forthright nature, and eager response to biblical scripture I said to my friend David, "This man could be a man of peace." God sovereignly led us to speak with him. I will continue to pray for him. We will see what God has in store!

Summary Questions for Reflection

1. Why do you think Cain rejected God's attempt to pursue a relationship with him? How does Abel's response to God reflect a different attitude? How are these same responses seen today?

2. If there is no "original sin," as believed by Sayyid Qutb, why do you suppose young children must be taught to tell the truth but don't need to be taught to lie?

3. What do you think is the role that Satan plays in our ability or inability to obey God's commands? Do you think Satan simply tries to make us stumble, or is his goal worse—does he actually want to destroy us?

4. Is sin just a local process, between us and God? If so, why do the effects of sin often spread beyond us, and from generation to generation? How do you think it might be possible to obtain a permanent fix for this problem?

CHAPTER 3

NOAH, JUDGMENT, AND THE FLOOD

God's assistance is not given to people who wait passively for something to happen.—Sayyid Qutb[1]

As it was in the days of Noah, so it will be at the coming of the Son of Man. For in the days before the flood, people were eating and drinking, marrying and giving in marriage, up to the day Noah entered the ark; and they knew nothing about what would happen until the flood came and took them all away. That is how it will be at the coming of the Son of Man.

(Matt. 24:37–39)

Hell: the Greatest Fear

A Pakistani friend told me about making the *Hajj* twice in a single year. He wanted to go "because on the Hajj you can ask God for whatever you want. I asked him for my biggest need, the fear of being sent to hell. I asked him to send me to heaven. I also asked for success in life, but that wasn't nearly as important to me."

Our path into the shadows continues by looking at the life of Noah and his part in God's judgment by means of the worldwide flood.

Noah: Setting the Stage

Other than living outside the garden of Eden, there is no evidence that Noah lived in a different location than Adam or Adam's immediate family. Using records from the Bible (Genesis): Noah was a direct descendant of Adam (nine generations down), and the grandson of Methuselah. According to the Bible, lifespans of all people before the worldwide flood were significantly longer. For example, Adam lived 930 years and Methuselah lived 969 years. Noah lived for 950 years, or 350 years after the flood which took place 600 years after Noah's birth. We are able to translate these years into our modern Gregorian calendar using the fixed known reference point when the Persian King Nebuchadnezzar destroyed Solomon's temple in the year 586 BC. This puts Noah's birth at 3078 BC and the year of the flood as 2497 BC (taking into account the difference between the lunar and Gregorian calendars).

Now, for the first strand in this chapter's rope, let's see how the stories about Noah compare in both the Qur'an and Bible.

Noah in the Qur'an

The Qur'an story about Noah is found primarily in Surah 11 (Hud), verses 25-49. It is also found in other locations in the Qur'an (7:59–64; 10:71–73; 21:76–77; 23:23–30; 25:37; 26:105–122; 29:14–15; 37:75–82; 51:46; 54:9–15; 69:11–12; and 71:1–28). In order to avoid repetition I will summarize the three most relevant passages below, from Surahs 11, 21, and 29.

Qur'an 11:25–49

[25]And We sent Noah unto his folk (and he said): Lo! I am a plain warner unto you. [26]That ye serve none, save Allah. Lo! I fear for you the retribution of a painful Day. [27]The chieftains of his folk, who disbelieved, said: We see thee but a mortal like us, and we see not that any follow thee save the most abject among us,

without reflection. We behold in you no merit above us—nay, we deem you liars. (Surah 11:25–27)

In verses 28–39 we see Noah repeatedly warning the people to worship and follow only Allah and that judgment would follow if they refused and dared him to bring on the judgment. Allah commands Noah to build an ark to be safe from the coming flood. The people outside ridiculed Noah and his project.

[40](Thus it was) till, when Our commandment came to pass and the oven gushed forth water, We said: Load therein two of every kind, a pair (the male and female), and thy household, save him against whom the word hath gone forth already, and those who believe. And but a few were they who believed with him. [41]And he said: Embark therein! In the name of Allah be its course and its mooring. Lo! My Lord is Forgiving, Merciful. (Surah 11:40–41)

In verses 42–43 the flood comes. Only Noah and his family (with the exception of one son who was labeled by God as "unrighteous") were saved.

And it was said: O earth! Swallow thy water and, O sky! Be cleared of clouds! And the water was made to subside. And the commandment was fulfilled. And it (the ship) came to rest upon (the mount) Al-Judi and it was said: A far removal for wrong-doing folk! (Surah 11:44)

In verses 45-49 Noah pleads with Allah for one of his sons who refused to enter the ark. God tells Noah that this unrighteous son is not really part of his family.

Qur'an 21:76–77

[76]And Noah, when he cried of old, We heard his prayer and saved him and his household from the great affliction. [77]And

delivered him from the people who denied Our revelations. Lo! They were folk of evil, therefore did We drown them all.

Qur'an 29:14–15

[14]And verily We sent Noah (as Our messenger) unto his folk, and he continued with them for a thousand years save fifty years; and the flood engulfed them, for they were wrong-doers. [15]And We rescued him and those with him in the ship, and made of it a portent for the peoples.

Noah in the Bible

The Bible story of Noah is found primarily in chapters 6–9 of the book of Genesis. Mankind had spread over all the earth. Evil and wickedness had also spread. This grieved God, who decided to eliminate all mankind except for Noah and his family (eight people in all—Noah, his three sons plus all four wives). God commanded Noah to build a wooden ark (ship) and gave specific details for its construction. He was then instructed to bring with him two of every kind of animal on earth. Noah was six hundred years old when the worldwide flood came. It started with forty days and nights of rain, until water covered the entire earth's surface plus seven-and-one-half feet higher. The water remained high for the next 150 days. Everything living on the earth perished. God promised never again to destroy the world by a flood. The rainbow became a sign of this promise from God.

In Isaiah 54 we see God's covenant with Noah connected with the future suffering of His servant, the Messiah:

> "To me this is like the days of Noah, when I swore that the waters of Noah would never again cover the earth. So now I have sworn not to be angry with you, never to rebuke you again. [10] Though the mountains be shaken and the hills be removed, yet my unfailing love for you will not be shaken nor

my covenant of peace be removed," says the LORD, WHO HAS COMPASSION ON YOU. [11] "Afflicted city, lashed by storms and not comforted, I will rebuild you with stones of turquoise, your foundations with lapis lazuli." (Isa. 54:9–11)

Note that this passage comes immediately after the prophetic sufferings of Christ detailed in Isaiah 52–53.

In the New Testament Noah is connected with the return of Christ in his end-times prophecy:

As it was in the days of Noah, so it will be at the coming of the Son of Man. [38] For in the days before the flood, people were eating and drinking, marrying and giving in marriage, up to the day Noah entered the ark. (Matt. 24:37–38)

In the book of Hebrews we see Noah's time on the ark as a story of righteousness by faith:

By faith Noah, being warned by God about things not yet seen, in reverence prepared an ark for the salvation of his household, by which he condemned the world, and became an heir of the righteousness which is according to faith. (Heb. 11:7)

Finally, we see Noah's ark story and rescue through the water connected with salvation and exemplified by water baptism today.

[18]For Christ also died for sins once for all, the just for the unjust, so that He might bring us to God, having been put to death in the flesh, but made alive in the spirit; [19]in which also He went and made proclamation to the spirits now in prison, [20]who once were disobedient, when the patience of God kept waiting in the days of Noah, during the construction of the ark, in which a few, that is, eight persons, were brought safely through the water. [21]Corresponding to that, baptism now saves

you—not the removal of dirt from the flesh, but an appeal to God for a good conscience—through the resurrection of Jesus Christ, [22]who is at the right hand of God, having gone into heaven, after angels and authorities and powers had been subjected to Him. (1 Pet. 3:18–22)

The Shadow When the Qur'an Is Compared to the Bible

Again, where are the shadows?

1. In the Qur'an one of Noah's sons refused to go with him in the ark and died in the flood—there is no evidence of this in the Bible.

2. In the Qur'an no details of the ark were given: design, dimension, building materials. This is elaborately detailed in the Bible.

3. In the Qur'an there are no details on the length of time of the flood.

4. Following the ark's safe arrival, in the Qur'an there is no mention of Noah building an altar or presenting a sacrifice.

5. In the Qur'an there is no "rainbow covenant" by God, where He promises never again to destroy the world by water.

6. Other than as a "sign to all peoples," in the Qur'an there is no meaning attached to the flood, such as connection with God's suffering Servant/Messiah (Isaiah 53–54); salvation and washing away of sins in baptism; or illustration of Christ's return in his end-times prophecy.

In summation, in the Qur'an, Noah and the worldwide flood was certainly a spiritual sign to all peoples. It was a call for repentance and judgment by God on all who refused to worship God. However, the spiritual significance ends there. Unlike the Bible, there is no connection with Christ—no rainbow covenant by God, no connection with the suffering Servant/Messiah, no salvation evidenced by the washing away of sins in baptism, and no connection with the return of Christ at the end of time. The shadow cast by the Qur'an on the Bible continues to grow.

Sayyid Qutb Themes

As with previous chapters, it is time for the second of our four strands. This chapter highlighting Noah relates most closely to one of our Qur'anic themes from Sayyid Qutb, number 14, which deals with God's judgment.

> 14. The Day of Judgment—Purpose and Value of Human Life in Islam. Paraphrasing Qutb, believing in the Last Day is really a belief in universal, divine justice. It announces that human life here on earth has purpose as well as value and order. It also affirms that all good deeds will one day be rewarded, even though the reward may not be apparent today.[2]

Sayyid Qutb presents a terrifying view of God's final judgment on all people. The Day of Judgment is also known in Islam as the Last Hour, the Last Day, or the Day of Reckoning. It includes portents (like a split moon) and trumpets. It is a fearful and terrifying time where all mankind is brought before God in judgment for their previous deeds and beliefs. Punishment is graphic, culminating with the residents of hellfire wishing they had obeyed God and His messenger (Muhammad).

According to Qutb, all mankind is gathered together in an awe-filled, overwhelming scene. All are divided into two groups. "Some among them will be wretched, and some happy" (Surah 11:105).[3]

Qutb further notes that God's time is different from ours. The coming of God's judgment may only be a moment, but actually it may last centuries or even millions of years.[4] A trumpet will be blown and then everyone gathered together.[5] Qutb goes on with a final scene from the Day of Reckoning: "And We set a just balance for the Day of Resurrection so that no soul is wronged in aught. Though it be of the weight of a grain of mustard seed, We bring it. And We suffice for reckoners" (Surah 21:47).[6]

Qutb adds that the fire of hell surrounds its occupants and touches every part of their faces. This will cause them to say, "I wish we had obeyed God and His messenger": "On the day when their faces are turned over in the Fire, they say: Oh, would that we had obeyed Allah and had obeyed His messenger!" (Surah 33:66).[7]

Associated Qur'an Story

For the third strand we have the following unique story from the Qur'an emphasizing the final judgment of God.

The Splitting of the Moon—from Surah 54 al-Qamr (the Moon)

Qutb believed this surah was revealed in Mecca. It contains fifty-five verses. Its theme is the judgment of God on past people groups who rejected His guidance. Its name comes from the first verse describing a physical catastrophe, the splitting of the moon:

The hour drew nigh, and the moon was rent in twain. (Surah 54:1)

Qutb indicated that this surah shows God's judgment on five ancient people groups:[8] the peoples of Noah, Lot, Pharaoh (of Egypt), and the pre-Islamic groups Ad and Thamud. The people of Ad were the major power brokers in southern Arabia. Ad was believed to be the great-great-grandson of Noah. The Ad people were followed by those of the Thamud, who migrated to northern Arabia and ruled in the eighth century BC.[9]

This physical splitting of the moon was considered a "sign" from God and scoffed at by the unbelievers as nothing but "magic":

And if they behold a portent they turn away and say: Prolonged illusion. (Surah 54:2)

Different views existed on this event. Some believed the splitting of the moon was allegorical. Others felt it would be a future event foreshadowing the final Day of Judgment. The traditional Islamic view is that the splitting of the moon was a literal, physical event that actually took place and was a miracle from God. This is the view held by Qutb as well as Ibn Kathir. It is also the view given in the two most respected Islamic Hadith collections, Sahih Bukhari and Sahih Muslim.

It started when the unbelievers of Mecca asked Muhammad to show them a miracle. Many reports exist that a visible gap in the moon was actually seen.

The surah's ending presents the Day of Judgment and the punishment meted out to all unbelievers, those who reject divine guidance (i.e., Islam):

On the day when they are dragged into the Fire upon their faces (it is said unto them): Feel the touch of hell. (Surah 54:48)

The contrast is that shown to the true believers (Muslims) in the final two verses:

[54]Lo! The righteous will dwell among the gardens and rivers, [55]firmly established in the favour of a Mighty King. (Surah 54:54–55)

Did this event, the splitting of the moon, actually happen? Was it a real miracle? Many believe it was. What about us in Christianity? Do we believe in miracles? Of course we do! Do we believe the moon physically split in the time of Muhammad? We leave that in the hands of God.

A New Perspective on Christianity: The Gospel of Barnabas

Once again, what follows is only a brief summary of this topic. For our fourth and final strand of this chapter on Noah, we have another new perspective on Christianity. This time we cover another supposedly reputable account of the life of Jesus, the Gospel of Barnabas. How does this topic connect with our chapter on Noah? Noah lived during a time of rampant unbelief, when most people chose to ignore God. They did not want to believe in God's revelations and commands. People have rebelled against God all through history. The Gospel of Barnabas was just one more attempt to discredit God's commands and cast doubt on the authenticity of the New Testament account of the life of Jesus.

The Gospel of Barnabas was supposedly authored by one of Jesus's followers, Barnabas. Upon examination, it is replete with historical, geographical, and religious contradictions. It claims that Jesus was not the Messiah and that he was not crucified on the cross. It is most likely a fourteenth-century Italian forgery that contradicts both the Bible as well as the Qur'an.

This third chapter ends with a mosque visit where an imam spoke about the coming Day of Judgment.

God Did Not Make Hell to Punish Us!

My son accompanied me during one mosque visit to northeastern Indiana. We had the privilege of interviewing a young man from a war-torn country previously known as Czechoslovakia. This Bosnian Muslim leader was grateful for the freedoms he now enjoyed in the United States.

During the course of the interview he shared his projected feelings when standing before Allah on the Day of Judgment. He said he would likely have two primary emotions: first would be "fear because Allah knew everything about us"; second was "hope because Allah loves us and did not create hell to punish us." He struggled as he tried reading from my English Scriptures. He was surprised and delighted when I told him I had a copy of the Bible in Bosnian in my briefcase. We then used it to read passages from Revelation 5 and Matthew 4.

He listened attentively when I shared my own journey of faith. I told of my changed life and hope in Christ because he died for me on the cross and rose again from the dead. I left him with a small box of chocolates as a gift from my wife to his. I believe he was most pleased when he accepted my offer to leave the Bosnian Bible with him. My prayer for this dear young man is that he read God's Word and come to an eternal knowledge of faith.

Summary Questions for Reflection

1. Connected with the Bible's story about Noah are God's rainbow covenant/promise, an altar to worship God, as well as a future promised Suffering Servant/Messiah. Why do you think those differences from the Qur'an might be important to consider?

2. God's final Day of Judgment reveals a terrifying scene. What physical and spiritual events are taking place in today's world that suggest this Day of Judgment might not be far off? What do you think we could or should be doing in preparation for that Day?

3. Why do you think some people give credence to the Gospel of Barnabas when its contents so obviously contradict both the Qur'an and Bible? What other inaccurate misconceptions about God and/or Jesus should we also be concerned about?

CHAPTER 4

JOB, THE WONDERS OF CREATION, AND GOD'S DIVINE JUSTICE

The Qur'an escorts the human soul throughout the cosmos. It inspires faith by gazing at light and darkness as well as by viewing the sun, moon, and stars.—Sayyid Qutb[1]

Then the Lord answered Job out of the storm. He said: "Who is this that obscures my plans with words without knowledge? Brace yourself like a man; I will question you, and you shall answer me.'" (Job 38:1–3)

Our odyssey into the shadows continues with the life of Job and his role in God's divine justice. Job begins with sacrifices made on behalf of his family. Personal disaster is followed by cheerless counsel from seeming friends. Job ultimately sees God in His revelation of creation and the universe.

Job: Setting the Stage

Biblical scholars believe Job to be possibly the oldest book in the Bible. Its first verse states Job lived in the land of Uz, probably related to Aram or Syria in Mesopotamia. Job likely lived after Noah and the flood but before the time of Abraham, giving him an approximate date of 2100 BC. This may have placed him in the Akkadian Empire under the rule of Sargon the Great.

Now let's see how the stories about Job compare in both the Qur'an and Bible.

Job in the Qur'an

Job is mentioned four times in the Qur'an. The two passages with the most detail appear below.

> [83]And Job, when he cried unto his Lord, (saying): Lo! Adversity afflicteth me, and Thou art Most Merciful of all who show mercy. [84]Then We heard his prayer and removed that adversity from which he suffered, and We gave him his household (that he had lost) and the like thereof along with them, a mercy from Our store, and a remembrance for the worshippers; (Surah 21:83–84)

In the above passage we find Job in an unnamed distress crying out to God for mercy. God answers Job and removes his distress. At least part of that distress was the loss of his people. God restored those who were lost and gave him back double their original number.

> [41]And make mention (O Muhammad) of Our bondman Job, when he cried unto his Lord (saying): Lo! The devil doth afflict me with distress and torment. [42](And it was said unto him): Strike the ground with thy foot. This (spring) is a cool bath and a refreshing drink. [43]And We bestowed on him (again) his household and therewith the like thereof, a mercy from us, and a memorial for men of understanding. [44]And (it was said unto him): Take in thine hand a branch and smite therewith, and break not thine oath. Lo! We found him steadfast, how excellent a slave! Lo! He was ever turning in repentance (to his Lord). (Surah 38:41–44)

In the above passage we see Job's suffering included thirst as well as the loss of his people. God instructed Job to kick the ground with his foot, and a refreshing stream of water rose up. God also gave Job back double the number of his lost people. God then ordered Job not to break his previous promises but to "strike" (what or who he was to strike, we do not know) with a bundle of grass. God then commended Job for his patience and endurance.

Job in the Bible

In contrast to the Qur'an's brevity, Job's story in the Bible is gargantuan. It comprises 1,070 verses in forty-two chapters. Here is a brief overview.

Timewise, the story of Job is possibly the most ancient in the entire Bible. The main character is the wealthiest and most famous man of his age. He was blameless in the sight of God and had seven sons and three daughters. He owned thousands of sheep, camels, oxen, and donkeys. He also had many servants. Although set locally, the incident is not local. It originates from a cosmic struggle between good and evil—between God and Satan, who convinces God to allow him (Satan) to test Job's faithfulness. God agrees and permits Job to be deprived first of his family and wealth, and later of his health.

In misery, Job had three friends who came to supposedly give comforting advice. They didn't! They all wound up telling him that he must have done something wrong to deserve his punishment by God. Even his own wife encouraged him to give up hope. Job continued to remain faithful to God. Toward the end of the book Job asks questions about God's character. Finally, God weighs in with a series of sixty-five questions, all emphasizing His own unique and awesome power and knowledge and sovereignty.

At the book's end, Job repents before God:

> [1]Then Job replied to the Lord: [2]"I know that you can do all things; no purpose of yours can be thwarted. [3]You asked, 'Who is this that obscures my plans without knowledge?'

Surely I spoke of things I did not understand, things too wonderful for me to know. [4]You said, 'Listen now, and I will speak; I will question you, and you shall answer me.' [5]My ears had heard of you but now my eyes have seen you. [6]Therefore I despise myself and repent in dust and ashes." (Job 42:1–6)

The book of Job begins and ends with Job presenting animal sacrifices to God because of sin—first for his sons and daughters, and then for his three comfortless friends. At the end, God more than restored all of Job's fortune.

The Shadow When the Qur'an Is Compared to the Bible

What is absent in the Qur'an's presentation of Job? First, there is no evidence of a cosmic conflict between God and Satan. There is also no focus on the character of God as the cause and solution for Job's problems. And finally, there is no theme of sacrifice as God's remedy for mankind's sin.

Sayyid Qutb Themes

For our second chapter strand we see the story of Job relating most closely to two of our Qur'anic themes from Sayyid Qutb, numbers 6 and 18, which deal with the beauty of God's creation.

6. Beauty and Wonder of God's Creation

According to Qutb and the Qur'an, all of nature—from the sun, moon, and planets down to the tiny atom—attest to the existence, truth, and majesty of God. According to Qutb, looking into the sky on a dark night, with their multitude of stars sending us light, allows us to perceive its singular beauty.[2]

Qutb also notes that beauty in nature makes hearts alive. Thinking about creation, such as in gardens, causes a person to praise the Maker of such beauty. The very best artists cannot match the colors of a single flower, or match its shades or delicate lines. God's creation is a miracle that is superior to all art.[3]

18. Illustrating Qur'anic Truths Using Various Scientific Topics—The Qur'an is mainly concerned with the human soul and the state of the human condition. Even so, scientific truths (meteorology, botany, zoology, physiology, mathematics, astronomy, and others) point to God through the Qur'an.

According to Sayyid Qutb, there are many signs everywhere in the universe that point to God's existence and power. All are able to see them, and they are visible both day and night. Through them people are invited to think about these signs.[4] These signs include visible astronomy and even our own day and night. According to Qutb, the most acceptable astronomical theory today is that constellations, stars, planets, and moons started as nebulae. These nebulae were torn apart and became circular in shape. The earth was part of the sun and came off it and then cooled.[5]

Even day and night have their place. According to Qutb, when night comes, the light goes and darkness takes over. Everyone everywhere sees this (except for those in the polar areas).[6] Also included are the weather as well as geophysics, and even all life on earth. Qutb notes that lightning, thunder, clouds, and thunderbolts are well-known occurrences.[7] He also notes that the Qur'an states that the mountains maintain the earth's balance so that it stays firm.[8]

According to Qutb, everything in the universe speaks to people about the presence of God. Just look at land around you (desert)—it is lifeless and dead without a single drop of water. Then with springs of water it comes to life, producing grain and fruit. Life is a miracle that no human can reproduce.[9]

Continuing our four-stranded rope model for each chapter, we now turn to a relevant and unique story from the Qur'an. Like the saga of Job, this is a story of divine justice.

Associated Qur'an Story

The Lost Necklace—from Surah 24 al-Nur (the Light)

This surah was revealed in Medina and has sixty-four verses. It takes its name from one of the most famous verses in the Qur'an, verse 35, which is known as the Verse of Light:

> Allah is the Light of the heavens and the earth. The similitude of His light is as a niche wherein is a lamp. The lamp is in a glass. The glass is as it were a shining star. (This lamp is) kindled from a blessed tree, an olive neither of the East nor of the West, whose oil would almost glow forth (of itself) though no fire touched it. Light upon light. Allah guideth unto His light whom He will. And Allah speaketh to mankind in allegories, for Allah is Knower of all things. (Surah 24:35)

Qutb states that this entire surah deals with the education of the Muslim community in general, and specifically with the problem of adultery.[10] He notes that in the early days of Islam the punishment for adultery comes from Surah 4, verse 15:

> As for those of your women who are guilty of lewdness, call to witness four of you against them. And if they testify (to the truth of the allegation) then confine them to the houses until death take them or (until) Allah appoint for them a way (through new legislation).

Thus, according to Qutb, in the early days of Islam punishment for an adulteress was confinement at home plus a verbal reprimand. For the adulterer it was only a verbal reprimand. In our current surah (24), new revelation came from God to increase the punishment. For those unmarried, punishment for adultery would be flogging, due to their sexual inexperience. For those married there was stoning. However, a false accusation of adultery would also incur punishment. That's the case with our current episode. Our Qur'an story follows.[11]

When Muhammad went out on military raids, lots would be drawn to see which one of his wives would accompany him. The lot for the raid on Bani al-Mustaliq fell to Aishah. Aishah traveled inside a howdah which was carried on the back of a camel as part of the caravan raid. One night, after stopping, Aishah got out of the howdah "for a certain purpose." At the time she was wearing a string of zafar[12] beads around her neck. When she got back to the howdah, she noticed her necklace was missing. She went out to search for it. When she got back to the caravan it had gone on without her. The servants responsible for taking Aishah's howdah on and off the camel failed to note that she was not inside the howdah. Aishah lay down and waited for someone to rescue her. Later, one of the camel riders who had fallen behind the caravan, Safwan ibn al-Mu'ttal of the Sulaym tribe, came up. He recognized who she was. He put her on his camel to ride while he went on foot. He brought her back to the caravan where it had stopped for the next night's journey. Unfortunately, the damage was done. She had been alone with another man unchaperoned. Tongues wagged.

The main accusers were Abdullah Ibn Ubayy as well as Mistah and Hamna, daughters of Jahsh. The accusations of adultery and the resulting case perplexed the entire Muslim community in Medina for a whole month. Muhammad consulted with Ali ibn Abi Talib and Usama ibn Zayd regarding whether or not he should divorce Aishah. Usama believed she was innocent and that the story must be a lie. Ali told Muhammad that God had imposed no matrimonial restrictions on him and that there were many other women besides Aishah. The quandary was resolved by a new revelation from God.

The falsity of the situation, and vindication by God, is reported in verses 11–20 of this surah. Specifically note verse 11:

Lo! They who spread the slander are a gang among you. Deem it not a bad thing for you; nay, it is good for you. Unto every man of them (will be paid) that which he hath earned of the sin;

and as for him among them who had the greater share therein, his will be an awful doom. (Surah 24:11)

Those who brought the false accusation were flogged.

For our final strand we look at a brief summary of another new perspective on Christianity: the other supposedly reputable accounts of the life of Jesus—the "other Gospels."

A New Perspective on Christianity: The Other Alleged Gospels

Like Job's three friends and their attempts to discourage Job from following God, this is a more modern attempt to discredit God's Word, the Bible. This section is a follow-up on Qutb's earlier comment in Chapter 3 about "one of the many Gospels written at this period."[13] The majority of these "many Gospels"[14] probably come from the Nag Hammadi library found in Egypt in 1945. These are mostly gnostic documents and have a marked absence of historical substance or narrative text. For example, the Infancy Gospel of Thomas shows Jesus making clay birds come to life and even killing other children for annoying him when he was younger.

After reading through about forty of these "other gospels," I have concluded that they do not even begin to compare with the substantive and organized texts of the biblical Gospels. They are of questionable value at best. At worse, they contradict what we know of Jesus from more authoritative texts.

Our chapter on Job concludes with a story about another man who also needed to endure—this time with a skin tattoo!

"This Too Shall Pass!"

"Dr. Ed, I'm thinking about a girl. Could you give me any clues in picking out a good wife?"

I had met this young Pakistani man two years ago over a chessboard at the local coffeehouse, and over the last two years this dear man and

I had a number of detailed conversations about Jesus and the Christian faith. Today he visited my home for the second time. A day earlier he had graduated, and he would be traveling north in a few days to stay with his brother. Although it was late July, the weather outside was pleasant. We felt a gentle breeze in our screened-in back porch.

I pondered his question. Since he was Pakistani, I asked, "Is she American?"

He replied, "Yes, but there's a problem. She says she is gay. But I like her and we get along together really well." I asked more about her. He said, "She comes from a strong Christian family but says Christianity is not for her anymore."

My wife joined us with the pot of tea.

After the past two years, this man had indicated that he had no further interest in Christ. He had given up on his Muslim faith but was fascinated with Hinduism. Most noticeable today was a new tattoo on his left forearm in Hebrew script. He said it meant, "This too shall pass."

"This too shall pass." In modern times it is one of the most popular tattoos to get. Wikipedia attributes the saying to ancient Persian Sufi poets Sanai and Attar of Nishapur. It was mentioned in English literature in 1813 by Jane Austen in *Pride and Prejudice*, and by the English poet Edward Fitzgerald in 1852. Later, President Abraham Lincoln used it in a speech given in September 1859 Jewish folklore popularized it as well, with a sage attributing it to King Solomon, "Gam Zen Yaavor." This is the one he prominently displayed. The saying intends to make one happy when they are sad and contemplative when they are happy. That theme flavored our afternoon tea.

Responding to his original request, I gave him a few principles I learned over the years about selecting a wife. The topic turned to "truth." My wife added that Jesus said He was the truth. I added in Urdu, his native language, the verse from John 14:6. My wife chimed in, "The end of that statement was, 'No one comes to the Father but through me [Jesus].'"

He then asked about the advisability of "pursuing wealth." My wife said that his parents in Pakistan must be very proud of both their sons. He looked embarrassed and said in a lower voice, "I'm sure they are more proud of my brother than of me." His new university degree was not a prestigious one like engineering. We mentioned from the Bible that "The love of money is the root of all kinds of evil" (1 Tim. 6:10), that Jesus said in Matthew 6 "Look at the birds of the air," "See how the lilies of the field grow," and finally, "seek first his kingdom and his righteousness and all these things will be given to you as well." (vv. 26, 28, 33). On this topic we also discussed idolatry. He looked down and said, "When I got these tattoos, I wanted to feel happy, but now when I see them I think they are idols taking my thoughts away from God." He felt he had done wrong. But he still wanted to get more tattoos!

Because he was also interested in birds, I promised to email him a story my wife wrote about a bird many years ago, "The King's Gift." She wrote it originally to help explain Jesus's good news to one of her Muslim girlfriends. He looked depressed. We told him that even though he was not a Christian, when he was in trouble he could still "call on the name of Jesus," which was powerful. He smiled.

After he left to go home, we prayed for this dear sensitive soul that Christ would draw him to Himself.

Summary Questions for Reflection

1. What advantages might be present if God chose to use sacrifice as a remedy for sin rather than mere punishment? Might there also be disadvantages?

2. How does the beauty and wonder of creation impact your view of God's character and His role in human suffering and judgment?

3. Why do you think some people give preference to the other alleged Gospels, even though they are obviously of inferior historic quality and content?

CHAPTER 5

ABRAHAM AND GOD'S WORLDWIDE COVENANT WITH HUMANKIND

One reflection of the Qur'an's uniqueness is how it relates every person and every feeling in the universe to a belief in the oneness of God. Every human insight confirms this belief.—Sayyid Qutb[1]

When Abram was ninety-nine years old, the Lord appeared to him and said, "I am God Almighty; walk before me and be blameless. I will confirm my covenant between me and you and will greatly increase your numbers." (Gen 17:1–2)

From a historical perspective, Judaism, Christianity, and Islam all claim the common bond of Abraham. From a spiritual perspective, they are united by the cross—as Jesus told the Jewish leaders:

Your father Abraham rejoiced at the thought of seeing my day; he saw it and was glad. (John 8:56)

Abraham: Setting the Stage

Abraham was born in Ur of the Chaldees (near modern-day Nasiriyah in southern Iraq), in Mesopotamia, approximately four hundred years after Noah and the flood. This gives a date of approximately 2100 BC, during either the Ur III Dynasty or Isin/Larsa Dynasties, and just before the great King Hammurabi of the First Dynasty of Babylon. Abraham was the tenth generation down as a direct descendant of Noah.

Let's see how the stories about Abraham compare in both the Qur'an and Bible.

Abraham in the Qur'an

We are introduced to Abraham's story in Surah 2:

> And (remember) when his Lord tried Abraham with (His) commands, and he fulfilled them, He said: Lo! I have appointed thee a leader for mankind. (Abraham) said: And of my offspring (will there be leaders)? He said: My covenant includeth not wrong-doers. (Surah 2:124)

Now we have six stories about Abraham, only two of which are also found in the Bible (4 and 6):

1. *Abraham and his son Ishmael built the Ka'ba (house of worship) in Mecca (Surah 2:125–132).* In verses 125–128 we see Abraham and his son Ishmael building the Ka'ba as a house of worship and dedicating its worship to God. In verses 129–132 Abraham asks God to send them another prophet to spread the message of Islam (who would be Muhammad).

2. *"How does God give life to the dead?" (Surah 2:258–260).* In these three verses another man disputed God's power with Abraham. Abraham told him that God is the One who gives life and death. He then related this story of a man passing by who wondered

the same thing about a seemingly dead village. God caused the man to die for a hundred years and then brought him back to life. God then told Abraham to kill and divide four birds and distribute their pieces on various hills. Abraham called to the birds and God brought them back to life.

3. *Abraham's journey from idolatry to monotheism (Surah 6:74–79).* In verses 74–79 we see Abraham confronting his own father Azar for wrongly worshipping idols. He shared his own journey out of polytheism. He said he first thought he could worship a star, then the moon, and finally the sun, but concluded they were not worthy to be worshipped since they all set and lost their power. Abraham concluded that God could not have any partners at all.

4. *Abraham, God's messengers, and the destruction of Sodom and Gomorrah (Surah 11:69–83).* In verses 69–73 angel messengers from God came to Abraham warning him of coming judgment on Sodom and Gomorrah—the cities where Lot lived. In verses 74–81 Abraham pleaded for Lot's people. They told Abraham it was too late and that Lot's people were doomed. When the angels came to Lot, Lot's neighbors wanted to sexually abuse the angels; Lot tried to stop them. Lot and his family fled, but Lot's wife remained and was destroyed with the others. In verses 82–83 the destruction is an accomplished fact:

> [82]So when Our commandment came to pass We overthrew (that township) and rained upon it stones of clay, one after another, [83]marked with fire in the providence of thy Lord (for the destruction of the wicked). And they are never far from the wrong-doers.

5. *Abraham argues with the people about idols—"Burn him!" (Surah 21:51–71).* Abraham confronted his father and people who were idol-worshippers. He destroyed all their idols but the largest one. The people were angry and asked Abraham, "Who

did this?" Abraham pointed to the largest idol and said, "Ask him!" The people were ashamed but decided in anger to burn Abraham. God made the fire cool, and it did not harm him. God protected Abraham and his nephew Lot.

6. *God commands Abraham to sacrifice his son Ishmael (Surah 37:99–111).* In verses 99–106 God commanded Abraham to take and sacrifice his son. When Abraham agrees and is about to kill his son when an angel stops him, since he had passed the test. He had proven his willingness to obey God.

> [107]Then We ransomed him with a tremendous victim. [108]And We left for him among the later folk (the salutation): [109]Peace be unto Abraham! [110]Thus do We reward the good. [111]Lo! He is one of Our believing slaves. (Surah 37:107–111)

Abraham in the Bible

Abraham's story in the Bible is more extensive than what appears in the Qur'an. It takes up almost half the book of Genesis. Abraham's story continues into the Psalms (via Melchizedek) and then to his connection with faith and Christ in the Gospels and throughout the remainder of the New Testament.

In Genesis 11 we are introduced to Abram through his father Terah, who had two other sons, Nahor and Haran. Haran had a son named Lot. But Abram's wife, Sarai, was barren. They lived in Ur of the Chaldees (modern-day southern Iraq). Haran died there and Terah decided to move the whole family westward from Ur, came to the land of Canaan (modern-day Palestine), and settled there. Terah died at the age of 205 on the way to Canaan.

Next comes God's magnificent and famous promise to Abram:

> The Lord had said to Abram, "Leave your country, your people and your father's household and go to the land I will show you.[2]

I will make you into a great nation and I will bless you; I will make your name great, and you will be a blessing.[3] I will bless those who bless you, and whoever curses you I will curse; and all peoples on earth will be blessed through you." (Gen. 12:1–3)

Abram obeyed and took his wife Sarai and his nephew Lot and traveled into Canaan. God continues the promise in the same chapter and Abram built an altar to God. Later, because they couldn't get along, Lot and Abram and their respective herds separated. Lot chose the green valley of the Jordan and moved there, to Sodom and Gomorrah— wicked and sinful places.

Genesis 14 recounts a battle where the kings of Sodom and Gomorrah were defeated and their possessions plundered; Lot and his family were also captured. Abram heard about the plight of his nephew and went to his rescue. Abram brought Lot, his family, and all their possessions back safely. Abram also rescued the people and possessions of Sodom. Then Abram met Melchizedek, the king of Salem, which meant "the King of Righteousness." Melchizedek was not an ordinary person; he was a priest of God Most High. Melchizedek, king of Salem, blessed Abram.

In Genesis 15 God repeated his promise to Abram and expanded it to include a physical son. God said Abram's physical descendants would be as numerous as the stars of the sky. Abram believed God, and this belief was counted to Abram as righteousness.

In Genesis 16 we see Sarai still barren. In order to have a child of her own Sarai concocts a plan whereby Abram would sleep with Sarai's Egyptian slave girl Hagar; the resulting child would belong to Sarai. When Hagar knew she was pregnant she despised Sarai her mistress. An angry Sarai complained to Abram, who told her she could do whatever she wanted with Hagar. Sarai treated her harshly and she fled into the wilderness. An angel found Hagar beside a spring and asked her where she was going? Hagar replied that she was running away from Sarai. The angel told Hagar to go back to Sarai and submit to her authority. God then gave Hagar a promise through the angel. God promised to bless Hagar's descendants and that they would be too numerous to count. God said she would have a son and call him Ishmael. When Ishmael was born, Abram was eighty-six years old.

In Genesis 17 God renews His promise to Abram and changes his name to Abraham, meaning "father of nations." God expands on His covenant, promising that nations and kings would come through him. God promised the land of Canaan as an everlasting possession. He also instructed Abraham to be circumcised as well as every male in his household as a sign of the covenant. God also changed Sarai's name to Sarah and promised a son through her. Abraham found this hard to believe and hoped God's blessing might come through Ishmael. God said He also planned to bless Ishmael: "But my covenant I will establish with Isaac, whom Sarah will bear to you by this time next year" (Gen. 17:21).

When Abraham was ninety-nine years old, he and his entire household were circumcised. Then Abraham had three visitors (angels), whom he entertained. They promised Sarah would have a son the following year. Then God, through the angels, told Abraham of His decision to destroy Sodom and Gomorrah because of their extreme wickedness. Lot, his wife, and two daughters were the only ones who left Sodom. Then God rained fire and brimstone on Sodom and Gomorrah, completely destroying the two cities. The angels told them not to look back, but Lot's wife disobeyed and was turned into a pillar of salt.

Abraham and Sarah again journeyed south. God caused Sarah to get pregnant. She gave birth to a son and named him Isaac. Hagar and Ishmael continued to live with Abraham. One day Sarah saw Ishmael mocking them. In anger, Sarah demanded that Abraham cast out Hagar and Ishmael; he acquiesced and sent the two away with food and water.

In Genesis 22 God gives Abraham the ultimate test, to sacrifice his son Isaac to God. An angel of the Lord stopped Abraham and told him that God has seen his willingness to obey. God reaffirmed His special covenant through Abraham to multiply his descendants and bless all the nations of the earth.

Later Abraham sent his servant north to find a wife for his son Isaac from among his relatives. The servant brought back Rebecca, who married Isaac. Abraham died at the age of 175.

Abraham is later connected to Melchizedek in the Psalms, where he prefigures the coming Messiah: "The Lord has sworn and will not change His mind, 'You are a priest forever, in the order of Melchizedek'" (Ps. 110:4).

Moving into the New Testament we see a more direct connection of Abraham with Christ in John 8:56–58. Jesus said to the Jewish leaders,

> 56"Your father Abraham rejoiced at the thought of seeing my day; he saw it and was glad." 57"You are not yet fifty years old," the Jews said to him, "and you have seen Abraham!" 58"I tell you the truth," Jesus answered, "before Abraham was born, I am!"

Also in the New Testament we see Abraham's connection with belief, righteousness, and circumcision in Romans 4:3: "What does the Scripture say? 'Abraham believed God, and it was credited to him as righteousness.'"

Even though Abraham initially had two sons, here is where the Bible makes it clear that God's everlasting spiritual covenant was to come through Isaac and not through Ishmael.

> 22For it is written that Abraham had two sons, one by the slave woman and the other by the free woman. 23His son by the slave woman was born in the ordinary way; but his son by the free woman was born as the result of a promise.24These things may be taken figuratively, for the women represent two covenants. One covenant is from Mount Sinai and bears children who are to be slaves: This is Hagar. Now Hagar stands for Mount Sinai

in Arabia and corresponds to the present city of Jerusalem, because she is in slavery with her children. ²⁶But the Jerusalem that is above is free, and she is our mother. (Gal. 4:22–26)

The book of Hebrews seals Christ's relationship with Melchizedek:

> ⁵In the same way, Christ did not take on himself the glory of becoming a high priest. But God said to him, "You are my Son; today I have become your Father." [Psalm 2:7] ⁶And he says in another place, "You are a priest forever, in the order of Melchizedek." [Psalm 110:4] (Heb. 5:5–6)

> ¹⁹We have this hope as an anchor for the soul, firm and secure. It enters the inner sanctuary behind the curtain, ²⁰where Jesus, who went before us, has entered on our behalf. He has become a high priest forever, in the order of Melchizedek. (Heb. 6:19–20)

In the next chapter of Hebrews we are also reminded that Abram gave Melchizedek a tithe of all the recovered spoils from the incident with Lot.

The Shadow When the Qur'an Is Compared to the Bible

So, what are the significant differences in the Qur'an and Bible accounts of Abraham?

What we learn from the Qur'an that is not in the Bible is Abraham's personal journey from idolatry to monotheism, God's protecting him from violent and angry idolaters, his being shown God's ability to give life to the dead, and Abraham and his son Ishmael building the Ka'ba in Mecca as a house of worship.

What we don't see in the Qur'an about Abraham is the following:

1. There is no worldwide covenant. Other than the Qur'an's promise to make Abraham a "leader for mankind" (Surah 2:124),

there is no promise from God for descendants beyond number—a multitude of nations—a blessing to all the families of the earth (Gen. 12–17).

2. There is also no "justification by faith" for Abraham that resulted in righteousness (Heb. 15:6).

3. In addition, there is no Melchizedek, no paying tribute (tithe) from the lesser to the greater (Heb. 7:7), and no prefiguring of Christ (Ps. 110:1–4; Heb. 5–7).

4. There is no circumcision as a sign of God's promise and a seal of the righteousness by faith (Rom. 4:11; Col. 2:11–12).

5. There is no illustration of law versus grace, illustrated by Hagar and Sarah (Gal. 4:21-26).

6. Finally, there is no sacrifice of Isaac, only the sacrifice of Ishmael, the "son of the slave woman," a "covenant of the flesh." Actually, in the Qur'an the name of Ishmael is not mentioned in the surah (37) in connection with this sacrifice. The only son mentioned by name in that surah is Isaac.

In summary, Abraham's story in the Qur'an includes descendants through both Ishmael and Isaac. It also contains stories of faith and commitment to monotheism as well as revelations about the power of God. But what is strikingly absent is the sacrificial role of Christ and justification by faith. It shows Islam truly as a salvation "by works."

Sayyid Qutb Themes

It's time for our second strand in this chapter highlighting the story of Abraham. This chapter relates most closely to two of our Qur'anic themes from Sayyid Qutb, numbers 5 and 16, which deal with the nature of worship and prayer in Islam.

5. Nature of Worship and Prayer in Islam—Worship: total submission to God alone. Prayer: celebrates the praise of God,

establishes a bond between a believer and his Lord, strengthens a believer's spirit, is one of the best deeds a believer can do and erases sin and error, involves regular and established daily prayer, and includes prostration and standing.

Worship and prayer are two sides of the same coin. Qutb writes that worshipping only God means complete submission only to God in all matters both now and in the life to come.[2] According to Qutb, worship means that every action should please God. Regularly established prayer celebrates God's praise and is the most perfect and complete type of worship.[3]

There are benefits to prayer. To paraphrase Qutb, prayer strengthens the spirit and sustains the heart and will to complete difficult duties. Prayer also creates a bond between God and believers. Prayer is one of the best deeds anyone can do. Therefore, it is an action that erases sin and error.[4] It makes us part of the great cycle of the universe.[5]

16. Islam—a Complete and Integrated System for Life

Qutb notes that the cornerstone of the Islamic faith is based on the principle of unity: a united universal faith as well as a unity of all prophets and messengers for all time. This unity is the backbone of Islam and legitimizes the Muslim community's claim to Abraham's legacy as the religion of God. It also unites all people in the spirit of real peace and love.[6]

Qutb reiterates that the foundation of the complete system of Islam is believing in one God. It's not just a separate belief but extends to all matters of life, including authority and morality. This cannot be fully taken in without understanding what every Muslim declares when he or she says, "I testify there is no god but God and that Muhammad is the messenger of God." All worship is only to God, as is all submission—not just during prayer but in every situation in life.[7]

Associated Qur'an Story

Continuing our chapter model of a four-stranded rope, for our third strand we have a Qur'an story dealing with the House of Worship in Islam allegedly built by Abraham and his son Ishmael. This story emphasizes the hopes of all Muslims as they see God protecting them and blessing their religion of Islam.

"The Year of the Elephant"[8]—from Surah 105 Al-Fil (The Elephant)

Our story explodes on the scene in AD 570 with Christian-background Ethiopia ruling southern Arabia through their governor Abrahah (not Abraham) in Yemen. It gives birth to Surah 105 of the Qur'an (al-Fil—the Elephant). It is a short surah (only five verses) and takes its name from the first verse.

> [1]Hast thou not seen how thy Lord dealt with the owners of the Elephant? [2]Did He not bring their stratagem to naught, [3]and send against them swarms of flying creatures, [4]which pelted them with stones of baked clay, [5]and made them like green crops devoured (by cattle)? (Surah 105:1–5)

Sixth-century polytheistic Arabia was a turbulent land. It was surrounded and dominated by foreign powers. Moving clockwise, northwest was the Eastern Roman (Byzantine) Empire. To the northeast lay the Persian Sassanid Empire, religiously Zoroastrian. Long-standing Roman–Persian wars culminated in a fifty-year peace treaty in AD 561, with tribute being paid to the Persians; the treaty broke down four years later. South of Arabia was the Ethiopian kingdom, governed from Yemen, whose control extended to southern Arabia.

Governor Abrahah wrote to the king of Ethiopia, saying he would build a magnificent church for him in Yemen (Sana). Trying to disrupt the worship practices of the polytheists, Abrahah ordered the Arabs to conduct their annual pilgrimage to his new church in Yemen rather than to their own Kaaba in Mecca. As Muslims believe this ancient sacred house was originally built by Abraham and his son Ishmael two thousand years earlier, the Qurayshi Arabs were angered and one of their tribe traveled to Yemen, relieved himself inside the church at night and then fled. This so enraged Abrahah that he swore he would march to southern Arabia and destroy the house of Mecca (*Kaaba*) stone by stone.

Abrahah gathered a large army of soldiers and many war elephants, with which he intended to pull down the Kaaba using chains. Abrahah rode in the lead, on a huge elephant named Mahmood. Arab soldiers responded to the call to defend their sacred house, but Abrahah defeated them. When Abrahah's army arrived outside Mecca, Mahmood, the elephant, refused to go further, and laid down. Abrahah's men beat the elephant, urging it to rise; the elephant refused. According to the Qur'an Allah sent birds like swallows, each carrying three small stones (one in each claw and one in the beak). The birds then pummeled Abrahah and his army. His soldiers fled in panic. Abrahah himself was severely wounded by this and died on the way back to Yemen.

According to the Islamic traditions (Hadith), Muhammad said Allah restrained the elephant from entering Mecca and protected the Kaaba. This defense of the sacred house built by Abraham and his son was one of the blessings bestowed by Allah on the Qurayshi people. This took place in the sacred Islamic month of Muharram. Fifty days later the prophet of Islam was born. That year highlights the Year of the Elephant. It reckoned times and dates in the Arabian Peninsula until the Islamic calendar was instituted in the times of Umar the second Caliph. That year still celebrates and inaugurates the hopes of all Muslims and highlights the blessings of Allah through Islam.

A New Perspective on Christianity: "Christians Believe in Three Gods"—The Trinity

We conclude this chapter by addressing one of the most tension-producing topics between Christianity and Islam: Do Christians believe in multiple gods when they believe in the Trinity? Again, what appears below is only a brief summary of this topic.

When relating to Muslims, hot issues are bound to surface. One of the most friction-producing is that Muslims see Christians as those "who ascribe partners to God." Some Muslims see these partners as Father, Son, and Holy Spirit. Others see this threesome as God, Jesus, and Mary. As a result, to all our Muslim friends we Christians are polytheists. In Islam, this is the unforgivable sin.

At those uncomfortable times our tendency is to clam up and avoid the issue. I think there is a better way: asking questions. I tried this useful question with one of my Muslim friends when this touchy topic arose:

"Which one existed first, God, His Spirit, or His Word?" My Muslim friend quickly replied, "Obviously God existed before anything else."

I followed with a comment, "That poses a problem for us. If God ever existed without His Spirit, He would be a dead God. If He ever existed without His Word, He would be a dumb God, unable to speak." My friend understood and smiled. He said, "Of course, all three had to exist at the same time." I smiled in return. (I first heard that question more than thirty years ago from a dear friend and mentor, a Lebanese pastor Rev. Fouad Elias Accad.)

For those Muslims who are seriously interested, there is a solid biblical basis for the Trinity. These all deal with the character of God and how that character is reflected in the person and works of Christ. A few passages are Matthew 28:19; John 14:16–17; Colossians 1:15-17; Hebrews 9:14; and 1 Peter 1:1–2. There are many others, starting as early as Genesis chapter 1.

It's always tempting to try and use analogies for the Trinity—such as water (as solid, liquid, and gas); egg (shell, yolk, and egg white); sun (heat, light, and plasma); the triangle; or even St. Patrick's shamrock. These are all attractive but all inherently wrong, since they lead to the heresy of modalism. Basically, the Trinity is a concept that is truly revealed and understood by God's Spirit.

I conclude with the remarks of associate pastor Haydn Lea from Queensland, Australia:

> Perhaps we must be content to admit that we cannot fully understand God's nature in our finitude. What we can understand and accept is that God exists eternally as one divine nature, substance, or essence, comprising three co-equal, co-eternal and consubstantial persons—the Father, the Son and the Holy Spirit. Each person is fully the one God, but is also distinct.[9]

Our chapter concludes with the following story.

Abraham, Jesus, and Time

During one mosque book interview an imam asked me the following: "Why is it, in Christianity that Abraham in the Old Testament of your Bible could go to God directly, but that now Christians have to go through Jesus? What is the reason for this difference?"

With a smile I replied, "There is no difference. Jesus came more than two thousand years ago. Those of us living now have to look back to what Jesus did for us on the cross. Abraham, and everyone else, had to look forward to Jesus and what he did. In fact, Jesus spoke about this very thing when he said to the Jewish leaders, 'Your father Abraham rejoiced at the thought of seeing my day; and he saw it and was glad'" (John 8:56).

I reminded the imam, "It is only we humans who are limited by time. God is above all that and exists in the past, present, and future." He grinned and agreed.

I further suggested, "In fact, I believe God has left His fingerprints in many places for our benefit. For example, Jesus's sacrifice of his life for us on the cross may even be prefigured in your Qur'an, such as Surah al-Safat 'Then We ransomed him with a tremendous victim' (momentous sacrifice – The Holy Qur'an A. Yusuf Ali) (Qur'an 37:107). I believe that this 'momentous sacrifice' provided by Allah may actually be pointing to Jesus."

A new thought for a new day. May God add His blessing to this important exchange of ideas!

Summary Questions for Reflection

1. Why do you think God made covenants (agreements) with mankind? Are they for His benefit or for ours? Does God ever break His agreements with us? Why or why not?

2. What do you think was the significance of Abraham's relationship with Melchizedek? How did it relate to the meaning of Melchizedek's name?

3. It appears impossible for two infinite and opposite contradictory forces to coexist at the same time. Try to imagine two such forces, like God's absolute justice (where every crime is punished) and God's absolute mercy (where every crime is forgiven). Imagine the tension of two ropes pulling on the corner of a tent. How have they become compatible and work together? How might this apply to our current chapter?

CHAPTER 6

JOSEPH AND THE JEWISH PEOPLE

Every human being is impacted by his or her environment and in turn impacts others. His feet may be firmly planted on earth, but his heart and soul soar through the heavens.—Sayyid Qutb[1]

"For I know the plans I have for you," declares the Lord, "plans to prosper you and not to harm you, plans to give you hope and a future." (Jer. 29:11)

Staccato of Antiaircraft Fire

We stayed with a family in the mountains overlooking Beirut. This was our first visit to Lebanon since a forced evacuation from the city eighteen years earlier. At that time, in July of 1982, we had lived through six weeks of the "Siege of West Beirut." On June 6, 1982, Israel invaded Lebanon with fifty thousand troops in Operation Peace for Galilee. Now I returned to Lebanon to attend a board meeting for a Lebanese Christian charitable organization. While here in Lebanon I was also asked to speak at the medical school of the American University of Beirut in my subspecialty of medical quality management.

About midnight we woke to the staccato of antiaircraft fire. That was a sound we hadn't heard for eighteen years. We rushed to the balcony and saw the sky lit by explosions. Israeli aircraft pounded a military unit just south of us. A few minutes later the air raid ceased and we went back inside and tried to sleep. Two hours later a similar episode occurred. Over the rest of that night two more air strikes took place. Our Lebanese friends had no sleep—they spent the night watching live television reports.

According to an Associated Press release dated February 8, 2000, 8:12 EST:

> Israeli warplanes struck across Lebanon early today, destroying three major power stations and targeting a guerrilla base in retaliation for recent Hezbollah attacks that have killed five Israeli soldiers.
>
> Fifteen civilians were reported wounded in the Israeli strikes.
>
> Large areas of Lebanon plunged into darkness because of the damage to the power grid or as a precautionary shut down of installations to protect them from further damage.
>
> The capital, Beirut, the town of Baalbek in the eastern Bekaa Valley and the cities of Sidon and Tyre in the south were blacked out for most of the night. Power was gradually restored to some areas.[2]

Next morning the tone was somber. Over breakfast, my wife and I prayed about whether or not I should go into the city proper to give my planned lecture at the medical school. We were Americans, and America was a longtime ally of Israel. How would the local population treat us? The Lord encouraged us from His Word not to live in fear. I chose to go. My wife accompanied me.

The two-hour bus ride (due to congested traffic) to the center of town gave us more time to reflect and pray. A sticker on the back of a bus seat advertised the phrase "No fear!" Driving through a Christian-predominant suburb we saw a cross painted on the side of a building. God let us know He was present.

The lecture was well attended. Afterward we stopped at a tiny diner on the street outside the school for a light lunch. The proprietor ushered us to one of his few tables. There was no electricity. Over a gas stove the owner used a candle in order to work. He was jittery and glanced at us several times as he prepared our sandwiches. After eating I got up to pay. Our host asked me in Arabic, "*Anta Yahudi*" (Are you Jewish)? I smiled and said "No!" He visibly relaxed.

We reflected on our host's obvious discomfort at the possibility of my being Jewish. Was it due only to the recent Israeli military action? Or did the animosity go deeper? Historical events, writings, and personal experiences confirm the latter.

We continue our journey into the shadow cast by the prophet of Islam by looking at the life of Joseph, the justice of God, and His involvement with the Jewish people.

Joseph: Setting the Stage

Joseph was the great-grandson of Abraham through Isaac, and the eleventh son of Jacob. He was born in Canaan/Palestine about 1916 BC and was sold into slavery in Egypt by his jealous brothers about 1898 BC when he was seventeen years old. During Egypt's Middle Kingdom Joseph may have served under the Pharaoh named Sesostris III, near the end of the 12th Dynasty.

Joseph in the Qur'an

Joseph's story in the Qur'an is found almost exclusively in the twelfth surah—Yusuf (Joseph), beginning with verse 4:

> [4]When Joseph said unto his father: O my father! Lo! I saw in a dream eleven planets and the sun and the moon, I saw them prostrating themselves unto me. [5]He said: O my dear son! Tell

not thy brethren of thy vision, lest they plot against thee. Lo!
Satan is for man an open foe. (Surah 12:4–5)

In verses 6–19 we see Joseph's jealous brothers plotting to either
kill him or permanently send him off to a distant land. They chose the
latter option and threw him into a well. They took his shirt, stained it
with animals' blood, and went weeping to their father. They said Joseph
had been killed by a wolf. Later they went back and took Joseph out
of the well. They then sold him to a passing caravan headed for Egypt.

[20]And they sold him for a low price, a number of silver coins;
and they attached no value to him. [21]And he of Egypt who
purchased him said unto his wife: Receive him honourably.
Perchance he may prove useful to us or we may adopt him
as a son. Thus we established Joseph in the land that We
might teach him the interpretation of events. And Allah was
predominant in His career, but most of mankind know not.
[22]And when he reached his prime We gave him wisdom and
knowledge. Thus We reward the good. [23]And she, in whose
house he was, asked of him an evil act. She bolted the doors
and said: Come! He said: I seek refuge in Allah! Lo! He is my
lord, who hath treated me honourably. Lo! Wrong-doers never
prosper. (Surah 12:20–23)

In verses 24–34 we see the unsuccessful plot of his owner's wife
attempting to seduce Joseph. When Joseph fled, she grabbed and tore
his shirt from the back. The back location of the ripped cloth was proof
to the husband that his wife had not told the truth. After additional
schemes she eventually had Joseph successfully imprisoned.

[35]And it seemed good to them (the men-folk) after they had
seen the signs (of his innocence) to imprison him for a time.
[36]And two young men went to prison with him. One of them

said: I dreamed that I was pressing wine. The other said: I dreamed that I was carrying upon my head bread whereof the birds were eating. Announce unto us the interpretation, for we see of those good (at interpretation). [37]He said: The food which ye are given (daily) shall not come unto you but I shall tell you the interpretation ere it cometh unto you. This is of that which my Lord hath taught me. Lo! I have forsaken the religion of folk who believe not in Allah and are disbelievers in the Hereafter. (Surah 12:35–37)

In verses 38–42 we see Joseph correctly predicting the fates of two fellow prisoners. One was restored to the king's service; the other was killed. To the rescued one Joseph asked to be remembered to the king. The surviving companion forgot, and Joseph was imprisoned for a few additional years.

In verses 43–49 Joseph interprets the king's (Pharaoh's) dream of the seven kine (cattle) and seven ears of corn and the coming years of plenty and famine.

In verses 50–53 we see Joseph inquiring of the king about the lady who wickedly tried to seduce him. She acknowledged her crime. Joseph is elevated to power.

[54]And the king said: Bring him unto me that I may attach him to my person. And when he had talked with him he said: Lo! Thou art today in our presence established and trusted. [55]He said: Set me over the storehouses of the land. Lo! I am a skilled custodian. [56]Thus gave We power to Joseph in the land. He was the owner of it where he pleased. We reach with Our mercy whom We will. We lost not the reward of the good. (Surah 12:54–56)

In verses 57–100 we see Joseph's brothers coming to Egypt to buy grain because of widespread famine. Joseph's half brothers had to deal directly with Joseph, who was in charge of Egypt's grain, but they did not recognize him. Using subterfuge Joseph induced them to return with his full brother. On their second visit to Egypt, this time accompanied by his full brother, Joseph revealed himself to them. Joseph told them not to be grieved by their past mistakes and assured them of God's forgiveness. He then told his brothers to go back to their home and bring back their father and all their possessions. His brothers went back and told their father, who had never given up hope that he (Joseph) was still alive. His brothers admitted their original sin against Joseph. They ask their father to intercede with Joseph on their behalf but do not ask Joseph directly. Reconciliation takes place.

Our story ends in verses 101–111 with Joseph's father and mother and all his brothers bowing down to him in fulfillment of his original dream. Joseph again pledges his obedience and submission to the God of the universe.

Joseph in the Bible

The Bible narration of Joseph is in the book of Genesis, chapters 37–50. Our story opens with Genesis 37:1–11. Joseph was the next-to-youngest of Jacob's twelve sons. Unfortunately, Joseph was also Jacob's favorite son, and the other brothers knew it. His father made him a special coat. Both of these facts made Joseph's brothers angry. Then Joseph had two special dreams which demonstrated his own favored status. He had to tell them to everyone. Even Jacob reproved Joseph for his prideful dreams.

In Genesis 37 Joseph's brothers had the perfect opportunity to get even with him. They threw him into a pit and sold Joseph to Midianite slave traders bound for Egypt. Then they took Joseph's special coat, dipped it in animals' blood, and showed it to their father, explaining that Joseph had been killed by a wild animal. Meanwhile, the Midianites sold him to Potiphar, the captain of Pharaoh's bodyguard. Chapter 38 has an interpolated story of another brother—Judah.

In Genesis 39 Joseph worked hard for Potiphar and was diligent. The Lord prospered Joseph, and he was promoted to be overseer of Potiphar's entire household. Potiphar's wife lusted after Joseph and unsuccessfully tried to get him to sleep with her. Joseph refused. She falsely accused Joseph before Potiphar, who had him imprisoned. Again, Joseph was diligent and God blessed him. He was put in charge of the other prisoners.

In Genesis 40 both Pharaoh's cupbearer and chief baker offended Pharaoh and were imprisoned. They had dreams which Joseph correctly interpreted. Then Pharaoh had two mysterious dreams of his own.

In Genesis 41:1–8 Pharaoh has two troubling dreams about the seven cows and the seven ears of grain. Pharaoh's wise men and magicians were unable to interpret the dreams. Joseph was brought to Pharaoh and correctly interpreted Pharaoh's dreams. He also suggested a solution to Pharaoh's dilemma. As a reward, Pharaoh put Joseph in charge of all Egypt. Joseph prepared Egypt for the coming seven years of famine.

In Genesis 42–43, back in Canaan, Jacob and his eleven sons and their families endured famine but had heard there was plenty of grain in Egypt. Jacob sent his sons twice to Egypt to purchase the needed grain.

In Genesis 44 Joseph recognized his brothers and concocted a subterfuge. He told the house steward to fill each man's sack with grain, but also to put his own special cup used for divination into the bag belonging to Benjamin, the youngest brother. When they left the city Joseph sent officials after them, accusing them of stealing his special divining cup. They were told the person responsible for the theft would remain in Egypt as Joseph's slave. The special cup was found in Benjamin's bag. Through all this Joseph forced his brothers to reflect on their much earlier crime of selling him into Egypt.

In Genesis 45–46 Joseph revealed himself to them, and then sent his brothers back to Canaan to bring their father and live permanently in Egypt. They settled in Goshen as shepherds. In Genesis 47 Pharaoh welcomed Jacob and his sons. In Genesis 48, before his death, Jacob blessed Joseph's two sons and said that from the youngest son would come "a group of nations" (v. 19). In Genesis 49 Jacob summoned his sons and gave each of them a special blessing. In Genesis 50 Joseph told his brothers of God's sovereignty and that He would work out everything for ultimate good. He also said that one day God would bring the Jews out of Egypt and go back to Canaan. It would be four hundred years before this promise of God took place.

The Shadow When the Qur'an Is Compared to the Bible

Again, what are the differences in the two accounts?

1. In the Qur'an version there is no direct repentance and asking forgiveness by Joseph's brothers for their previous crime.

2. There is also no assertion of God's absolute sovereignty over evil and His plan to work things out for ultimate good.

3. In the Qur'an version there is also no promise of a future return of the Jews to their promised land of Canaan.

4. Neither is there the promise of a "group of nations" that would come through the line of Manasseh.

5. Finally, in the Qur'an version there is no "type of Christ" seen in Joseph's life of suffering so that others might be spared.

As a recap, Joseph's story in the Qur'an includes many of the basic facts recorded in the Bible—Joseph's jealous brothers, their selling him into slavery in Egypt, his temptation to immorality by a woman, his unjust imprisonment, his ability to interpret dreams, and his rise to power in Egypt as a result. There is also his final meeting with his brothers in Egypt and the fulfillment of his original dream.

But once again there are significant omissions in the Qur'an's story. There is no direct repentance and asking forgiveness of Joseph by his brothers. There is no evidence of God working out everything for ultimate good. There is no plan for the Jewish return to Canaan and no promise of a "group of nations" that would come through the line of Manasseh. Finally, there is no "type of Christ" exemplified in the sacrificial life of Joseph.

Sayyid Qutb Themes

It is time to weave in two of our nineteen Qur'anic themes from Sayyid Qutb. The ones most closely related to the story of Joseph are numbers 10 and 12. These deal with practical Islam (family, economics, and justice as a deterrent force), as well as how to relate to people of earlier revelations, like Jews and Christians.

> 10. Social Systems in Islam: Care for the Poor, Role of Women, Justice, Economics, Marriage, Family, and Divorce (protecting the interests of weaker individuals)

In this section Qutb focuses on the importance of home, a correct view of women, marriage, family, divorce, economics, and justice. Capital punishment is seen as a deterrent force in society. Qutb affirms that men and women have equal status before God. According to Qutb, God gave mankind, both men and women, a place of honor. They have equal status in being honored by God.[3] It was God's goal to bring mankind into existence, as well as to have them populate and take care of the earth.[4]

According to Qutb, we have here the Islamic view of the home—a place of rest. Islam wants everyone's home to be a place of safety, rest, ease, and security. It was never intended to be a place of conflict.[5] Qutb states that the marriage bond is meant to be both permanent and firm.[6] He further notes that when a marriage relationship is so strained that it can no longer be maintained, there is no possibility for a happy family life; in that case it is better for the couple to separate. Islam does not bind married people with chains. It tries to maintain affection and compassion, as well as duty. But if those elements cannot cause the couple to be reconciled, it does not condemn them to a permanent life of hate and a marriage that is only superficial.[7]

In Islam, there is a restriction on the number of times divorce and remarriage to the same partner may occur; Qutb addresses this limit.[8] Qutb writes that the first divorce puts the entire marriage relationship to the test. The second divorce provides a final opportunity to reevaluate the situation before becoming final. The third divorce demonstrates the complete breakdown in the marriage and shows that continuing the relationship is untenable.[9]

Regarding economics, Qutb says that the Islamic system is based on the foundational principle that God is the creator of everything and the absolute master. A proviso of God's agreement with mankind is that every believer must look out for the welfare of each other and that they all share the benefits of what God has provided. This does not signify Marxist ownership but rather, reasonable private ownership.[10]

Regarding justice, God controls the universe and everything He does in people's lives reflects justice.[11] Qutb continues that capital punishment is a strong deterrent against the commission of further crimes.[12]

11. Relating to People of Earlier Revelations (Jews and Christians)—Islam is tolerant and does not force itself on anyone. Non-Muslims may share their faith provided that they do not try to win Muslims to their faith and not insult Islam.

Qutb discusses the major issue separating Islam from people of earlier religions (namely Jews and Christians): Christians erroneously believe in the Trinity, claiming that Jesus was God Himself.[13]

Qutb also notes that Islam is very tolerant of other faiths and does not force itself on anyone. It's OK for non-Muslims who live in a Muslim-controlled state to share their faith with others, but they must not try to convert Muslims from their faith, and they must not insult Islam. The Qur'an forbids abusing those people, but it is very clear that those who live in Muslim countries must not criticize Islam or distort its facts.[14]

Associated Qur'an Story

In weaving in the third strand of our rope for this chapter, the following story from the Qur'an emphasizes the Muslims' interaction between polytheism and monotheism and most closely concerns this chapter's theme about Joseph. Joseph also had to deal with the challenges of polytheism while relating closely to people of another religious belief.

The Prophecy of the Byzantines' Victory and "The Bet"—from
Surah 30 al-Rum (The Byzantines/Romans)

This surah has sixty verses and was revealed in Mecca. It takes its name from the first four verses:

[1]A., L., M. [2]The Romans have been defeated [3]in the nearer land, and they, after their defeat will be victorious [4]within ten years—Allah's is the command in the former case and in the latter—and in that day believers will rejoice. (Surah 30:1-4)

The Surah's theme has largely to do with time, and specifically, the end times. It also deals with the contrast between monotheism and polytheism. This story from the Qur'an is unique because it results from an actual prophecy. Here, context and timing are everything. At the time this surah was revealed, the Eastern Roman Empire, ruled from Byzantium (Constantinople or modern-day Istanbul) was crumbling. The Western Roman Empire had already ended more than a hundred years earlier when the Goths sacked Rome. The Byzantines were nominally Christian. Their major opponent was Persia, largely polytheistic.

Verse 2 speaks of the recent Persian victory at the Battle of Antioch (in Syria) over the Byzantines in AD 613. The Quraysh in Mecca were polytheistic and overjoyed with the triumph of Persia (also polytheistic) over the monotheistic Byzantines. They were especially pleased because this represented a defeat, by proxy, of the monotheistic religion preached by Muhammad in Islam.

Sayyid Qutb gives more details about our story.[15] When verse 4 of the Surah predicted a future victory by the Byzantines, "within ten years" (" within a few years" in Arabic), some of the polytheists from Mecca taunted Abu Bakr and challenged him to a bet. Abu Bakr agreed and wagered four young camels that this victory would come within seven years. When six years had gone, Abu Bakr went to Muhammad and asked him what he should do. Muhammad went to the polytheists asking them how they defined "a few years." They told him "less than ten." Muhammad then advised Abu Bakr to increase the bet and extend it for two additional years. The Qurayshi polytheists agreed. The Byzantines were indeed victorious in AD 622 and Abu Bakr won his bet. Note again the importance of timing in this Surah as well as context—the Islamic prohibition on betting did not take place for several years until after the Muslims emigrated from Mecca to Medina.

A New Perspective on Christianity: The World Jewish Conspiracy and The Protocols of the Elders of Zion

The fourth and final strand in our rope about Joseph deals with the ancient people of Egypt relating to their Jewish neighbors.[15]

Tea with Friends

While enjoying afternoon tea with a Muslim couple, my wife and I blandly discussed politics with our guests. The wife suddenly took the opportunity to practice her broken English, saying, "I love Hitler because he killed Jews. We are only sorry he didn't finish the job." Pin-drop silence. We were speechless. The husband tried to smooth things over while letting his wife know this topic was out of bounds. Was this just a chance comment? I don't think so.

Again, what appears below is only a brief summary of this topic. What follows is another root in the long-standing animosity of Muslims toward Jews—a document known as *The Protocols of the Elders of Zion*.

In his work *In the Shade of the Qur'an*, Qutb wrote that Zionism exploited atheism for its own ends and tried to destroy the foundation of human life. He said this is stated in the *Protocols of the Elders of Zion* and that Zionism's ultimate aim is to control humanity. Qutb asserted that their aim is also to destroy Islam.[16] Qutb further stated that the *Protocols* wants to strip humanity of all its values, except for those that are animal and carnal.[17]

Above, Qutb wrote about a supposedly long-standing Zionist Jewish plan whose goal is to dominate the world and ultimately destroy Islam. He also wrote that this plan is supported by a document he identified as the *Protocols of the Elders of Zion*.[18]

The *Protocols of the Elders of Zion* turns out to be a forged and plagiarized short booklet in which world Jewish leaders allegedly prepared and planned a world takeover by Jews that started three thousand years ago in the time of the Jewish King Solomon. The forgery was initiated at the start of the twentieth century with the Russian secret police in an attempt to thwart the mystical monk Rasputin and keep him from negatively influencing the Russian Tzar from making needed moderate governmental changes in policy. It's a story filled with intrigue and deception. It was debunked by the *London Times* in 1921. Unfortunately, it is still widely believed to be genuine throughout the Muslim world. Jews worldwide are portrayed as evil conspirators and plotters. It still hinders the existence of the state of Israel to this day. It fooled the American industrialist Henry Ford and was widely used by Adolph Hitler.

This chapter about Joseph ends with the following story about an imam's sermon on the justice of God.

"Allah does not believe in individuality or in tranquility, but in justice!"

On one of my research visits, my Christian friend John and I traveled two hours by car to an Indiana mosque. The massive gray onion-shaped dome on the building's top assured us we were at the right place. We were early. After an hour's wait, we met the imam in the parking lot. Wearing a tan-colored one-piece robe, he smiled warmly, shook both our hands, and welcomed us inside.

It was Ramadan, Islam's holiest month, where every Muslim fasts from all food and drink from dawn to dusk. They hospitably offered us cookies and water, which we politely declined out of respect for our hosts not being able to join us. Their Friday prayers were set to start in a few minutes. The imam said we would talk more afterward.

Along with the others we took off our shoes and entered their carpeted worship area. John and I sat on folding chairs to the side and in back of the others. This promised to be a unique visit. This was the smallest mosque attendance I had ever witnessed. Only five men were present (not counting the imam). In addition, one woman took her place behind us.

The imam made his way to the front and donned a black outer robe and a black turban for his head. These were the marks of a Muslim Shiite cleric.

Eighty-five percent of the Islamic world identify as Sunni Muslims; only about fifteen percent are Shiites. The conflict between Sunni and Shiite Islam arose after the death of the prophet of Islam, Muhammad. Most believed the Islamic leadership or Caliphate (from *Caliph*—or successor) passed from Muhammad to one of the earliest adherents to Islam, Abu Bakr. This was considered the usual pathway (or *sunnah*, in Arabic), giving rise to Sunni Islam. There were others, however, who believed the leadership should have gone to Muhammad's son-in-law Ali. These adherents were known as the party of Ali (in Arabic, the word for "party" is *shiia* or *shiiat Ali*). Today this group is known as Shiite Islam.

The Muslim call to prayer for both Sunni and Shiite Islam is nearly the same, with the exception of the frequent addition in Shiite Islam of the phrase *Wa Ali wali-Allah* (and Ali is the representative of

Allah). The prayer form itself also has frequent prostrations (standing, bending, and kneeling with forehead touching the carpet). The only obvious differences in the prayer form I could see between Sunni and Shiite Islam were slightly differing spoken phrases as well as standing with arms held down rather than folded across the chest. The actual *khutbah* in today's mosque visit also had frequent attributions to the *Imam Khomeini* (Grand Ayatollah Ruhollah Khomeini; Iran, 1902–1989).

The imam began today's sermon with, "Allah does not believe in individuality or in tranquility, but in justice!" He urged the Muslims present not to ask Allah for temporal blessings such as beauty or success. Rather, they should ask for permanent ones such as individual character. When the prayers and sermon were finished everyone greeted the imam and left the carpeted prayer area to put on their shoes and leave. The imam then sat down at a table to speak further with me and John, to complete our planned interview.

As our time drew to a close the *imam* asked a few questions about Christianity. I then asked John to tell the imam why Jesus was personal to him. He gave a God-honoring word of personal testimony. This included details of his daughter's illness, near death, and rescue by God. The imam then shared about his own wife's recent illness and death. John and I reached over to touch him and tell him how sorry we were. John prayed for him. I quoted a verse in his native language of Urdu from John 14:6, as well as leaving him with the traditional Aaronic blessing from Numbers 6:24: "The Lord bless you and keep you. . . ."

Summary Questions for Reflection

1. Other than the obvious reason of "fear," what possible reason might have existed to explain Joseph's brothers' lack of asking his forgiveness in the Qur'an? Why might the Qur'an's story have also neglected to include God's promise to the Jews of their future returning to Canaan?

2. What do you think was the significance of Abu Bakr's bet with the Byzantines in our Qur'an story recorded earlier in this chapter?

3. What do you think are the likely reasons for the modern-day effects of the *Protocols of the Elders of Zion*?

CHAPTER 7

MOSES, THE PASSOVER, AND GOD'S WRITTEN LAW

One attribute of God's is that He is the sole ruler in the cosmos. No human being can possess anything in the universe—God owns it all. This becomes the core issue of faith - the oneness of God.
—*Sayyid Qutb*[1]

By faith Moses, when he had grown up, refused to be known as the son of Pharaoh's daughter. He chose to be mistreated along with the people of God rather than to enjoy the pleasures of sin for a short time. He regarded disgrace for the sake of Christ as of greater value than the treasures of Egypt, because he was looking ahead to his reward. (Heb. 11:24 26)

O ur study of the shadow cast by the prophet of Islam continues as we look at the life of Moses and his role in the Passover and God's written law. Moses is the prophet Muhammad most liked to be compared to. Moses is also the Old Testament prophet Muslims most likened to their own prophet, since they both were lawgivers, warriors, and statesmen.

Moses: Setting the Stage

Moses lived four centuries after Joseph. He was born the son of Hebrew slaves in Egypt. To protect him from death at the hands of the Egyptians his mother placed him in a wicker basket and released him in the Nile River. Moses was rescued by Pharaoh's daughter, and was raised and educated as her adopted son. She named him Moses because "I drew him out of the water" (Exod. 2:10).

At age forty Moses killed an Egyptian for mistreating a Hebrew slave. He then fled Egypt and lived for the next forty years as a shepherd in Midian. At age eighty God appeared to Moses in a burning bush and sent him back to Egypt to rescue the Israelites from slavery. After a series of ten God-ordered, devastating plagues the pharaoh allowed the Hebrew slaves to go free. The last plague was God's angel of death passing over Egypt and killing every firstborn son in each household where lamb's blood had not been painted over the doorway as a faith response. This event has been celebrated by Jews each year since that time as the Passover. Their departure from Egypt, the Exodus, took place around 1446 BC and was probably during the rule of Amenhotep II, the seventh Pharaoh of the 18th Dynasty during Egypt's Middle Kingdom period.

Moses in the Qur'an

Unlike the story of Joseph, which is found primarily in one surah, Moses's story is retold numerous times in many different surahs. Moses is mentioned more times than any other prophet in the Qur'an and also is mentioned in the greatest number of surahs (thirty-four out of the 114). Moses's story is also singular because he is the prophet Muhammad most often liked to be identified with. Here is an example:

> [114]And verily We gave grace unto Moses and Aaron, [115]and saved them and their people from the great distress, [116]and helped them so that they became the victors. [117]and We gave them the

clear Scripture [118]and showed them the right path. [119]And We left for them among the later folk (the salutation): [120]Peace be unto Moses and Aaron! [121]Lo! Thus do We reward the good. [122]Lo! They are two of our believing slaves. (Surah 37:114–122)

We see a similar summary in Surah 32:

[23]We verily gave Moses the Scripture; so be not ye in doubt of his receiving it; and We appointed it a guidance for the Children of Israel. [24]And when they became steadfast and believed firmly in Our revelations, We appointed, from among them, leaders who guided by our command. [25]Lo! Thy Lord will judge between them on the Day of Resurrection concerning that wherein they used to differ. (Surah 32:23–25)

Because the story of Moses is found many places throughout the Qur'an, I present summaries from four of the most relevant passages, from Surahs 2, 7, 18, and 28.

Surah 2:47–73

We see the Children of Israel severely oppressed by the Egyptians. God delivered them by dividing the sea and drowning Pharaoh's army. Then God told Moses to come away for forty nights, when he received the scripture from God on Mount Tur (Sinai). During that time the people worshiped the "calf." Moses came back and rebuked them. He told them to repent and God would forgive them. The people said they would never believe until they could see God plainly. God then amazed them with thunder and lightning. God sent them manna (bread from heaven) and quail to eat and enjoy. But the people continued to rebel and sin against God. God sent a plague on the people. Then they were thirsty, and God told Moses to strike the rock. Twelve springs of water gushed up—one for each of the twelve tribes of Israel. The people continued to rebel against God, so He turned them into apes.

In response the people urged Moses to intercede to God for them again. God told them to sacrifice a yellow heifer. They did as they were commanded, but not with enthusiasm.

Surah 7:103–174

In verses 103–132 we see Moses interacting with Pharaoh by showing his miraculous signs to Pharaoh and his sorcerers. Moses threw down his staff and it became a snake. He then put his hand into his shirt. When he pulled it out it turned completely white. In a contest, Pharaoh's sorcerers did the same tricks, but Moses's snake swallowed theirs. Then the sorcerers of Pharaoh bowed down and chose to worship the God of Moses. In anger Pharaoh said he would cut off the sorcerers' hands and feet on opposite sides and have them crucified. Pharaoh said he would kill the Israelites' male children. God then promised punishment for the Egyptians.

> [133]So We sent against them the flood and the locusts and the vermin and the frogs and the blood—a succession of clear signs. But they were arrogant and became a guilty folk. [134]And when the terror fell on them they cried: O Moses! Pray for us unto thy Lord, because He hath a covenant with thee. If thou removest the terror from us we verily will trust thee and will let the Children of Israel go with thee. (Surah 7:133–134)

In verses 135–137 God blessed the Children of Israel while He drowned Pharaoh's army.

> And we brought the Children of Israel across the sea, and they came unto a people who were given up to idols which they had. They said: O Moses! Make for us a god even as they have gods. He said: Lo! Ye are a folk who know not. (Surah 7:138)

In verses 139–141 God chastised the Israelites for seeking other gods.

And when We did appoint for Moses thirty nights (of solitude), and added to them ten, and he completed the whole time appointed by his Lord of forty nights; and Moses said unto his brother, Aaron: (before he went up): Take my place among the people. Do right, and follow not the way of mischief-makers. (Surah 7:142)

In verses 143–144 Moses went up on the mountain (Mount Tur) to speak directly with God, who showed Moses His glory and told him about his assigned mission.

And We wrote for him, upon the tablets, the lesson to be drawn from all things and the explanation of all things, then (bade him): Hold it fast; and command thy people (saying): Take the better (course made clear) therein. I shall show thee the abode of evil-livers. (Surah 7:145)

In verses 146–150 God tells Moses the importance of people following His signs. While Moses was gone the people took their ornaments and made a calf's image to worship. It seemed to make a sound as wind blew through it. They worshipped it but later repented of their disobedience. When Moses came back, he was saddened by their evil. He put down the stone tablets and grabbed his brother by the hair. Aaron said, "The people made me do it."

In verses 151–160 Moses prays to God asking forgiveness for himself and his brother Aaron. Moses tells the people of God's anger at their worshipping the calf. He also said that God would forgive them if they turned to God in repentance. Moses then took up the tablets with God's commands and chose seventy of his people, then he worships God in prayer. Next Moses tells them about the coming of the prophet of Islam. Moses commands them to follow this "Prophet who can neither read nor write" whom they will find mentioned in their own scriptures (Torah). When the people were hungry and thirsty God commanded Moses to strike the rock and twelve springs of water came out for them. God gave them clouds for shade and also manna and quail to eat.

In verses 161–173 Moses rebuked the people for their rebellion and failure to properly keep the Sabbath. God turned those who rebelled into apes. Moses also reminded the people that God is forgiving and merciful. To remind the people of His power, God shook Mount Tur (Sinai) over their heads and promised to test people with both prosperity and adversity.

Surah 18:60–82

In this passage we see three seemingly unrelated stories involving Moses following a companion (named Khidr in the Islamic traditions, or Hadith). Moses asked this companion to teach him higher learning and wisdom. The companion wanted to teach Moses patience and agreed—if Moses would promise not to question any of his actions. Moses agreed.

They came first to a boat containing fishermen. Moses's companion damaged the boat so that it sank. Upset, Moses asked his companion what he was doing. Was he trying to drown the people? Being rebuked, Moses replied that he had forgotten his promise and asked to be forgiven. Next they met a young man who his companion proceeded to kill. Again Moses was upset and asked, "You just killed an innocent person. What were you thinking?" The companion again reproved Moses for questioning his actions. Finally they came to a town. Being hungry, Moses and his companion asked the inhabitants for food, but they were refused hospitality. They then saw a wall in the town about to collapse. Moses and the companion repaired the wall and went on their way. In frustration Moses asked, "Why didn't you ask them for any pay for what we did?"

Moses's companion replied, "Enough! It's time for us to part." Then the companion explained each of the three situations. In the first case, the companion said the boat could be easily fixed and the fishermen could use it for profit; otherwise, the local king would have confiscated it for himself. In the second story, the young man who was killed had been a rebellious son; God wanted to give the parents a better son later in exchange. In the final story, the wall contained a treasure belonging to two orphans who would later find it and own the treasure. These stories illustrate God's ultimate knowledge and that we should not question His ways, as Moses questioned his companion's.

Surah 28:3–46

In verses 3–28 we see Pharaoh trying to kill the Israelite male newborns. Moses, as a newborn, was put by his mother into the Nile (presumably in a water-resistant basket) in order to save his life. The wife of Pharaoh rescued the child and raised Moses as her own. Moses's birth mother was given the job of suckling the newborn. When Moses grew up he saw an Egyptian fighting with a Jew, and Moses killed the Egyptian. When his deed became known Moses fled to the land of Madyan (Midian). Moses saw two women shepherdesses trying to water their flocks but being prevented by other men. Moses intervened and the women's flocks were allowed to water. The young women asked their father to employ Moses as a shepherd. Moses stated his intention to marry one of the daughters. The father agreed if Moses promised to work for him for eight years. Moses agreed.

> [29]Then, when Moses had fulfilled the term, and was traveling with his housefolk, he saw in the distance a fire and said unto his housefolk: Bide ye (here). Lo! I see in the distance a fire; peradventure I shall bring you tidings thence, or a brand from the fire that ye may warm yourselves. [30]And when he reached it, he was called from the right side of the valley in the blessed field, from the tree: O Moses! Lo! I, even I, am Allah, the Lord of the Worlds. (Surah 28:29–30)

In verses 31–42 Moses and his brother Aaron showed the two signs of God to Pharaoh and his sorcerers (the rod becoming a snake and the hand turning white). In arrogance, Pharaoh commanded one of his chiefs to bake bricks and build him a tower tall enough so he could climb up to see Moses's god. God brought judgment on Pharaoh and drowned him and his followers in the sea.

And We verily gave the Scripture unto Moses after We had destroyed the generations of old; clear testimonies for mankind, and a guidance and a mercy, that haply they might reflect. (Surah 28:43)

In verses 44–46 we see a merciful God using Moses as one who warns future people.

Moses in the Bible

The Bible narration of Moses is found mostly in the Old Testament books of Exodus, Leviticus, Numbers and Deuteronomy. Because the story is long, I will provide a summary and include only a few of the most relevant passages.

The story begins at the end of the book of Genesis. Joseph and his extended family lived and worked and multiplied in Egypt for four hundred years. Unfortunately, most of that time was spent in slavery because the Egyptians feared the Israelites might eventually take over. The oppression was severe, and the people cried out to God for deliverance. God answered by saving an Israelite newborn. God had his mother place him in a tarred wicker basket and released it in the river. God directed the basket to the daughter of Pharaoh, who named the baby Moses and raised him as her own child.

The child grew and was educated as Egyptian royalty. As an adult, Moses killed an Egyptian who was mistreating an Israelite. When the deed became known Moses fled the wrath of Pharaoh and went into the desert. For the next forty years Moses was a shepherd for the priest of Midian. He married and had children.

One day, while tending the flock, Moses saw a burning bush that was not consumed by the fire. He went to investigate. God spoke to Moses from the burning bush.

In Exodus 3 God told Moses he would use him to rescue the Israelites from the Egyptians and then bring them out of Egypt to a land flowing with milk and honey. Moses rightly felt inadequate, but God promised him His presence for the task.

> [13]Moses said to God, "Suppose I go to the Israelites and say to them, 'The God of your fathers has sent me to you,' and they ask me, 'What is his name?' Then what shall I tell them?" [14]God said to Moses, "'I AM WHO I AM.' This is what you are to say to the Israelites: 'I AM' has sent me to you." [15]God also said to Moses, "Say to the Israelites, 'The Lord, the God of your fathers—the God of Abraham, the God of Isaac and the God of Jacob—has sent me to you.'" (Exod. 3:13–15)

In Exodus 4 God gave Moses explicit instructions where to go, what to say, and what to do. God even gave Moses two miraculous signs to show Pharaoh which would demonstrate God's power—the staff becoming a snake and his hand turning white with leprosy. Moses left and met his brother Aaron in Egypt.

> [1]Afterward Moses and Aaron went to Pharaoh and said, "This is what the Lord, the God of Israel, says: 'Let my people go, so that they may hold a festival to me in the wilderness.'" [2]Pharaoh said, "Who is the Lord, that I should obey him and let Israel go? I do not know the Lord and I will not let Israel go." (Exod. 5:1–2)

In Exodus 5:3–10:29 Moses demanded that Pharaoh allow the Israelites to go. Pharaoh refused and then made the Israelites' task of making bricks more difficult by forcing them to gather their own straw but maintain their daily quota of bricks. The Israelites were angry with Moses for their increased workload. Moses went back to Pharaoh with the same demand: to let the Israelites leave Egypt and worship God. Pharaoh continued to refuse because his heart had been hardened by God. Through Moses, God brought nine plagues that affected all Egypt—except for where the Israelites lived in Goshen. God turned all the water to blood so that all the fish died. Then there were frogs, then gnats, and then swarms of insects. This was followed by boils; then darkness; and then thunder, fire, and hail destroying the crops and livestock. Next came locusts eating all that remained.

> ¹Now the Lord had said to Moses, "I will bring one more plague on Pharaoh and on Egypt. After that, he will let you go from here, and when he does, he will drive you out completely. ²Tell the people that men and women alike are to ask their neighbors for articles of silver and gold." ³The Lord made the Egyptians favorably disposed toward the people, and Moses himself was highly regarded in Egypt by Pharaoh's officials and by the people. (Exod. 11:1–3)

The Israelites would effectively plunder the Egyptians, who were already anxious for the Israelites to leave and were afraid of the power of their god.

Now we see arguably one of the most significant events in Jewish history: the Passover. In Exodus 12:1–12 God commanded Moses to tell each Jewish family to take a one-year-old male lamb or goat on the fourteenth day of the first month of their year and sacrifice it at twilight. They were to take some of the blood and place it on the sides and top of the doorframes of their houses. They were to roast the lamb and eat it that night with bitter herbs and bread made without yeast. They were to be prepared for a quick exit from Egypt in the morning. God's Spirit was going to pass through Egypt in judgment and kill every firstborn male in each house where no blood had been painted on the doorposts—but pass over each Jewish home and leave them safe.

God brought this final plague to pass, and Pharaoh agreed to let the Israelites go. They left Egypt and took the bones of Joseph with them (as Joseph had requested at the end his life; Gen. 50:25). God went before the Israelites as a pillar of cloud by day and a pillar of fire by night to show them the way.

In Exodus 14 Pharaoh had a change of heart and chased after the Israelites. The Israelites were afraid when they saw the approaching Egyptian forces, but God protected them with a "pillar of cloud" that both hid them from the Egyptians and lit their way forward (vv. 19–20). Then God divided the waters of the Red Sea using Moses and a strong wind. All the people crossed over in safety. When the Egyptians pursued, the waters returned and drowned all of Pharaoh's forces.

In Exodus 15–19 the Israelites wandered in the wilderness while the people complained of hunger and thirst. God provided water and food for them in the form of a grain from heaven (manna) as well as quail. The people continued to grumble. Finally God brought them to Mount Sinai where He planned to give them His law. On top of Mount Sinai, in Exodus 20:1–17, God wrote the Ten Commandments in stone for Moses to take down to the Israelites.

In Exodus 21–39 God gave more details of His laws, and with His own fingers wrote His law on stone tablets. For forty days Moses was with God. God also gave Moses details of a tabernacle/tent of worship He wanted them to build, and details of the sacrifices they were to present.

During the forty days of Moses's absence, the people were afraid he wasn't coming back. They influenced Aaron to make a golden calf, which they proceeded to worship with much revelry. God told Moses to go down and confront this idolatry. Moses did and threw down and broke the stone tablets. He destroyed the golden calf and made the people eat the rubble. God brought about the deaths of many of the rebellious people.

In Exodus 40 God commanded Moses to set up the tabernacle and they prepared for worship by anointing Aaron and his two sons as priests. God gave details of how the worship was to take place. God's cloud was over the tabernacle by day and a fire by night.

After the first set of stone tablets was destroyed Moses went back up Mount Sinai and God replaced the tablets. When God instructed the Israelites to enter the promised land of Canaan, they were afraid of the people there, who looked like giants to them. Because of their rebellion, God forbid them to enter. Instead they wandered in the wilderness for the next forty years until all that previous generation who were twenty years old and up died. During those forty years Moses also disobeyed God, in an act of anger against the Israelites (Num. 20:1–13), and was told he also could not enter the Promised Land.

The book of Leviticus gives extensive details about the sacrificial system. Included here is also the basis for why sacrificial atonement is necessary. This is particularly evident in Leviticus 16 with a visual transference of sins from the people to the scapegoat—the one that took the blame. The book of Deuteronomy contains Moses's farewell speech to the Israelites forty years later as they were about to enter the land promised them by God. Moses also told the people about a special prophet God would one day send, who would bring about God's ultimate kingdom.

In Deuteronomy 18:15–18 God promised Moses that He would one day send another very special prophet, like Moses, who would tell people exactly what to do. That special prophet was identified by the New Testament writers as God's Messiah, Jesus the Christ.

> He said to them, "This is what I told you while I was still with you: Everything must be fulfilled that is written about me in the Law of Moses, the Prophets and the Psalms." (Luke 24:44)

> [22]For Moses said, "The Lord your God will raise up for you a prophet like me from among your own people; you must

listen to everything he tells you. [23]Anyone who does not listen to him will be completely cut off from among his people." [24]Indeed, all the prophets from Samuel on, as many as have spoken, have foretold these days. (Acts 3:22–24)

At the end of the book of Deuteronomy Moses died at the age of 120 and was buried by God.

The Shadow When the Qur'an Is Compared to the Bible

Moses's story in the Qur'an includes many of the basic facts recorded in the Bible. But there are six striking absences.

1. When Moses is first called by God, he is given the task of delivering the Israelites from bondage. However, Moses knows he will be asked by the Israelites who this god is who is delivering them. He wants to be able to tell them the god's name. In the Bible God distinctly tells Moses, "I am who I am. Tell them that 'I am' has sent you." In the Qur'an it is different—God simply tells Moses "I am Allah." To the ancient Israelites, the name "I am" had great significance. The Jews knew that "I am" was a reference to God. In the New Testament the name "I am" is clearly associated with Jesus. Note that when the Jews questioned Jesus about his person and authority, he used the phrase "I am." In addition, Jesus illustrated it. In the Gospel of John, Jesus used the "I am" word picture seven times:

   In John 6:48 Jesus said, "I am the bread of life."

   In John 8:12 and 9:5, "I am the light of the world."

   In John 10:7: "I am the door of the sheep."

   In John 10:11: "I am the good shepherd."

   In John 11:25: "I am the resurrection and the life."

   In John 14:6: "I am the way, the truth, and the life."

And finally, in John 15:1: "I am the true vine and my Father is the vinedresser."

In addition, in John 8:58 Jesus said, "Before Abraham was born, I am"—making His deity clear to the Pharisees. All this is missing in the Qur'an.

2. In the Qur'an there are only nine plagues that God visited on the Egyptians, but ten in the Bible. In the Qur'an the tenth plague is missing—arguably the most important plague of all: the death of the firstborn. There is no Passover, and thus no need for an atoning sacrifice.

3. Although in the Qur'an Moses did spend forty days alone with God on the mountaintop, but other than Moses being given a "book" by God there is no mention of the Ten Commandments.

4. During the forty days, in the Qur'an there is no mention of the extensive sacrificial system presented in the Bible. Other than obedience and simply asking forgiveness for sins, there is no permanent means for having sins removed.

5. In the Qur'an there is no mention of the tabernacle or the Holy of Holies. In contrast, Hebrews 9:11–14 says:

> [11]When Christ came as high priest of the good things that are already here, he went through the greater and more perfect tabernacle that is not man-made, that is to say, is not a part of this creation. [12]He did not enter by means of the blood of goats and calves; but he entered the Most Holy Place once for all by his own blood, having obtained eternal redemption. [13]The blood of goats and bulls and the ashes of a heifer sprinkled on those who are ceremonially unclean sanctify them so that they are outwardly clean. [14]How much more, then, will the blood of Christ, who through the eternal Spirit offered himself

unblemished to God, cleanse our consciences from acts that lead to death, so that we may serve the living God!

6. In the Bible there is a clear prediction of a coming prophet who the New Testament writers identified as Jesus the Messiah. This also is absent in the Qur'an.

In summary, what are the missing puzzle pieces in the Qur'an's account of Moses? There is no "I am." There is no Passover. There are no Ten Commandments. There is no sacrificial system of atonement for sins. There is no tabernacle or Holy of Holies. There is no prediction of the coming of Christ. Could the pattern revealed by this shadow be any more obvious?

Now, for our second of our four rope strands, let's examine Sayyid Qutb's "Nineteen Qur'anic themes" that are relevant to the story of Moses.

Sayyid Qutb Themes

This seventh chapter highlighting the story of Moses relates most closely to two of Qutb's nineteen Qur'anic themes, 2 and 13. These two themes deal with God's revealing Himself to mankind through His words, as well as the struggle and opposition of taking God's message throughout the world.

2. Nature of God's Revelation, and the Miraculous Nature of the Qur'an—Need to interpret the Qur'an based on the historical context and time of revelation (Progressive Revelation)

According to Qutb, the book revealed to the Muslim community (Qur'an) is God's final message to mankind. It confirmed the previous message in terms of faith and their main content. However, it is God's final message and the ruling text.[2] Islam only has one miracle that proves it is true—the Qur'an itself. The Qur'an maps an entire system for life, addressing the mind, heart, and all human needs. It is available to be read by all generations and is always valid. Qutb notes that physical miracles are available and witnessed only by one generation. Even so, most of those who see miracles fail to believe in them.[3]

13. Nature and Purpose of Jihad and its Progressive Nature Based on Time of Revelation (Greater and Lesser Jihad—God wants all people to have the opportunity to respond to the message of Islam)

In this section Qutb clarifies this threateningly relevant topic. According to Qutb, Islamic *jihad* is primarily defensive in nature, when all Islam is being threatened. However, it is also a means to guarantee that every person on earth has the privilege of responding to the message of Islam. He further stresses the progressive revelatory nature of *jihad* in response to evolving historical life situations for the early Muslim community in seventh-century Arabia that has applicability for today's world. Also central to Qutb's views on *jihad* is "freedom of belief," which he calls "man's most precious human right."[4]

Qutb notes that *jihad* began with the strict instructions that Muslims were only to fight against those who were fighting them. Muslims were not to be the aggressors.[5]

Fight in the way of Allah against those who fight against you, but begin not the hostilities. Lo! Allah loveth not aggressors. (Surah 2:190)

What about forced religious conversion? Qutb states that forcing anyone to convert religiously is the worst possible violation of human rights. It is worse than murder, regardless of how the religious conversion took place.[6] He further notes that the most basic of all human rights is freedom of belief. Any limitation to that right must be opposed, even to the point of taking life.[7]

Qutb says that later they were permitted to fight: "Sanction is given unto those who fight because they have been wronged; and Allah is indeed able to give them victory" (Surah 22:39).[7] Qutb states that this became a requirement to fight against those who fought against them, again citing Surah 2:190 (above). Qutb summarizes:

> The prophet of Islam spent more than a dozen years at first simply advocating his message and not fighting. He was not to take up arms but to forbear and be patient. Then he was given permission to leave (emigrate) and then to fight. God commanded him to fight only those who fought against him and not with those who stayed away from a fight. Later on, he was ordered to fight those who did not believe until they would submit to God.[9]

Associated Qur'an Story

The following story from the Qur'an emphasizes the absolute unity of God.

One Third of the Entire Qur'an—From Surah 112 Al-Ikhlas

[1]Say. He is Allah, the One! [2]Allah, the eternally besought of all! [3]He begetteth not, nor was begotten; [4]and there is none comparable unto Him. (Surah 112:1–4)

With only four verses this is one of the shortest surahs in the Qur'an. It is also arguably one with the greatest significance.

In the Hadith of Sahih Bukhari, one man heard another Muslim reciting this surah over and over. Dismayed by the man's actions, he complained to the prophet of Islam. Muhammad defended the man, declaring that this single surah was equal to one third of the entire Qur'an. Qutb further emphasized that this was the most fundamental principle of Islam: God's absolute oneness. He noted that this surah contains an explanation of human existence and a way of life itself. The prophet of Islam was ordered by God to declare this truth to the entire world.

Qutb explains the Arabic word used here, *ahad*. He portrays it as more precise than the usual term for "one," *wahid*. He writes that *ahad* connotes a continuous and absolute unity without any equals at all. Qutb states, in fact, that there is no real or permanent existence except for God. He further notes that this surah was so important that the prophet of Islam recited it as one of the surahs he used to start and end each day.[10]

A New Perspective on Christianity: Was Muhammad Prophesied in the Bible?

There are two major Bible passages that Muslims believe are prophecies of their own prophet Muhammad—one from the Old Testament and one from the New. In the next chapter, Chapter 8, about David and Solomon, is covered Part II of this same question—the minor/other Bible passages. Once again, what appears below is only a brief summary of this topic.

Part 1: The Major Bible Passages

The two most common Bible passages many Muslims believe refer to Muhammad appear below. Two passages lead the pack, one from the Old Testament and one from the New:

> The Lord your God will raise up for you a prophet like me from among your own brothers. You must listen to him. (Deut. 18:15)

> And I will ask the Father, and He will give you another Counselor [or, comforter] to be with you forever. (John 14:16)

It is most important to remember the adage, "A text without a context is a pretext." When we look at difficult Bible passages without examining their context, we are ripe for mistakes such as our Muslim friends make. It is so here likewise. When we examine the book of Deuteronomy as well as the New Testament Gospel of John in light of the entire Bible—and specifically, how the words "brothers" and "comforter" are overwhelmingly used—their meanings become clear.

In Deuteronomy, "brothers" signifies fellow Israelites, fellow Jews. It could not possibly mean Muhammad. For the New Testament word of "comforter" in John 14, the context also allows for only one person— one who is eternal, lives within us, and convicts the world of "sin, righteousness, and judgment": Jesus of Nazareth, God's Messiah who died on the cross and rose again from the dead three days later.

In conclusion, was Muhammad prophesied in our Bible? I would still give the same reply I first gave to my Bangladeshi friends thirty years ago. "Our Bible does have many places where a singular prophet is foretold. Would you like to look at some of those together?"

There are still other Bible passages that are less commonly referred to by Muslim apologists as being biblical prophecies of Muhammad. Even though they are not dealt with in this chapter they are still important, and we will address them in the next chapter. These include the Abrahamic covenant in Genesis 12–17; Deuteronomy 33:1–2; Isaiah 11:1–2; 21:13–15; 29:11–12; 42:1–4; and Haggai 2:7.

This chapter concludes with the following story about the importance of reading God's Word.

I've Never Read the Bible!

Between fifty and seventy-five shoeless Muslims stood shoulder to shoulder, arranged in horizontal lines. Each person faced the direction Mecca. My Christian friend Brently and I sat in the back of the mosque during this Jumah service (Friday sermon and prayers). Four complete cycles of standing, sitting, and kneeling took place. Finally, each sitting person in unison turned toward their right shoulder and said *"As-Salaamu-Alaykum"* (Peace Be upon You). They repeated this toward the left shoulder. Everyone stood up and smiled, greeted their neighbors, and the Friday service was finished.

Several people came back to greet us. One was an older Palestinian gentleman born in Lebanon—the real Lebanon, not the one in Indiana. He wanted to help with my Qur'an book project. After completing an interview he wanted to know, "Tell me, what is your overall motivation for doing this project?" I then shared my personal testimony and verse of Scripture (1 Pet. 3:18).

At the end I asked if he had ever read the Bible. He said, "No." He brightened when I mentioned an extra Arabic Injeel (New Testament) I had in my briefcase. I gave it to him. May this man read God's words of life. As Jesus said in John 6:44, "No one can come to me unless the Father who sent me draws him." May it be so!

Summary Questions for Reflection

1. What do you think is the significance of Jesus identifying himself in the Gospels with the "I am" of the Old Testament?

2. What do you think might be the significance of the Qur'an's having neglected to include the story of the Exodus Passover, Moses's house of worship/Holy of Holies, and the sacrificial system to remove people's sins?

3. Concerning the absolute unity of God, which do you think existed first: God, His Spirit, or His Word? Why do you think this question is important to discuss?

4. There is clearly a special person prophesied by God in the Bible to come who would lead all people into His truth. Most Muslims believe Muhammad was that person. But if they are not correct and Muhammad was not that person, what implications does that hold for the only other remaining candidate—the Palestinian carpenter from Nazareth?

CHAPTER 8

DAVID AND SOLOMON AND THE UNIQUE WORSHIP OF GOD

True goodness means giving something away. This means distributing money, possessions, love, effort, and yes, even one's own life if needed. A greedy person cannot be good because he wants to possess and not give to others.—Sayyid Qutb[1]

David said, "My son Solomon is young and inexperienced, and the house to be built for the Lord should be of great magnificence and fame and splendor in the sight of all the nations. Therefore I will make preparations for it." (1 Chr. 22:5)

Twenty-five years ago we spent a two-week vacation in Israel. Our rented minibus stopped at the Temple Mount, one of the holiest sites for all Jews, Christians, and Muslims. Below us was the Wailing Wall, one of the last remnants of Solomon's temple. Stone steps led up. Gazing higher we saw the ten-story gilded Dome of the Rock. This structure houses the same stone mentioned in the Bible (2 Sam. 24:16-25), as the threshing floor of Araounah later became the location of the temple, the center of Jewish worship.

Solomon's temple was destroyed twice—the first time by Nebuchadnezzar in 586 BC, and the second time by the Roman invasion of Palestine in AD 70. Over it, the Dome of the Rock was built in AD 691 by the Caliph Abd al-Malik. It is an octagonal structure 115 feet high and sixty-six feet in diameter. The golden dome has ornate tile and artwork. There are 360 degrees of surrounding Arabic calligraphy telling the story of Muhammad's Night Journey where Muslims believe he ascended into heaven.

Going inside, we encountered a huge stone surrounded by wooden scaffolding. Under the stone was a small carpet-covered prayer area. We couldn't see the stone's top surface but later saw professional photographs in the *Biblical Archaeological Review*. The photographs show a curious 1½ x 2½-cubit depression in the stone which some people think may have held the ark of the covenant. Today, under Islamic control, non-Muslims are no longer allowed access to the inside of the Dome of the Rock.

We continue our journey into the shadow cast by the prophet of Islam by looking at the lives of David and Solomon, and the worship of God.

David and Solomon: Setting the Stage

King David and his son Solomon lived approximately five hundred years after the time of Moses. David was a direct descendant of Abraham, fourteen generations down (Matt. 1:17). We also read in the Old Testament:

> In the four hundred and eightieth year after the Israelites had come out of Egypt, in the fourth year of Solomon's reign over Israel, in the month of Ziv, the second month, he began to build the temple of the Lord. (1 Kings 6:1)

Using our current system of dating, the Exodus took place in 1446 BC (see Chapter 7). Moving 480 years forward to the start of

Solomon's temple brings us to 966 BC. Solomon would have been born approximately 1000 BC, and David probably thirty to forty years earlier.

During his reign, Solomon controlled the trade routes coming out of Arabia, India, and Africa. Other major powers in the area included Africa to the south, in the 3rd Intermediate Period of Egypt, with its 21st Dynasty ruled by Pharaoh Smendes. To the north was the Phoenician Empire along the coast and the Middle Assyrian Empire. Further north, in Asia Minor, was the sunset of the ancient Hittite Empire. To the northeast was Elam (ancient pre-Iran). In Asia was the Zhou Dynasty of China and the Indus Valley Civilization. All the above took place during the early Iron Age.

David and Solomon in the Qur'an

David

David is mentioned nine times in the Qur'an. The first four passages are the most substantive. The initial one chronicles David's battle with Goliath.

> So they routed them by Allah's leave and David slew Goliath; and Allah gave him the kingdom and wisdom, and taught him of that which He willeth. And if Allah had not repelled some men by others the earth would have been corrupted. But Allah is a Lord of Kindness to (His) creatures. (Surah 2:251)

In the next two passages, both David and Solomon were given knowledge and other special abilities, such as understanding the language of birds.

> [78]And David and Solomon, when they gave judgment concerning the field, when people's sheep had strayed and browsed therein by night; and We were witnesses to their

judgment. [79]And We made Solomon to understand (the case); and unto each of them We gave judgment and knowledge. And We subdued the hills and the birds to hymn (His) praise along with David. We were the doers (thereof). [80]And We taught him the art of making garments (of mail) to protect you in your daring. Are ye then thankful? (Surah 21:78–80)

[10]And assuredly We gave David grace from Us, (saying): O ye hills and ye birds, echo his psalms of praise! And We made the iron supple unto him. [11]Saying: Make thou long coats of mail and measure the links (thereof). And do ye right. Lo! I am Seer of what ye do. (Surah 34:10–11)

A fourth passage shows David settling a dispute between two brothers. The details of the story are very similar to one told in the Bible following King David's sin with Bathsheba (see 2 Samuel 11–12). In this story (Surah 38:17–26) David hears the case of two brothers arguing. One brother had ninety-nine ewes and the other only one. The brother with the ninety-nine demanded the single one. David understood that God had used this story to convict him of his own sin in life.

The other five passages only briefly mention David. Two of the five show David being given the Psalms by God (Surahs 4:163; 17:55). One has David cursing those who lacked true faith (Surah 5:81). Another has David being given knowledge by God (Surah 27:15). The final passage shows David given grace and the ability to make chain armor (Surah 34:10–11).

Solomon

In the Qur'an God gave Solomon wisdom but also supernatural powers, such being able to interpret the language of birds and power over the *jinn* (spirits).

⁸¹ And unto Solomon (We subdued) the wind in its raging. It set by his command toward the land which We had blessed. And of everything We are aware. ⁸²And of the evil ones (subdued We unto him) some who dived (for pearls) for him and did other work, and We were warders unto them. (Surah 21:81–82)

In the next passage we see the story of the ants, the hoopoe bird, and the transported throne of the Queen of Sheba (Surah 27:15–44). Solomon interacts with the animals and wonders where the hoopoe bird is. He then sends a letter to the Queen of Sheba in Yemen, telling her of the wonders of Islam. The Queen of Sheba took presents to Solomon but had a magnificent throne which she tried to keep secret from Solomon. Solomon had one of his spirit beings (*jinn/ifrit*) magically transport it from Yemen to Jerusalem. This amazed the Queen of Sheba and resulted in her submission to God in Islam. (More details of this story are given in our Associated Qur'an Story at the end of this chapter.)

Next we see Solomon's power over the wind and his being able to travel with it. We also see the death of Solomon finally being made known by the destructive power of a simple worm.

¹²And unto Solomon (We gave) the wind, whereof the morning course was a month's journey and the evening course a month's journey, and We caused the fount of copper to gush forth for him, and (We gave him) certain of the jinn who worked before him by permission of his Lord. And such of them as deviated from Our command, then We caused to taste the punishment of flaming Fire. ¹³They made for him what he willed: synagogues and statues, basins like wells and boilers built into the ground. Give thanks, O House of David! Few of My bondmen are thankful. ¹⁴And when We decreed for him, nothing showed his death to them save a creeping creature of the earth which gnawed away his staff. And when he fell the jinn saw clearly how,

if they had known the Unseen, they would not have continued in despised toil. (Surah 34:12–14)

David and Solomon in the Bible

David

In the Bible, the story of David begins in 1 Samuel 16 and extends through 1 Kings 2. Parts of the story are also contained in the book of 1 Chronicles. Our narration starts with the prophet Samuel being commanded by God to anoint a new king over Israel, after King Saul's disobedience toward God. Samuel went to the family of Jesse, who had eight sons. David, the youngest son, was chosen and anointed.

David's fame was launched by his duel with the Philistine giant Goliath.

> [48]As the Philistine moved closer to attack him, David ran quickly toward the battle line to meet him. [49]Reaching into his bag and taking out a stone, he slung it and struck the Philistine on the forehead. The stone sank into his forehead, and he fell face down on the ground. [50]So David triumphed over the Philistine with a sling and a stone; without a sword in his hand he struck down the Philistine and killed him. (1 Sam. 17:48–50)

David's importance in the Israelite kingdom continued to grow and prosper. At the same time, Saul's popularity declined. Saul's jealousy turned to hatred and an increasing desire to pursue and kill David. But God's Spirit protected David. At one point David had the opportunity to kill his adversary Saul but refused out of respect for the Lord's "anointed."

For a number of years Saul's jealousy drove him to pursue David unsuccessfully (1 Sam. 18–31). Finally, in a battle with their enemies, the Philistines killed Saul and his sons. David was then crowned king of Israel.

Over the next years God established David's rule in Jerusalem (2 Sam. 1–6) and gave him wives as well as sons and daughters. Then we see David's desire to build a special temple to God's honor and glory. Through Nathan the prophet, God communicates to David that he is not the one to build the temple; this job God plans for David's son Solomon. God does promise to establish David's lineage in a permanent everlasting kingdom.

Over the next forty years God gave David more wives and sons and daughters. Some of David's sons rebelled, resulting in more treachery, warfare, and bloodshed. David is also famed for his devotion to God. Most of the Psalms are attributed to his authorship.

> [10]Then David rested with his fathers and was buried in the City of David. [11]He had reigned forty years over Israel—seven years in Hebron and thirty-three in Jerusalem. [12]So Solomon sat on the throne of his father David, and his rule was firmly established. (1 Kings 2:10–12)

Jesus the Messiah connected himself with King David when he asked the religious leaders a question:

> [41]While the Pharisees were gathered together, Jesus asked them, [42]"What do you think about the Christ? Whose son is he?" "The son of David," they replied. [43]He said to them, "How is it then that David, speaking by the Spirit, calls him 'Lord'? For he says, [44]"'The Lord said to my Lord. "Sit at my right hand until I put your enemies under your feet."' [45]If then David calls him 'Lord,' how can he be his son?" [46]No one could say a word in reply, and from that day on no one dared to ask him any more questions. (Matt. 22:41–46)

Solomon

The story of Solomon starts with 1 Kings 1 and flows through chapter 11; it is also contained at the end of 1 Chronicles and continues into 2 Chronicles. God gave Solomon riches, wealth, wisdom, insight, understanding, and peace. From 1 Kings 4 we see that Solomon was known as the wisest person of the east, including Egypt. He was known far and wide for his thousands of proverbs, as well as songs and extensive knowledge of botany and zoology. People came from many surrounding nations just to hear his wisdom. God also gave Solomon the task of building His temple, in preference to his father David. From 1 Kings 6 we know that the foundation of the temple alone took Solomon four years to build, then seven more years to build the temple proper.

Solomon's story includes an encounter with the Queen of Sheba in 1 Kings 10 and her traveling to Solomon to test his knowledge. She was so impressed by what she found that she gave him large gifts of gold, precious gems, and spices.

King Solomon's fame and political influence continued to spread far and wide. In 1 Kings 10 we see Solomon's great wisdom and riches as well as fourteen hundred chariots and twelve thousand horses. He was so rich that silver was considered as common as stones and cedar was as common as trees.

> [41]As for the other events of Solomon's reign—all he did and the wisdom he displayed—are they not written in the book of the annals of Solomon? [42]Solomon reigned in Jerusalem over all Israel forty years. [43]Then he rested with his ancestors and was buried in the city of David his father. And Rehoboam his son succeeded him as king. (1 Kings 11:41–43)

The authorship of three books of the Bible is attributed to Solomon—Proverbs, Ecclesiastes, and the Song of Solomon.

The Shadow When the Qur'an Is Compared to the Bible

When comparing the Bible and Qur'an renditions of David and Solomon, what is notably absent from the Qur'an?

1. There is no evidence of King Saul's enmity for David (Talut in the Qur'an is Saul). This resulted in David's repeated flights from Saul and his struggles for survival that lasted for years. It also resulted in Saul's losing his kingship and David's establishing his own lineage.

2. There is no evidence of David's concern and respect for God's "anointed."

3. There is no evidence of David's or Solomon's involvement in building God's temple. This extensive and meaningful structure was central to all of God's worship by the Israelites, as well as their means of paying for sin through animal sacrifice.

4. In the Qur'an there is no evidence of Jesus the Messiah's connection with King David.

5. And finally, in the Qur'an there is no evidence of God's purpose in using David's lineage to establish a permanent everlasting kingdom.

In summary, it is clear that God's "anointed" is more than merely a physical king. He also represents more than just a physical temple. This "anointed" individual will also be the means for permanently eradicating sin. Isn't it interesting that the word *messiah* in Hebrew and *masih* in Arabic both mean "anointed one?"

Now let's examine two of the key Sayyid Qutb Nineteen Qur'anic themes that are relevant to the story of David and Solomon.

Sayyid Qutb Themes

This chapter about David and Solomon relates most closely to two of Qutb's nineteen Qur'anic themes, 9 and 19, dealing with the supernatural in Islam as well as the importance of poetry and art.

9. Nature of the Supernatural in Islam (Angels, Jinn, Heaven, Hell, and Miracles)

In this section Qutb discusses the nature of the supernatural in Islam, which includes angels, *jinn* (spirits), heaven, hell, and miracles. According to Qutb, belief in angels and the spiritual world is what differentiates man from animals. Animals view the world via the senses and instinct whereas man sees a world beyond.[2]

Qutb believes that angels are another type of God's creation with specific characteristics and jobs. We only know about angels what God has already told us.[3] Paraphrasing Qutb, the nature of the *jinn* (demons), like *Iblis* (Satan) and his offspring being totally given to evil, remains unknown to us, except for what God tells us through the Qur'an and Hadith. On this basis we know that the *jinn* were created from fire and can live on the earth's surface, or even outside the earth. They move faster than humans. Also, some of them are good believers and some totally disbelieve. They can see humans, but humans cannot see them in their original forms. They can also tempt believers to stray but have no real power over true believers. A *jinn* stays around a believer, but when that believer remembers God, the *jinn* leaves. When a believer is focused on worldly matters, the *jinn* can tempt him. All demonic plots are ineffective when a believer reminds himself of God. Just like humans, the *jinn* will be resurrected and face judgment before God. They are either rewarded with heaven or punished in hell. Compared to angels, *jinn* are very weak and powerless.[4]

Also, according to Qutb, the key to understanding all evil is that Satan makes bad deeds look good.[5]

Qutb also compares heaven and hell. According to Qutb, heaven is a place of total and everlasting comfort with shade and fruit. This is in contrast with the suffering of unbelievers. Each of these, however (comfort, shade, and fruit vs. suffering), is the correct destiny of both groups.[6] The fire of hell is huge enough to hold all its inhabitants. Here they are captured and there is no hope of escape. There is no cool air to breathe and no chance to minimize their suffering. If they call out for help, they are given dirty water to drink—others describe it as "boiling oil." If anyone's face comes near it, their face will be burned. What do you think it will do to a person's throat or stomach if they attempt to drink it?[7]

Islam readily acknowledges the existence of miracles. However, Qutb highlights that in Islam there is an even greater miracle: the existence of the Qur'an itself. Qutb notes that the message of Islam was designed by God to be available to all communities and all times. It was never intended for only a particular group or location. God made the Qur'an His miracle. A physical miracle impresses the local audience, but is only a part of history. In contrast, the miracle of the Qur'an is still present more than thirteen centuries later.[8]

19. Islamic Views of Poetry and Art—OK when looking at life from an Islamic viewpoint and to achieve an Islamic objective

In Islam, both poetry and art are intimately associated with King Solomon. Here Qutb deals with an apparent contradictory question: Are poetry and art permissible in Islamic society? On the surface, the answer appears to be "No!"—especially in light of some of the disappointing experiences the prophet of Islam experienced with other artists and poets, especially those coming from pre-Islamic Arabia.

According to Qutb, poets (artists too) follow their own emotions and desires and have no clear objective. It's whatever strikes their fancy at the time. They live in a world of their own imagination. In contrast, Islam wants people to face the facts of life and for their dreams to become a reality. Islam changes all feelings in such a way that they work together to produce a perfect model for the world.[9]

But Qutb looks deeper at this question. According to Qutb, Islam does not prohibit all of poetry and art, as some people seem to think. It only prohibits poetry and art that give way completely to emotions, desires, and fanciful dreams. Poetry and art are permissible when they support and encourage the noble feelings and practice of Islam.[10]

Associated Qur'an Story

A third strand from our rope includes the following story from the Qur'an Surah 27—the Ant. We have already alluded to this story earlier in the chapter.

Solomon, the Hoopoe, and the Queen of Sheba: A Story of Knowledge beyond Our Perception —from Surah 27 Al-Naml (the Ant)

This surah has ninety-three verses believed to be revealed in Mecca. It gets its name from verse 18:

Till, when they reached the Valley of Ants, an ant exclaimed: O ants! Enter your dwellings lest Solomon and his armies crush you, unperceiving.

Qutb says this surah highlights knowledge, particularly that which lies beyond the reach of our normal perception and known only to God.[11] However, sometimes God gives this special knowledge to some of His servants, like King David and his son Solomon. For example, Solomon was taught by God the language of the birds and how to control the *jinn* (spirits). This story begins with verses 15–16 of the surah:

[15]And We verily gave knowledge unto David and Solomon, and they both said: Praise be to Allah, Who hath preferred us above many of His believing slaves! [16]And Solomon was David's heir. And he said: O mankind! Lo! We have been taught the language of birds, and have been given (abundance) of all things. This surely is evident favour.

Our current story focuses on Solomon's interaction with the *jinn*, the hoopoe, and the Queen of Sheba. The hoopoe is a bright-colored bird with a fan-like crest on its head. Qutb reminds us that the *jinn* are spirits created by God from fire. They can see humans but we cannot see them.

One day Solomon's large retinue of animals and birds and *jinn* were gathered before his court. We continue from verse 17:

> [17]And there were gathered together unto Solomon his armies of the jinn and humankind, and of the birds, and they were set in battle order.

But the hoopoe was missing and Solomon was upset:

> [20]And he sought among the birds and said: How is it that I see not the hoopoe, or is he among the absent? [21]I verily will punish him with hard punishment or I verily will slay him, or he verily shall bring me a plain excuse. (Surah 27:20-21)

Later the hoopoe came in and explained its absence in verses 22–23:

> [22]But he was not long in coming, and he said: I have found out (a thing) that thou apprehendest not, and I come unto thee from Sheba with sure tidings. [23]Lo! I found a woman ruling over them, and she hath been given (abundance) of all things, and hers is a mighty throne.

The hoopoe told Solomon that this queen (of Sheba) and her people worshipped the sun. Solomon then prepared a special letter for the queen, demanding that she and all her people should repent and worship only the one true God (in Islam). Solomon sent this letter with the hoopoe, which delivered it to the queen. Immediately she agreed with the command and ordered all her people to stop worshipping the sun and from then on worship only God.

According to our Qur'an story, the queen wanted to placate King Solomon and sent him many presents, but she desired to keep her own magnificent throne locked away and hidden from him. Solomon heard about the throne and was angry at the gifts, returning them.

Then the queen and some of her court traveled to Solomon to declare her allegiance openly to God alone. Before the queen arrived, Solomon wanted to impress her. He asked his own retinue:

> He said: "O chiefs! Which of you will bring me her throne before they come unto me, surrendering?" (Surah 27:38)

One of the *jinn*, who boasted of his own strength, promised to bring it within a few hours (v. 39) but this was not quick enough for Solomon. Another one who said he had knowledge of the book was able to transport the queen's throne in the blink of an eye (v. 40) and brought it before Solomon. The symbolism here is that spiritual knowledge is more important than physical strength.

The queen entered Solomon's palace, whose floor was transparent. She was extremely impressed by all she saw and experience. She responded in verse 44:

> [44]It was said unto her: Enter the hall. And when she saw it, she deemed it a pool and bared her legs. (Solomon) said: Lo! It is a hall, made smooth, of glass. She said: My Lord! Lo! I have wronged myself, and I surrender with Solomon unto Allah, the Lord of the Worlds.

We now move to the final strand in this chapter's rope. This is the second part of the topic we covered in chapter 7, when we examined the major Bible passages of Deuteronomy 18:15 and John 14:16 that Muslims traditionally use when they think that their prophet must have been prophesied in our Christian Bible. In this chapter we look at Part 2 of that same question, but this time look at the minor Bible passages Muslim apologists normally refer to in evaluating that same question.

A New Perspective on Christianity: Was Muhammad Prophesied in the Bible?

(Part 2: The Minor Bible Passages)

We had referred to other Bible passages in the previous chapter that are less commonly referred to by Muslim apologists as being biblical prophecies of Muhammad. These include the Abrahamic covenant in Genesis 12–17, as well as Deuteronomy 33:1–2; Isaiah 11:1–2; 21:13–15; 29:11–12; 42:1–4; and Haggai 2:7. Thorough examination of each of these passages—looking at the context in light of the entire Bible—reveals that only one person was able to fulfill them. And that person was not Muhammad, the prophet of Islam.

I end this chapter with the following story about a dream and asking God for the desires of your heart, just as Solomon did in 2 Chronicles 1:7–13.

If God Came to You in a Dream and Said You Could Ask Him for Anything, What Would You Ask For?

We had an outdoor barbecue with a few of my son's Middle Eastern friends. Drinking tea following the meal I posed the following question: "If God came to you in a dream and said you could ask Him for anything, what would you ask?"

Without hesitation, a friend from Saudi Arabia gave a single word "heaven." Another Saudi friend said, "to be accepted by God." The third young man came from a poor region of Iran. He said, "I'd like a chunk of change—maybe a million dollars."

I next asked my wife for her answer. Referring back to the first man's saying "heaven," she said, "Since heaven is already secure for me, I'd ask for wisdom in helping others." My son added, "Since heaven is also secure for me, I'd ask God to make it secure for others."

Summary Questions for Reflection

1. The focus of this chapter, as well as the fulfillment of prophecy, centers on a special person known as God's "anointed." What do you think is the significance that the Hebrew word for "anointed" is *Moshiach*, and in Arabic *Masih*—and that both are translated into English as "Messiah"?

2. Who do you think God values more: an individual with extra spiritual knowledge (like Solomon) or someone with extra spiritual character (like David)? And why? Which person do you think has a greater influence on the lives of future generations?

3. What might be the spiritual significance of being a son of the bondwoman compared to the son of the freewoman? How might that influence inheritance laws?

CHAPTER 9

JONAH, JUDGMENT, AND GOD'S COMPASSION FOR THE LOST

In any community whenever a heart of faith combines with a desire to work, that individual inherits the land. When those two elements separate, an imbalance is created and despotic oppression results.—Sayyid Qutb[1]

For as Jonah was three days and three nights in the belly of a huge fish, so the Son of Man will be three days and three nights in the heart of the earth. (Matt. 12:40)

Mercy on the Day of Judgment

Discussing compassion with an African friend, we looked at this Bible passage from Lamentations 3:22–23: "Because of the Lord's great love we are not consumed, for his compassions never fail. They are new every morning; great is your faithfulness." My friend went on to explain the importance of showing mercy on Judgment Day: "Allah will say, 'I was hungry and you did not feed me. I was thirsty and you gave me nothing to drink. I was sick and you didn't take care of me,'" he told me.

That opened a door for me to share with him the words of Jesus, who said much the same thing in the *Injeel* (New Testament). He wanted to look at it. Together we read Matthew 25:31–46, the parable of separating the sheep from the goats on Judgment Day. My friend laughed in both amazement and pleasure at the words of Jesus.

Continuing to pursue the shadow cast by the prophet of Islam, we look at the life of Jonah and God's compassion on lost souls.

Jonah: Setting the Stage

Jonah lived in the village of Gath-Hepher in Galilee (2 Kings 14:25). This story took place during the reign of King Jeroboam, of the northern kingdom of Israel. Our story centers on the Assyrians—longtime enemies of the Jews. For many years the hated Assyrians had oppressed and mistreated Jonah's Jewish people. In 760 BC Jonah was ordered by God to go to the capital of the Assyrian Empire, Nineveh, telling them to repent of their wickedness or be destroyed. Nineveh was located on the east bank of the Tigris River, near modern-day Mosul in southern Iraq. Jonah refused to go and help this hated enemy of his people. He was afraid they might indeed repent and that God would forgive them. Jonah wanted to see them destroyed. So he fled by ship to Tarshish, a Phoenician port on the coast of southern Spain at the western end of the Mediterranean Sea. God pursued Jonah and had him swallowed by a huge fish (possibly a whale). Once Jonah had repented of his attitude, God ordered him again to go to Nineveh; this time he went. The entire city repented of its evil ways and was spared by God. Even so, one hundred and fifty years later, in 612 BC Nineveh was destroyed by the invading Babylonians and Medes, who toppled the Assyrian Empire.

At the time of Jonah, the Assyrian Empire was at the height of its power. The Etruscan civilization was in Italy. Greece had just celebrated the first Olympiad in 776 BC and Egypt was ruled by the Kushites from the south (modern-day Sudan) during the 25th Egyptian Dynasty.

Our journey into the shadows continues with the Qur'an and Bible versions of the story of Jonah.

Jonah in the Qur'an

Jonah appears in the Qur'an six times. In five surahs he is mentioned briefly. The longest and most detailed account is below.

> [139]And Lo! Jonah verily was of those sent (to warn). [140]When he fled into the laden ship, [141]And then drew lots and was of those rejected; [142]And the fish swallowed him while he was blameworthy; [143]and had he not been one of those who glorify (Allah) [144]he would have tarried in its belly till the day when they are raised; [145]Then We cast him on a desert shore while he was sick; [146]and We caused a tree of gourd to grow above him: [147]And We sent him to a hundred thousand (folk) or more [148]and they believed; therefore We gave them comfort for a while. (Surah 37:139–148)

Jonah in the Bible

In the Bible, our story comprises the entire book of Jonah, with four chapters and forty-eight verses. Jonah is also referred to by Jesus in the New Testament.

In the first chapter we are introduced to Jonah when God commanded him to go to the capital city of the Assyrian Empire and preach to it about its wickedness. Fleeing from God, Jonah went the other direction, getting on a ship bound for the western end of the Mediterranean. God then brought about a great storm that was about to sink the ship. Jettisoning the ship's cargo, the desperate sailors cast lots in an attempt to find out who was responsible for this disaster. The lot fell on Jonah. Jonah admitted his guilt. He said the only solution was to throw him bodily into the sea, which the sailors did; the sea calmed in response. God then provided a large fish (possibly a whale) that swallowed Jonah. Jonah was inside the fish for three days and three nights.

The significance of Jonah's being inside the fish for three days and three nights was a prefiguring of what would one day happen to God's Messiah. In Matthew 12:39 Jesus told the religious leaders that this was the "sign of Jonah." He said this sign pointed to His own death on the cross and resurrection three days later.

In Jonah 2, the prophet prayed to God and cried out for help. God answered and had the fish vomit Jonah onto dry land.

In the third chapter, God's command to go to Nineveh came a second time. This time Jonah obeyed. Nineveh was huge—it took three days to cross the city. Jonah preached God's message. The whole city believed and fasted before God. The king of Nineveh and all the people repented of their evil deeds, and God spared them.

In Chapter 4 Jonah waited outside Nineveh, hoping the city might be destroyed. He was in the hot sun and God caused a plant to grow and provide him with shade. Jonah complained to God because He had decided not to destroy the Ninevites. Then God caused a worm to destroy the shading plant—then Jonah complained because his shade was gone. God asked Jonah if it was right for him to complain about the fate of the plant. Jonah replied, ""It is," he said. "And I'm so angry I wish I were dead" (Jonah 4:9). The book ends with God's response to Jonah in verses 10–11:

> [10]But the Lord said, "You have been concerned about this plant, though you did not tend it or make it grow. It sprang up overnight and died overnight. [11]And should I not have concern for the great city of Nineveh, in which there are more than a hundred and twenty thousand people who cannot tell their right hand from their left—and also many animals?"

The Shadow When the Qur'an Is Compared to the Bible

There are many similarities in the two stories. In both, Jonah flees from God's command and is swallowed by a large fish. Jonah prayed to God for forgiveness. God answered and caused the fish to vomit Jonah onto dry land. Jonah went and preached to a large city as God commanded. The people repented and God relented from destroying the city.

However, the differences in the two versions are striking. To begin with, in the Qur'an there is no specific mention of the time Jonah would spend inside the fish. According to the Qur'an, the length of time was contingent on Jonah's repentance. If he failed to repent, his confinement could have lasted until the Day of Judgment (Qur'an 37:144). In the Bible, although Jonah's release was timed with his repentance, it was prefigured by God to correspond with Jesus's future death and resurrection: "For as Jonah was three days and three nights in the belly of a huge fish, so the Son of Man will be three days and three nights in the heart of the earth" (Matt. 12:40).

The next major difference dealt with the shade plant God caused to grow. In the Qur'an, its purpose was to help Jonah recover from his ordeal inside the fish. In the Bible, its purpose was to help Jonah understand God's compassion for lost people.

In summary, what are the shadows in the Qur'an's story of Jonah when compared to the Bible? In the Qur'an the focus is on Jonah's repentance and not on his understanding of God's compassion for the lost. Most important, in the Qur'an there is no connection with Jesus the Messiah's future death on the cross and resurrection three days later. Yes, there is light from the sun. But there is also shadow which partially obscures the sun.

Sayyid Qutb Themes

Now for our next rope strand: Sayyid Qutb's nineteen Qur'anic themes. The theme most relevant to the story of Jonah deals with God's message of judgment.

4. God's Messengers and a Unified Message for All Mankind—
Fear God, Worship Him Alone, and Obey His Messengers

According to Qutb, God sent to every community a messenger
with a unified message. This message was not for one group of people
only. Nor was it for a specific time in history. Rather, it was a message
for all humankind and for all time. Failure to heed God's messengers
and failure to believe in God's message results in God's judgment and
destruction. He quotes from the Qur'an:

> And for every nation there is a messenger. And when their
> messenger cometh (on the Day of Judgment) it will be judged
> between them fairly, and they will not be wronged. (Surah 10:47)

According to Qutb, the Islamic faith is a declaration of freedom for
all people—freedom from serving other creatures (including man himself
and his own desires). Islam declares that all godhead and lordship in the
universe belong only to God. Islam was not just a message for the Arabs
but for all humans. It frees them from having to serve anyone else.[2]

According to Qutb, the message of Islam is the same one given by
all of God's messengers: to fear God alone and obey His messenger. In
each generation, all people demanded to be shown a miracle by the
messenger proving that he (the messenger) was from God.[3]

With that, we come to the third strand in our rope—a unique story
from the Qur'an that involves nonviolent confrontation of those who
oppose you.

Associated Qur'an Story

The Treaty of Al-Hudaybiyyah—from Surah 48 Al-Fath (the Victory)

This surah was revealed in Medina and has twenty-nine verses. It takes
its name from the first verse:

> Lo! We have given thee (O Muhammad) a signal victory.
> (Surah 48:1)

Our Qur'an story begins with Muhammad having a dream.[4] He saw himself entering Mecca and performing *tawaf* (circumambulating the sacred Kabah). Accompanying him were companions, some with heads shaved and others with hair shortened. When Muhammad related his dream, his friends rejoiced. As a result of the dream, he and fourteen hundred other Muslims traveled to Mecca in AD 628. At that time, the Qurayshi people of Mecca were at war with Muhammad and his fellow Muslims. But Muhammad did not come prepared for war. Instead, he brought sacrificial camels. Muhammad and the other Muslims intended to worship.

Muhammad's riding camel suddenly sat down and refused to go further. The location was a well at al-Hudaybiyyah, on the western edge of Mecca. Muhammad concluded God wanted them to stop there. But the well only provided minimal water and soon ran dry. He put his hands into the well, and suddenly there was enough water to satisfy the needs of his entire group.

From here, Muhammad sent four successive emissaries into Mecca asking permission to peacefully perform their worship at the Kabah. Each emissary was rebuffed and treated roughly. Finally, he sent one of his companions, Uthman. Uthman failed to return. After several weeks a rumor spread that he had been killed. In response, Muhammad and his entire fourteen hundred made a severe pledge: there at al-Hudaybiyyah, they vowed to fight to the death until they could freely worship in Mecca. In Islamic history books this pledge is known as *Bayat al-Ridwan* (the Pledge Earning God's Pleasure). This is recorded in verses 18–19:

> [18]Allah was well-pleased with the believers when they swore allegiance unto thee beneath the tree, and He knew what was in their hearts, and He sent down peace of reassurance on them, and hath rewarded them with a near victory; [19]and much booty that they will capture. Allah is ever Mighty, Wise. (Surah 48:18-19)

Uthman was not killed. He had only been imprisoned and was later allowed to return. However, when the Qurayshis of Mecca heard about the special pledge and saw the determination of Muhammad and his followers they lost heart. They sued for peace. Muhammad quickly accepted their terms. An agreement was drawn up and signed, the Treaty of al-Hudaybiyyah, which allowed for free and safe access for Muslims to come and worship at the Kabah. They agreed that the peace treaty was to last for ten years.

Two years after this famous treaty, Mecca peacefully surrendered to Muhammad and to the religion of Islam.

The Treaty of al-Hudaybiyyah has always been seen by Muslims as a major turning point in Islamic history. Qutb further notes that it is a tangible witness that Islam did not always spread by means of the sword, as is commonly believed by those who are not Muslims.

This chapter's story on Jonah showcases God's heart of compassion for a lost group of people—a truth foundational to the Christian faith. This gives rise to our fourth interwoven rope strand as we explore another new perspective on Christianity

A New Perspective on Christianity: Emperor Constantine and the Council of Nicaea

The First Council of Nicaea was an ecclesiastical gathering in AD 325, highlighting truths foundational to the Christian faith. These truths were restated and reaffirmed at the time of the Emperor Constantine. What actually did and did not take place at this important meeting is often misunderstood and a source of potential friction between Muslims and Christians. Referring to the First Nicene Council, Qutb wrote:

> Constantine, the Roman Emperor, held one of three famous synods, attended by 2,170 bishops. They differed a great deal about Jesus. Each group expressed a certain view. Some said that he was God who descended to earth in person, giving life to whomever He willed and caused others to die, before returning

to heaven. Some said that he was God's son, while others claimed that he was one of the three entities forming the Godhead: the Father, the Son and the Holy Spirit. A different group claimed that he was one of three deities: God was one, Jesus another and his mother the third. However, another group said that Jesus was God's servant, messenger, spirit and word. Others made yet different claims. All in all, no more than 308 agreed on any one view. The Emperor decided to support that view, expelling all those who did not agree, and persecuting those who opposed it, particularly those who advocated God's oneness.[5]

Some errors need correction. First, Constantine only presided over one of the seven "ecumenical" synods or councils (not three, as listed by Qutb), the first one in AD 325. The next of the seven church councils took place in Constantinople in AD 381. The last of the seven was slightly more than four hundred years later in AD 787, but also in Nicaea. Second, there were not "2,170 bishops" in attendance but only 318. Qutb did get one thing right: the major reason for this first council was to clarify the misunderstanding about the relationship of Jesus Christ to God, the Father.

Consulting the actual records of the minutes taken of the First Council of Nicaea by the respected church historian Eusebius, what actually did and did not take place was discussed and binding decisions were made. The relationship of Jesus Christ to God the Father was reaffirmed in the Nicene Creed and restated in the more modern Apostles' Creed. Note that the deity of Christ had never been in doubt; that was already firmly believed and taught from the first century AD. The two other agenda topics discussed by his council was setting the official date of Easter, and firming up various church doctrinal issues such as forbidding self-made eunuchs, hasty ordination of new converts, clergy from keeping female friends in their houses, clergy from loaning money, and kneeling in prayer on the Lord's Day and during the days of Pentecost. They also included bishop ordinations, approving individual excommunications, preferences given to certain regional churches, dealing with lapsed baptized believers who desire to return to the faith, crimes disqualifying church leaders, administering sacraments, and church attendance for those desiring to change churches.[6]

In summary, the First Nicene Council was called by the Roman Emperor Constantine in AD 325. The council largely dealt with the heresy which sought to demote Jesus Christ from his rightful place as a co-equal member of the godhead. The Nicene Creed resulting in the modern Apostles' Creed was the result. Other smaller issues were addressed such as setting the annual calendar date for Easter as well as some church doctrinal laws. The deity of Christ and the canon of Scripture were never in question.

This ninth chapter about Jonah concludes with the following story about the final Day of Judgment,

It Will Be a Terrible Day!

During a Friday mosque visit in northern Indiana, I looked on from the back. I estimated between 125 and 150 present—not a white face in the crowd. The imam declared, "One day we will all stand before God on the Day of Judgment. It will be a terrible day. We will either go to *jenna* (heaven) or to *nar* (the fire). I hope you will all go to heaven!" I silently prayed, "That's also my prayer for each person here."

After the *khutba* and repeated common prayer ritual, the crowd got up to leave. The imam came over to greet me and my Christian traveling companion, Andrew. He asked what we were there for. I explained my purpose. He said, "I wish we had known sooner that you were coming." The imam had another meeting to attend but made arrangements for me to interview an elderly African-American Muslim convert.

This older gentleman was also accompanied by another younger Muslim who appeared to be of Asian origin. We were able to complete a shortened form of the survey, since the older man was in a hurry. Before we left, I asked if my friend Andrew could take one or two minutes to tell why Jesus was personal to him. He agreed. Andrew shared how Jesus had saved him and changed his life and delivered him from an addiction to computer games.

I left our older Muslim friend with a copy of a previous book I had written about the Islamic Hadith as well as a box of chocolates. To me there seemed to be little or no personal interest in what we had discussed. However, the man's younger Asian companion was definitely interested and asked if he could also get a copy of my book. I gave one to him, as well as my business card, and invited him to contact me. He thanked me and said he would read the book. "Cast your bread upon the waters for after many days you will find it again." May it be so, Lord!

Summary Questions for Reflection

1. Why do you think it is important to understand God's compassion for lost and dying souls?

2. What do you think is the significance of the Bible's connecting the life of Jesus with the Sign of Jonah?

3. How does understanding the Qur'an's story of the Treaty of al-Hudaybiyyah help Christians better understand their Muslim friends?

CHAPTER 10

ZECHARIAH AND JOHN THE BAPTIST: PREPARING FOR THE COMING MESSIAH

All individuals are responsible for themselves and choose their own life situations. They may either move ahead in life or regress. They may either have honorable positions or suffer humiliation.—Sayyid Qutb[1]

But the angel said to him: "Do not be afraid, Zechariah; your prayer has been heard. Your wife Elizabeth will bear you a son, and you are to give him the name John. He will be a joy and delight to you, and many will rejoice because of his birth." (Luke 1:13–14)

The shadow cast by the prophet of Islam is lengthening. Now we look at the lives of Zechariah and John the Baptist and their preparation for the coming Messiah. Please note that this Zechariah should not be confused with the Old Testament Zechariah, author of the book named for him.

Zechariah and John the Baptist: Setting the Stage

At the time of Zechariah and his son John the Baptist, Solomon's second temple was still standing in Jerusalem. The famed Library of Alexandria was present in Egypt and the Great Pyramid of Giza was 2,500 years old. The Colosseum in Rome had yet to be built. The Roman Empire was the major superpower of the day but was regularly challenged to the east by the Parthian Empire. Egypt had already been conquered by Rome. South of Egypt in Africa was the Kush Empire. To the northeast in Europe were barbaric Germanic tribes. To the northwest was the kingdom of Sarmatia. To the far southeast was the Indo–Parthian Empire. To the north of the Indo–Parthian Empire, China was ruled by the Han dynasty.

The main languages spoken in Palestine at the time were Latin (by the Romans); Aramaic (by the common people); Hebrew (by the religious Jews); and Greek (by the educated, which included the Romans), due to the Greek Hellenistic influence of Alexander the Great.

Locally, the Romans used Herod the Great, an Idumean Jew, to govern the populace. Zechariah was born in the first century BC in northern Palestine in Hebron. He was of the priestly line of Aaron and served on a rotating basis as a priest in Herod's temple in Jerusalem. He and his wife Elizabeth had a son who they named John; we know him as John the Baptist. He was the one who announced the coming of Jesus the Messiah. John's mother Elizabeth was an older cousin of Mary the mother of Jesus.

Now, on to Zechariah and his son John the Baptist.

Zechariah and John the Baptist in the Qur'an

Zechariah (Zakariya), and his son John the Baptist (Yahya), are present in four surahs of the Qur'an. In two of these surahs they are merely mentioned. The two significant passages appear below.

In Surah 3 verses 37–41 we see Zechariah as a guardian to Mary. Zechariah was amazed that God had miraculously provided Mary with needed food. Elderly Zechariah then prayed, asking God for a son of his own who would be righteous. Through an angel, God promised this would come to pass. But Zechariah was incredulous because his own wife was barren. Through an angel, Zechariah was told that because he was amazed, he would not be able to speak at all for three days and three nights.

In the second Qur'an passage, in Surah 19:2–6, Zechariah prays to God for a son, since he himself was elderly and his wife was barren. God responds in verse 7:

> [7](It was said unto him): O Zachariah! Lo! We bring thee tidings of a son whose name is John; We have given the same name to none before (him).

In verses 8–14 God tells Zechariah that he will not be able to speak for three days because of his inability to believe in this promise. The passage ends in verse 15:

> Peace on him the day he was born, and the day he dieth and the day he shall be raised alive!

Zechariah and John the Baptist in the Bible

In the Bible, Zechariah and John are seen primarily in Matthew 3, 11, and 14; Luke 1; and John 1. We are introduced to Zechariah at the beginning of Luke's monumental work.

Zechariah

> [5]In the time of Herod king of Judea there was a priest named Zechariah, who belonged to the priestly division of Abijah; his wife Elizabeth was also a descendant of Aaron. [6]Both of them were righteous in the sight of God, observing all the Lord's commands and decrees blamelessly. [7]But they were childless because Elizabeth was not able to conceive, and they were both very old. (Luke 1:5–7)

We see Zechariah entering the temple to burn incense. An angel of the Lord appeared to him, telling him not to be afraid. The angel then told him that his prayers for a child would be answered and that his barren wife Elizabeth would bear him a son that he would name John. The angel said that John would cause many to return to God and would be a forerunner in the spirit and power of Elijah. Zechariah asked the angel how this could be possible because he and his wife were both old. The angel replied that he was Gabriel, and that because Zechariah did not believe his report, he would be unable to speak until the child was born. After this Zechariah could not speak and Elizabeth became pregnant.

Still in Luke 1 Elizabeth gave birth. The child was named John and suddenly Zechariah was able to speak.

> [67]His father Zechariah was filled with the Holy Spirit and prophesied: [68]"Praise be to the Lord, the God of Israel, because he has come to his people and redeemed them. [69]He has raised up a horn of salvation for us in the house of his servant David [70] (as he said through his holy prophets of long ago), [71]salvation from our enemies and from the hand of all who hate us—[72]to show mercy to our ancestors and to remember his holy covenant, [73]the oath he swore to our father Abraham: [74]to rescue us from the hand of our enemies, and to enable us to serve him without fear [75]in holiness and righteousness before him all our days. [76]And you, my child, will be called a prophet of the most high; for you will go on before the Lord to prepare the way for him, [77]to give his people the knowledge of salvation through the forgiveness of their sins, [78]because of the tender mercy of our God, by which the rising sun will come to us from heaven [79]to shine on those living in darkness and in the shadow of death, to guide our feet into the path of peace." [80]And the child grew and became strong in spirit; and he lived in the wilderness until he appeared publicly to Israel. (Luke 1:67–80)

John the Baptist

We are introduced to John the Baptist at the start of his public ministry:

> [1]In those days John the Baptist came, preaching in the wilderness of Judea [2]and saying, "Repent, for the kingdom of heaven has come near." [3]This is he who was spoken of through the prophet Isaiah: "A voice of one calling in the wilderness, 'Prepare the way for the Lord, make straight paths for him.'" (Matt. 3:1–3)

Elsewhere in Matthew 3 we see John dressed in camel's hair and leather belt. People came to him from all over Judea, confessing their sins and getting baptized. John confronted the religious leaders who came to him for baptism, warning them to flee from the wrath to come. He told them to instead bring fruit that shows their true repentance.

John affirmed that he was only pointing to God's Messiah, toward the true Light (John 1:6–8). John was not the Messiah, or Elijah, or "the prophet" (John 1:20–21)—only "one calling in the desert" and preparing for the coming of the Messiah (John 1:23). He said that he, himself, was not worthy to untie the shoes of the Messiah.

Jesus then came to John to be publicly baptized. As Jesus came out of the water the heavens opened and the Spirit of God descended upon Jesus in the form of a dove. A voice from God was heard: "This is my Son, whom I love; with him I am well pleased" (Matt. 3:17).

Next, in the gospel of Matthew we see the details of John's imprisonment by King Herod. Herod arrested John because he had opposed Herod's marriage to his living brother's wife. The queen-wife's daughter danced before Herod and made him promise to have John the Baptist beheaded. John's body was brought to his disciples, who buried it and then reported to Jesus.

Before John's death, while he was still in prison, he sent his own disciples to inquire about Jesus. In reply, in Matthew 11:4–6 Jesus quoted from the book of Isaiah, stating that he was giving sight to the blind, making the lame walk, healing the lepers, making the deaf hear, and raising the dead back to life. Therefore, Jesus concluded, "Blessed is the man who does not fall away on account of me" (v. 6).

In verses 7–12 Jesus spoke to the multitudes about John. He quoted from Malachi 3:1, proclaiming that John was the foretold messenger who was preparing for the coming of the Messiah. He also said that entering God's kingdom would only come about with struggle.

The Shadow When the Qur'an Is Compared to the Bible

The similarity in the two versions is obvious—John was born to Zechariah and his barren wife in their old age. But there are three significant differences in the two presentations.

1. In the Qur'an the sign from God given to Zechariah of his coming child would be three days and nights of being unable to speak. In the Bible, this time was much longer: many months—the duration of his wife's pregnancy.

2. In the Qur'an Zechariah was given the guardianship of Mary, the mother of Jesus, when she was a young child. This is absent in the Bible. Of interest is that this story about Mary's guardianship by Zechariah also appears in the second-century non-canonical apocryphal Protoevangelium of James. Could there be a common source?

3. There is no mention in the Qur'an of John the Baptist being a forerunner of the coming of God's Messiah. Details of this forerunner were given in the Bible by Zechariah's praise and prophecy (Luke 1:68–79 above). In this praise Zechariah also quoted from the Old Testament prophet Isaiah in 40:3: "A voice of one calling: In the desert prepare the way for the Lord; make

straight in the wilderness a highway for our God." This prophet was known as the coming Messiah—God Himself come to earth in the flesh. All this is absent in the Qur'an.

In summary, what is notably absent is the centrality of the One for whom John the forerunner was preparing the world—Jesus the Messiah, the Lord, God come to earth in the flesh, the one Zechariah in his final speech said came "to give his people the knowledge of salvation through the forgiveness of their sins" (Luke 1:77).

Sayyid Qutb Themes

This chapter highlighting Zechariah and John the Baptist relates most closely to one of our nineteen Qur'anic themes from Sayyid Qutb—number 15, dealing with destiny and God's ultimate control over everything.

15. Destiny and God's Ultimate Control over Everyone and Everything

Qutb confirms the core Islamic belief and teaching that God is in complete control of everyone and everything in the universe. Qutb also reminds Muslims everywhere of the importance of the commonly used phrase *Insh-Allah*—if God wills! He also stresses the remembrance that we all will one day ultimately return to God.

Qutb adds that every act a human does or does not do, and every breath he takes, is obedience to God's will. The veil obscuring the future hides everything but the present. No matter how smart we are, we cannot see beyond the veil. For this reason, no person should ever say he is definitely going to do something without attaching the intention to God's will.[2]

Qutb adds that the most basic parts of the Islamic ideology—creation, education, and honor—come only from God. And to Him we will all return.[3]

[8]Lo! Unto thy Lord is the return. (Surah 96:8)

Associated Qur'an Story

The third strand of our rope brings us to the following Qur'an story closely associated with this chapter's theme of Zechariah and John the Baptist. Its topic is true justice.

The Stolen Shield—from Surah 4 Al-Nisa (the Women)

This is the second longest surah in the Qur'an. It was revealed in Medina shortly after Surah 60 (al-Mumtahana) and has 176 verses. The surah takes its name from verse 3:

> [3]And if ye fear that ye will not deal fairly by the orphans, marry of the women, who seem good to you, two or three or four; and if ye fear that ye cannot do justice (to so many) then one (only) or (the captives) that your right hands possess. Thus it is more likely that ye will not do injustice. (Surah 4:3)

After the *hijra*, a new community was being built along Islamic lines. As with many Medinan surahs, this one deals with social problems the Muslim community had to face. These social problems dealt with the topics of women, orphans, inheritance, marriage, and family rights in general.[4] They also dealt with those who claimed to be Muslims, but really weren't— "the hypocrites."

At this early stage of this community's life, not all Muslims fully understood the principles of Islam and the need to put them into practice. Qutb notes that our current Qur'an story comes from twelve verses (105–116) addressing one such misunderstanding.[5] The incident involved the theft of some body armor, a shield. Loyalty to clan and blood relations caused blame to be shifted from one of their own number onto that of an innocent Jew.

A group of the *Ansar*,[6] including Qatada ibn al-Nu'man and his uncle Rifa'ah, joined Muhammad on one of his military expeditions. On this expedition, a shield belonging to Rifa'ah was stolen. Suspicion rested on another of the Ansari clan, Bashir ibn Ubayriq as being the culprit. When the thief saw what was happening, he took the shield and placed it in the home of a Jew, Zayd ibn al-Samin. Ibn Ubayriq told some of his clan what he had done. They immediately went to Muhammad telling him that Zayd ibn al-Samin was the thief. They urged their prophet to condemn the Jew and to exonerate their relative ibn Ubayriq. Muhammad did. Then, according to Qutb, God revealed the truth to Muhammad, who cleared the Jew from the false charge. Bashir ibn Ubayriq then left Medina and joined the unbelievers. This resulted in verses 115–116 of the surah:

> [115]And whoso opposeth the messenger after the guidance (of Allah) hath been manifested unto him, and followeth other than the believer's way, We appoint for him that unto which he himself hath turned, and expose him unto hell—a hapless journey's end! [116]Lo! Allah pardoneth not that partners should be ascribed unto Him. He pardoneth all save that to whom He will. Whoso ascribeth partners unto Allah hath wandered far astray.

Qutb notes that this story did not take place merely to acquit an innocent man from wrongly paying the penalty for theft. The story was much broader and showed a standard that cannot be changed just to suit a desire or to support one's own family and friends. According to Qutb this story about justice truly illustrates the spirit of Islam.[7]

Now it's time for another controversial topic, as we go directly to the individual John the Baptist was preparing the way for.

A New Perspective on Christianity: The Deity of Christ

I was in central Indiana for a mosque visit. After the *khutba* I was introduced by the local imam to his congregation and asked to tell a little about the Qur'an project I was working on. He called me to the front and gave me his microphone. After I finished, I went to the back of the mosque. I was immediately surrounded by local Muslims, who had questions for me. I answered some of their inquiries but spent most of the time listening.

One of those standing around didn't ask a question. He was a young man of Pakistani origin. He was not angry, just a little confused. He looked down and slowly spoke: "Jesus never said that he was God!" I asked if this was a question he had for me or only a statement. He repeated, "Jesus never said that he was God!"

I replied, "Yes, there are lots of misunderstandings between Muslims and Christians."

A Muslim next to him said, "Just ask Dr. Hoskins a question!" Again the young man repeated his original comment.

Before he left I greeted him in Urdu (his native language) and gave him part of the Aaronic blessing from Numbers 6:24, "The Lord bless you and keep you." I finished by giving him a message from Jesus in Urdu (John 14:6): "I am the way, and the truth, and the life."

Over the years I have heard this same objection by Muslims more than once: "Jesus never said that he was God!" Qutb addressed this issue in detail.[8] He begins with a quote from the Qur'an:

[116]And when Allah saith: O Jesus, son of Mary! Didst thou say unto mankind: Take me and my mother for two gods beside Allah? He saith: Be glorified! It was not mine to utter that to which I had no right! If I used to say it, then Thou knewest it. Thou knowest what is in my mind, and I know not what is in Thy mind. Lo! Thou, only Thou, art the Knower of Things Hidden. Behold! God will say: "O Jesus the son of Mary! 'Didst

thou say unto men, worship me and my mother as gods in derogation of God'?" He will say: "Glory to Thee! Never could I say what I had no right (to say). Had I said such a thing Thou wouldst indeed have known it. Thou knowest what is in my heart, though I know not what is in Thine. Thou, only Thou, art the Knower of Things Hidden." (Surah 5:116)

Qutb wrote that if any one of God's servants claimed to be God, while knowing that he was only God's servant, he would be perpetrating a terrible offense, something no normal human being could do. Do we even think it is possible for Jesus to do such a thing, someone God chose to bear His message?[9] To this rhetorical question Qutb implies a definite "No!"

What appears below is only a brief summary of this topic, approached from three sides. What did Jesus say about himself in the Bible? Second, what did others say about him? And finally, what did Jesus do to either prove or disprove his deity? Jesus said that He and the Father were One. The Jews picked up stones to kill him. They knew what He was saying: that He was equal to God. Jesus also identified Himself multiple times with the great "I Am" of the Bible. From the context this was clearly identifying Himself with God the Father. Jesus most commonly referred to Himself as the Son of Man. From Daniel's dream in Daniel 7 the Jews clearly identified this statement with God. Before Pilate, at the end of the gospel of Matthew, Jesus clearly admitted that He was the Christ, the Son of God (Matt, 26:63).

Others besides Jesus attested to his divinity. The spirit world—both angels and demons—attested to Christ's divinity. His disciples also, as well as John the Baptist, did the same.

Finally, Jesus's actions also demonstrated his divinity. He gave sight to the blind, made the lame to walk, cured leprosy, cured a woman's bleeding disorder, and raised the dead to life. Probably most impressive of all, he died on the cross and rose from the dead three days later.

Of equal importance to Jesus's claim to personal deity is the next objection by Qutb—the death of Jesus Christ on the cross! That comes in our next chapter. *This* chapter concludes with the following story about the difficulties Muslims and Christians have in getting along together.

"Rich and poor, strong and weak, all stand together in prayer"

Harlan, my Christian traveling companion, and I visited a mosque in southern Indiana. The roof's steeple appeared to have once been topped by a cross. Before entering this former church, we removed our shoes and entered the prayer area. We sat on folding chairs in the back and waited in silence for other Muslims to arrive for their Friday *Jumah* prayers. Eventually about sixty men showed up. A few unseen women talked to each other in the partitioned room behind us.

"*Allahu Akbar*! (God is most great!) *Allahu Akbar*!" announced the call to prayer. When it ended the imam stood in front at the pulpit. The *khutbah* began. "Rich and poor, strong and weak, all stand together in prayer." Taking about twenty minutes, the imam explained first in Arabic and then in English the importance of the mosque and why Allah loved those best who were responsible for building mosques during their lifetimes. He stressed the importance of all Muslims working together in community.

When the *khutbah* was finished all the Muslim men crowded together in neatly arranged lines for the formal rote prayers involving bending and kneeling and prostrating and standing. The imam also chanted from the Qur'an which included the first surah (al-Fatihah— the Opening) as well as the Verse of Light (from 24:35)—"Allah is the light of the heavens and the earth. . . ."

When the service ended, the imam came to the back and greeted me and Harlan. I gave him my business card and a copy of the letter I had sent a week earlier requesting an interview. He took us to an adjoining office.

During the interview the imam asked why I thought it was so hard for Christians and Muslims to get along. I answered that we each had a common enemy: that enemy was Satan, and not each other. He smiled and wanted to know more. Harlan told of his personal journey to faith and why Jesus was personal to him. I also shared my story of coming to know Christ through serious heart disease when I was young. I quoted two verses about Jesus.

Nearing the end of our time I added, "I believe everyone should go back and look at original documents and that is why I have read the Qur'an seven times." I asked if he had ever read the *Injeel* (New Testament)? He said, "Not really." I said I had a copy of the *Injeel* in both English and Arabic in my briefcase and that he could have it if he wanted. He did. As we left I gave him a small gift of chocolates from my wife for him to take home to his family. I prayed for him leaving him with the Aaronic blessing from Numbers 6:24-26: "The Lord bless you and keep you. . . ." As we drove off, Harlan and I prayed for this dear man. May he read the Scriptures we left and may God open his eyes!

Summary Questions for Reflection

1. In the Bible John the Baptist is confirmed as the forerunner of the Messiah, who would be God come to earth and central to forgiveness of sins. If this is true, how should we respond personally to this Messiah?

2. Many claim today that Jesus was no more than a prophet of God. The claims of those around Jesus who knew him best believed and told others that he was much more. If that is not true, what do we do with all the evidence? Can we, in good conscience, simply ignore it?

3. Finally, if what Jesus, and others, said about himself is not true, then how can we consider Jesus to be a prophet of God at all?

CHAPTER 11

MARY THE MOTHER OF JESUS—HER PROMINENCE AND HER PAIN

Women are more impetuous by nature and tend to be more suggestible and pliant. This gentle and easygoing manner is actually a necessary advantage in their roles of motherhood.—Sayyid Qutb[1]

Then Simeon blessed them and said to Mary, his mother: "This child is destined to cause the falling and rising of many in Israel, and to be a sign that will be spoken against, so that the thoughts of many hearts will be revealed. And a sword will pierce your own soul too." (Luke 2:34–35)

Women Have Different Hopes, Dreams, and Perceptions

My family and I were guests in the home of an Arab Gulf couple. My son and I ate with the men, while my wife and daughter ate a separate meal with the women. During the ladies' meal, Charlene asked an important question she had always wondered about. She wanted to hear a Muslim woman's concept of heaven. So she asked,

"I know what heaven is supposed to hold for Muslim men. But I have always wanted to know what there is for you, for women."

One of the women said, "You know, I've always wanted to know that too. I asked the imam of our mosque. He said he didn't know either, but 'it must be so wonderful that it can't be described!'" She beamed as she spoke. Charlene smiled outwardly but inside shed tears that her friend was satisfied with such empty reassurance.

We continue our journey into the shadow cast by the prophet of Islam by looking at the life of Mary the mother of Jesus, and the emotional pain she experienced watching her precious son suffer.

Mary the Mother of Jesus: Setting the Stage

In Mary's time, Rome was the world's leading superpower and ruled Palestine. Aramaic was spoken by the common people. Mary was born in northern Galilee in the village of Nazareth. Her betrothed husband Joseph was also from Nazareth. Even though a virgin, Mary gave birth to a son, Jesus, 150 kilometers south of Nazareth in Bethlehem, in fulfillment of Bible prophecy. This was done at the order of Rome in response to a worldwide census:

> In those days Caesar Augustus issued a decree that a census should be taken of the entire Roman world. (Luke 2:1)

Let's look at how the story of Mary is told in both the Qur'an and the Bible.

Mary in the Qur'an

The story of Mary in the Qur'an is located primarily in two surahs: Surah 3 (The House of Imran) and Surah 19 (Maryam—the surah named after her). In Surah 3 we see the birth of Mary and her being given into the care of the Zakariya, one of the Jewish temple priests. In this surah Mary is told by the angels that God has chosen her and purified her. God has honored her by causing her, a virgin, to give birth to a child who would be God's Word in the person of Jesus.

(And remember) when the angels said: O Mary! Lo! Allah giveth thee glad tidings of a Word from Him, whose name is the Messiah, Jesus, son of Mary, illustrious in the world and the Hereafter, and one of those brought near (unto Allah). (Surah 3:45)

In verses 48–49 we see God's purpose for Jesus:

[48]And He will teach him the Scripture and wisdom, and the Torah and the Gospel, [49]and will make him a messenger unto the Children of Israel, (saying): Lo! I come unto you with a sign from your Lord. Lo! I fashion for you out of clay the likeness of a bird, and I breathe into it and it is a bird, by Allah's leave. I heal him who was born blind, and the leper, and I raise the dead, by Allah's leave. And I announce unto you what ye eat and what ye store up in your houses. Lo! Herein verily is a portent for you, if ye are to be believers.

In verses 50–51 Jesus came to confirm the Torah as a sign from God. In Surah 19 Mary gave birth to Jesus:

[20]She said: How can I have a son when no mortal hath touched me, neither have I been unchaste? [21]He said: So (it will be). Thy Lord saith: It is easy for Me. And (it will be) that We may make of him a revelation for mankind and a mercy from Us, and it is a thing ordained. [22]And she conceived him, and she withdrew with him to a far place. [23]And the pangs of childbirth drove her unto the trunk of a palm-tree. She said: Oh, would that I had died ere this and had become a thing of naught, forgotten! (Surah 19:20–23)

In verses 27–29 Mary takes her new baby Jesus back to her own people.

27Then she brought him to her own folk, carrying him. They said: O Mary! Thou hast come with an amazing thing. 28O sister of Aaron! Thy father was not a wicked man nor was thy mother a harlot. 29Then she pointed to him. They said: How can we talk to one who is in the cradle, a young boy?

She is briefly mentioned two other times. In the first instance she acknowledges that she must endure slander against her character:

And because of their disbelief and of their speaking against Mary a tremendous calumny; (Surah 4:156)

The second passage states that God breathed into her of His Spirit, which allowed her to testify to others of God's truthfulness.

And Mary, daughter of 'Imran, whose body was chaste, therefor We breathed therein something of Our Spirit. And she put faith in the words of her Lord and his scriptures, and was of the obedient. (Surah 66:12)

Mary in the Bible

In the Bible, Mary's story is much broader. She is first mentioned, although not by name, in a Bible prophecy 750 years before the birth of Christ.

The king of Assyria had sent troops to conquer Jerusalem. Isaiah the prophet told King Ahaz of Judah that God was sending him a special sign of God's care and protection:

Therefore the Lord himself will give you a sign: The virgin will conceive and give birth to a son, and will call him Immanuel. (Isa. 7:14)

The child's name, Immanuel, means "God with us." In the first chapter of the gospel of Matthew we see Mary giving birth to Jesus in Bethlehem, near Jerusalem. Mary was pledged in marriage to Joseph but was found to be pregnant before the marriage. Joseph wanted to divorce her quietly so not to disgrace her. An angel from God appeared in a dream to Joseph, telling him not to be afraid to take Mary as a wife since the pregnancy came from the Holy Spirit. The angel told Joseph that Mary would have a son and they would name him Jesus, because he would save his people from their sins. Joseph did as he was commanded.

In the second chapter of Matthew we see eastern magi (wise men—possibly astronomers) following a bright star, guided by God, who journeyed many miles to find a special child. The magi first came to the Jewish King Herod in Jerusalem, who sent them to find the child in Bethlehem. Herod was jealous of this newborn king who might one day threaten to usurp his throne and sent soldiers to find and kill the child. We see Mary and her husband Joseph, with the baby Jesus, fleeing Bethlehem by night and escaping into Egypt. Mary, Jesus, and Joseph stayed in Egypt for several years until the death of Herod. Then they returned and traveled north to live in the Galilean town of Nazareth.

An additional view we have of Mary comes from the gospel of Luke before Jesus's birth. She visited her cousin Elizabeth, the wife of Zechariah. Upon seeing Elizabeth, Mary burst out in a special praise to God—known for the last two thousand years as the Magnificat—focusing on God's magnificent character:

The Magnificat of Mary (from Luke 1:46–55)

My soul glorifies the Lord and my spirit rejoices in God my Savior,

for he has been mindful of the humble state of his servant.

From now on all generations will call me blessed,

for the Mighty One has done great things for me—holy is his name.

His mercy extends to those who fear him, from generation to generation.

He has performed mighty deeds with his arm;

He has scattered those who are proud in their inmost thoughts.

He has brought down rulers from their thrones but has lifted up the humble.

He has filled the hungry with good things but has sent the rich away empty.

He has helped his servant Israel, remembering to be merciful to Abraham and his

descendants forever, just as He promised our ancestors.

Our next glimpse of Mary comes eight days after Jesus's birth, when Joseph and his wife Mary took Jesus to the temple to be ritually circumcised. There they met an elderly religious man named Simeon. Upon seeing the child, Simeon praised God:

> [29]Sovereign Lord, as you have promised, you may now dismiss your servant in peace. [30]For my eyes have seen your salvation, [31]which you have prepared in the sight of all nations: [32]a light for revelation to the Gentiles, and the glory of your people Israel. (Luke 2:29–32)

Then Simeon turned to Mary and said:

> [34]This child is destined to cause the falling and rising of many in Israel, and to be a sign that will be spoken against, [35]so that the thoughts of many hearts will be revealed. And a sword will pierce your own soul too. (Luke 2:34–35)

We next see Jesus at age twelve when his parents took him to Jerusalem to celebrate the Feast of Passover. After Passover was over, Jesus's parents lost track of him and started searching. They found Jesus in the temple three days later.

> [48]When his parents saw him, they were astonished. His mother said to him, "Son, why have you treated us like this? Your father and I have been anxiously searching for you." [49]"Why were you searching for me?" he asked. "Didn't you know I had to be in my Father's house?" [50]But they did not understand what he was saying to them. [51]Then he went down to Nazareth with them and was obedient to them. But his mother treasured all these things in her heart. (Luke 2:48–51)

Eighteen years elapse; we next see Mary and Jesus attending a wedding in Galilee, as documented in the Gospel of John. Mary, Jesus, and his disciples were invited to the wedding. When the wine ran out, his mother Mary came to Jesus telling him about the lack. Jesus replied, "my hour has not yet come." Mary turned to the servants, "Do whatever he tells you" (see John 2:1–5). Jesus proceeded to turn plain water into wine needed for the celebration. This was Jesus's first miracle.

Our next and final look at Mary comes three years later, following Jesus's arrest, trial, and execution at the hands of the Roman authorities. The "sword" described thirty-three years earlier by the old man Simeon was indeed piercing her own heart:

> [25]Near the cross of Jesus stood his mother, his mother's sister, Mary the wife of Clopas, and Mary Magdalene. [26]When Jesus saw his mother there, and the disciple whom he loved standing nearby, he said to her, "Woman, here is your son," [27]and to the disciple, "Here is your mother." From that time on, this disciple took her into his home. (John 19:25–27)

The Shadow When the Qur'an Is Compared to the Bible

Following in our spirit of searching the shadows, what is missing in the Qur'an's account of the life of Mary that is present in the Bible account?

1. There is no Immanuel: "God with us."
2. There is no salvation or savior to pay for the sins of others.
3. There is no Magnificat.
4. There is no evidence of a mother "treasuring" the thought that her son would need to be found in his Father's (God's) house.
5. There is no Simeon and no mention of the sword-piercing Mary experienced as she watched her own son crucified.

Let's look at this from a modern mother's viewpoint. After they had seen Mel Gibson's 2004 movie *The Passion of the Christ*, one of my son's Muslim friends discussed the film with his own mother. He explained that although it looked like Jesus died, it was really someone else (like Judas) who had been substituted in Jesus's place. His mother said, "*Jesus's mother* thought it was him!"

Sayyid Qutb Themes

We now look at one of the nineteen Sayyid Qutb Qur'anic themes which closely relates to our chapter on Mary the mother of Jesus.

1. Nature of God, His Attributes, and the Absolute Importance of His "Oneness"

This is the cornerstone of Islam. It is best epitomized by one of the shortest and most often repeated surahs in the Qur'an—Surah 112:

[1]Say: He is Allah, the One! [2]Allah, the eternally besought of all! [3]He begetteth not, nor was begotten; [4]and there is none comparable to Him. (Surah 112:1–4)

This is viewed from a different perspective in another short surah:

[1]Say: O disbelievers! [2]I worship not that which ye worship; [3]Nor worship ye that which I worship. [4]And I shall not worship that which ye worship. [5]Nor will ye worship that which I worship. [6]Unto you your religion, and unto me my religion. (Surah 109:1–6)

Qutb notes that the prophet began each day by reciting these Surahs 112 and 109 in his voluntary prayer before starting the dawn prayer. This was highly significant.[2]

Hand-in-glove with this is a summary of God's attributes from another surah:

[2]The revelation of the Scripture is from Allah, the Mighty, the Knower, [3]The Forgiver of sin, the Acceptor of repentance, the Stern in punishment, the Bountiful. There is no God save Him. Unto Him is the journeying. (Surah 40:2–3)

Qutb reminds us of God's attributes: He is almighty, all-knowing, forgives sins, accepts repentance, is severe in retribution, and limitless in bounty. There is no god other than Him. And to Him we will ultimately return.[3] Qutb summarizes the one overriding rule throughout the universe: there is no god but God and all living beings are His servants. Their faith, views, and even their whole lives will not be made right unless that principle is made absolutely clear.[4]

Associated Qur'an Story

The third strand in our four-strand rope comes from a unique Qur'an story illustrating the chapter theme of Mary. Mary's life, including the Magnificat, is uniquely scripted to reflect submission to the will of God and to prayer and praise. That is also a major theme of the following story from the Qur'an.

The Night Journey—from Surah 17 al-Isra (the Night Journey)

This surah of 111 verses was revealed in Mecca. From it originates a two-part journey that took place in one night a year before the flight (*hijra*) of Muhammad from Mecca to Medina.[5] The surah takes its name from the first verse:

> [1]Glorified be He Who carried His servant by night from the Inviolable Place of Worship to the Far distant place of worship the neighborhood whereof We have blessed, that We might show him of Our tokens! Lo! He, only He, is the Hearer, the Seer. (Surah 17:1).

The "sacred mosque" was the mosque of Muhammad in Mecca. The "farthest mosque" was the location of the current al-Aqsa mosque in Jerusalem. Traditionally, in the first part of this night journey (*Isra*), Muhammad was carried by a heavenly winged horse, named Buraq, to Jerusalem. There, Muhammad led other prophets in prayer. At the al-Aqsa mosque the angel Gabriel allegedly tested Muhammad by bringing him three vessels—one of milk, one of water, and one of wine—and was told to choose. Muhammad chose milk and was commended by Gabriel, since he had chosen the *fitrah* (natural instinct). These details, including those for the second part of the night journey, come from the Hadith, such as those by Sahih Bukhari and Sahih Muslim as well as the writings of Muhammad's biographer, Ibn Ishaq, and others.

Before the ascent to heaven, Muhammad's chest was opened by Gabriel and his heart was washed with *zamzam* water to purify him and fill him with knowledge and faith. Then, during this second part of the night journey (*Miraj*, literally "ladder") he was transported through each of the seven heavens, where he met a different prophet of God at each level. At the first level he met Adam. Then he met John the Baptist. Next was Jesus, then Joseph, then Idris (believed by many to be Enoch of the Bible), then Aaron, then Moses, and finally Abraham. He finally came to the very throne of God where Muhammad received the command for he and his followers to perform the five daily prayers. At first, Muhammad was commanded to have fifty daily prayers. At Moses's recommendation Muhammad returned and was able to bargain this down to the current five.

Remembrance of this night journey is one of the most significant events in the Islamic calendar and celebrated throughout the Muslim world.

The issue of this night journey started in controversy. Some Muslims, when they heard this surah and learned about Muhammad's seemingly fantastic night journey, decided to stop being Muslims. They sought the advice of Muhammad's prominent follower (who also became the first Caliph following Muhammad's death) Abu Bakr. Abu Bakr said the story of the night journey was no more fantastic than Muhammad's receiving revelations from God. "I believe him," Abu Bakr said.

This surah contains issues of individual and social behavior, such as forbidding adultery and unnecessary killing. It further encourages care for children and the veneration of parents. As is true of all Qur'an surahs, it also addresses the importance of God's oneness. The surah begins and ends by praising God.

> And say: Praise be to Allah, Who hath not taken unto Himself a son, and Who hath no partner in the Sovereignty, nor hath He any protecting friend through dependence. And magnify Him with all magnificence. (Surah 17:111)

Finally, we explore possibly the most controversial topic of all to our Muslim friends—the crucifixion of Christ.

A New Perspective on Christianity: Jesus Was Not Crucified and Did Not Die on the Cross

My wife finished a friendly discussion with a Muslim girlfriend about our major beliefs about Jesus. Her Muslim friend responded, "We Muslims believe most of what you believe, but here is the main difference—it all comes down to the 'crucification'!" Even though she used an incorrect word, her meaning was abundantly clear.

Sayyid Qutb also discussed this issue when he wrote that Christians differ about the crucifixion. According to Qutb, some say that Jesus died on the cross, was buried, and then rose from the tomb three days later and was finally taken to heaven. Others say it was Judas who betrayed him and was made to appear like Jesus and that it was Judas who was actually crucified in his place. Again, the Qur'an gives the final word:

> And because of their saying: We slew the Messiah, Jesus son of Mary, Allah's messenger—they slew him not nor crucified him, but it appeared so unto them; and lo! Those who disagree concerning it are in doubt thereof; they have no knowledge thereof save pursuit of a conjecture; they slew him not for certain. (Surah 4:157)

> (And remember) when Allah said: O Jesus, Lo! I am gathering thee and causing thee to ascend unto Me, and am cleansing thee of those who disbelieve and am setting those who follow thee above those who disbelieve until the Day of Resurrection. Then unto Me ye will (all) return, and I shall judge between you as to that wherein ye used to differ. (Surah 3:55).

Over the last two millennia controversy over this topic has generated both heat and light. In 2004, actor Mel Gibson produced and directed *The Passion of the Christ,* dealing with the last twelve hours of Jesus's life. This movie about Christ's crucifixion grossed more than six hundred million dollars and was nominated for three Academy Awards. Due to its perceived anti-Semitic content, the film was not aired in Israel. As gruesome as Mel Gibson's portrayal of Christ's crucifixion appears, it is completely consistent with the accounts of the canonical gospels.

Altogether, given the first-century eyewitness confirmation of the crucifixion of Jesus (the four canonical Gospels), as well as the first- and second-century non-Christian historical accounts (Tacitus and Josephus), most reputable scholars of antiquity concur. The British New Testament scholar James Dunn, commenting about the baptism of Jesus and his crucifixion, states: "these two facts in the life of Jesus command almost universal assent and rank so high on the 'almost impossible to doubt or deny' scale of historical facts that they are often the starting points for the study of the historical Jesus."[6] The evangelical-turned-agnostic Bart Ehrman states that "the crucifixion of Jesus on the orders of Pontius Pilate is the most certain element about him."[7] John Dominic Crossan, the Irish-American historical scholar, states that "the crucifixion of Jesus is as certain as any historical fact can be."[8] Finally, there is the "boots on the ground" fact that eleven of the twelve disciples of Jesus went to their deaths proclaiming the truths behind his crucifixion. No one dies for something they know to be false!

But did Jesus die from the crucifixion process? Writing in one of the most reputable medical journals of our time, the *Journal of the American Medical Association*, physician William Edwards and his two colleagues concluded Jesus must have died from cardiovascular collapse, hypovolemic shock, exhaustion, and asphyxia.[9] As a physician myself, I completely agree with their conclusions. Yes, Jesus was crucified and died as a result. I am also reminded of the Arab mother discussing Mel Gibson's *The Passion* noted earlier in this chapter: "*His mother thought it was him!*"

This chapter ends with the following story about another woman—one who had just died.

Prayers for the Dead

My Christian friend David and I showed up at this Indiana mosque about a half hour before the Friday *Jumah* prayers. We sat in back, waited, observed, and prayed—we were asking God to bring us a "man of peace" (Matt. 10; Luke 10). The tennis-court-sized room faced Mecca and only had a few folks present. An older middle-aged gentleman drew near, greeted us, and politely asked who we were. We explained that we were Christians who loved Muslims. This man was joined by his college-aged son, whose eyebrows went up as he asked me, "How long have you been a Muslim?" I said I was a Christian who was also an author who wrote books for Christians, helping them to better understand how to relate to their Muslim friends. The son was fascinated and wanted to know more. I gave the two of them my business card and a copy of my last book, *A Muslim's Mind*. We talked a little about that book's topic, the Islamic Hadith. As the *Jumah* prayers started, the son gave me his phone number and twice asked me to contact him. I said I would. More and more people filtered into the mosque until all told there were about two hundred present—packed in like sardines.

The *khutba* accompanying the prayers focused on the Day of Judgment and what we would say to Allah when we met him. The imam then said we would be saying special funeral prayers (*janaa'iz*) for a lady in their Muslim community who had just died. The men in back spread about ten feet apart, and four other men carried in the shrouded woman's body on a board. When the prayers ended, the imam encouraged everyone to follow him immediately to the cemetery for the burial. He said you should go if you wanted to get "the maximum number of points" for your good deeds.

As the crowd thinned, three other men approached us. Only one of them stayed to participate in my interview process. After finishing, I left him with a small box of chocolates and a copy of *A Muslim's Mind* as a simple thank you. We put on our shoes and left. I followed up with the son, although I never received a response. I wondered, would anyone from that mosque have new thoughts about God and Christ? Our job as Christians is to trust God and show up, leaving any results to Him.

Summary Questions for Reflection

1. What do you think is the significance of Jesus being called "Immanuel" in the book of Isaiah (7:14)?

2. How does Mary, Jesus's mother, describe God's character in her Magnificat (praise to God)? How does Mary's Magnificat support the concept of God's Oneness?

3. My wife has watched our own children suffer at times from various illnesses and injuries. If someone attempted to convince her it was not her own child she was watching, she was so emotionally involved she would know it was them, even if she couldn't see their faces—by sounds they might make, or the way they made a hand motion or twisted their bodies. What does this say about Mary watching her own child suffer?

CHAPTER 12

JESUS AND THE GOSPEL OF THE KINGDOM OF GOD

The birth of Jesus, the son of Mary, was the most extraordinary episode in the history of humanity.—Sayyid Qutb[1]

May the God of peace, who through the blood of the eternal covenant brought back from the dead our Lord Jesus, that great Shepherd of the sheep, equip you with everything good for doing His will, and may He work in us what is pleasing to Him, through Jesus Christ, to whom be glory for ever and ever. Amen. (Heb. 13:20–21)

Before diving in here, let me tell a remarkable story, where the person of Jesus transformed a previous killer's life.

"No more killing. No more stealing. No more lying."

Just over a decade ago I was on a business trip to a country in South Asia. I met a man in a friend's house at night; his former job was training suicide bombers for Al-Qaida. As we talked, he told me about a dream he had ten years earlier. In the dream, he was flying in an airplane and on his way to carry out a suicide mission. Suddenly Jesus appeared to him above the plane, stretched out his arms, and wrapped them around him. Jesus told him, "No more killing. No more stealing. No more lying."

The next day, he asked many friends about the meaning of this dream. They all told him the dream came from Satan. My friend didn't think so. He quit working for Al-Qaida. He sought out and began a Bible correspondence course. The first lesson was on the Ten Commandments—don't kill, steal, or lie. This confirmed to him he was on the right track.

Another friend directed him to a doctor working in one of his country's hospitals. After reading the Bible for a few years with this doctor, he committed his life to Christ. Today he tells other Muslims about his hope in Jesus.

When I asked him how we could pray for him, he said, "First let me tell you what we don't need. We don't need your money, and we don't need your sword. But please do pray for us, that we would stay true to the teachings of the Bible." I assured him that I would.

Jesus: Setting the Stage

At the time of Jesus, Rome was the world's leading superpower and ruled Palestine. Under the direction of Rome, Herod the Great ruled the local populace. Solomon's second temple was still standing in Jerusalem. The famed Library of Alexandria was present in Egypt and the Great Pyramid of Giza was 2,500 years old. Jesus was born around the turn of the century (some historians believe this could have been as early as 4 BC) in Bethlehem, in response to Bible prophecy.

> But you, Bethlehem Ephrathah, though you are small among the clans of Judah, out of you shall come for me one who will be ruler over Israel, whose origins are from of old, from ancient times. (Mic. 5:2)

The main languages spoken in Palestine at the time were Latin (by the Romans), Aramaic (by the common people), Hebrew (by the religious Jews), and Greek (by the educated). We believe Jesus spoke all four.

Our journey into the shadows concludes with the story of Jesus.

Jesus in the Qur'an

Jesus is clearly unique in the Qur'an. He is named three times more often than Muhammad. Let's look at this singular person. The verses and passages below are not comprehensive, but they do form the bulk of what the Qur'an says about Jesus.

> [45](And remember) when the angels said: O Mary! Lo! Allah giveth thee glad tidings of a Word from Him, whose name is the Messiah, Jesus, son of Mary, illustrious in the world and the Hereafter, and one of those brought near (unto Allah). [46]He will speak unto mankind in his cradle and in his manhood, and he is of the righteous. [47]She said: My Lord! How can I have a child when no mortal hath touched me? He said: So (it will be). Allah createth what He will. If He decreeth a thing, He saith unto it only: Be! And it is. [48]And He will teach him the Scripture and wisdom, and the Torah and the Gospel, [49]and will make him a messenger unto the Children of Israel, (saying): Lo! I come unto you with a sign from your Lord. Lo! I fashion for you out of clay the likeness of a bird, and I breathe into it and it is a bird, by Allah's leave. I heal him who was born blind, and the leper, and I raise the dead, by Allah's leave. And I announce unto you what ye eat and what ye store up in your houses. Lo! Herein verily is a portent for you, if ye are to be believers. [50]And (I come) confirming that which was before me of the Torah, and to make lawful some of that which was forbidden unto you. I come unto you with a sign from your Lord, so keep your duty to Allah and obey me. [51]Lo! Allah is my Lord and your Lord, so worship Him. That is a straight path. (Surah 3:45–51)

According to the Qur'an Jesus was born of a virgin, Mary. It says Jesus was highly exalted in this life, and in the next world would be seated next to God. God taught Jesus the book and wisdom as well as the law (Torah) and Gospel (*Injeel*—good news). God sent Jesus as a messenger to the Children of Israel. As a child Jesus formed birds out of clay and then breathed life into them. He also performed miracles, healing those born blind as well as lepers. He also brought the dead back to life. All Jesus's miracles were done by the permission of God. His message was to fear and worship God alone and to obey him (Jesus).

> [52]But when he became conscious of their disbelief, he cried: Who will be my helpers in the cause of Allah? The disciples said: We will be Allah's helpers. We believe in Allah, and bear thou witness that we have surrendered (unto Him). [53]Our Lord! We believe in that which Thou hast revealed and we follow him whom Thou hast sent. Enroll us among those who witness (to the truth). [54]And they (the disbelievers) schemed, and Allah schemed (against them): and Allah is the best of schemers. [55](And remember) when Allah said: O Jesus! I am gathering thee and causing thee to ascend unto Me, and am cleansing thee of those who disbelieve and am setting those who follow thee above those who disbelieve until the Day of Resurrection. Then unto Me ye will (all) return, and I shall judge between you as to that wherein ye used to differ. (Surah 3:52–55)

Here the Qur'an says Jesus had disciples, those who would help him in his task. The disciples declared that they were Muslims. Allah said He would raise Jesus up to be with Him.

> Lo! The likeness of Jesus with Allah is as the likeness of Adam. He created him of dust, then He said unto him: Be! And he is. (Surah 3:59)

According to the Qur'an, Allah created Jesus from dust just as He created Adam.

> [157]And because of their saying: We slew the Messiah, Jesus son of Mary, Allah's messenger—they slew him not nor crucified him, but it appeared so unto them; and lo! Those who disagree concerning it are in doubt thereof; they have no knowledge thereof save pursuit of a conjecture; they slew him not for certain. [158]But Allah took him up unto Himself. Allah was ever Mighty, Wise. [159]There is not one of the People of the Scripture but will believe in him before his death, and on the Day of Resurrection he will be a witness against them. (Surah 4:157–159)

As we have repeatedly seen, the Qur'an clearly denies the crucifixion of Jesus. The Jews boasted that they killed Jesus by crucifying him. The Qur'an declares this never happened. It only appeared so.

> O people of the Scripture! Do not exaggerate in your religion nor utter aught concerning Allah save the truth. The Messiah, Jesus son of Mary, was only a messenger of Allah, and His word which He conveyed unto Mary, and a spirit from Him. So believe in Allah and His messengers, and say not "Three"— Cease! (it is) better for you! —Allah is only One God. Far is it removed from His Transcendent Majesty that He should have a son. His is all that is in the heavens and all that is in the earth. And Allah is sufficient as Defender. (Surah 4:171)

Here the Qur'an affirms that Jesus was only a messenger from God, as well as God's Word and a spirit from Him.

> They indeed have disbelieved who say: Lo! Allah is the Messiah, son of Mary. Say: Who then can do aught against Allah, if He had willed to destroy the Messiah son of Mary, and his mother

and everyone on earth? Allah's is the Sovereignty of the heavens and the earth and all that is between them. He createth what He will. And Allah is Able to do all things. (Surah 5:17)

In this passage the Qur'an affirms that those who say that Jesus is God have blasphemed.

> [72]They surely disbelieve who say: Lo! Allah is the Messiah, son of Mary. The Messiah (himself) said: O Children of Israel, worship Allah, my Lord and your Lord. Lo! Whoso ascribeth partners unto Allah, for him Allah forbidden paradise. His abode is the Fire. For evil-doers there will be no helpers. [73]They surely disbelieve who say: Lo! Allah is the third of three; when there is no God save the One God. If they desist not from so saying a painful doom will fall on those of them who disbelieve. (Surah 5:72–73)

Here the Qur'an again says it is blasphemous to say that God and Jesus are one and the same. Jesus told his fellow Israelites to worship only God. The Qur'an also affirms that anyone who attributes any partners to God will be denied entrance to heaven. In fact, the fire will be their eternal dwelling place. The Qur'an says it is also blasphemy to say that God is one of a trinity.

> And We caused Jesus, son of Mary, to follow in their footsteps, confirming that which was (revealed) before him in the Torah, and We bestowed on him the Gospel wherein is guidance and a light, confirming that which was (revealed) before it in the Torah—a guidance and an admonition unto those who ward off (evil). (Surah 5:46)

The Qur'an reaffirms that God sent Jesus to confirm the law (Torah) that came before him. God gave the gospel to Jesus, which provides guidance and light.

¹¹⁰"When Allah saith: O Jesus, son of Mary! Remember My favour unto thee and unto thy mother; how I strengthened thee with the holy Spirit, so that thou spakest unto mankind in the cradle as in maturity; and how I taught thee the Scripture and Wisdom and the Torah and the Gospel; and how thou didst shape of clay as it were the likeness of a bird by My permission, and didst blow upon it and it was a bird by My permission, and thou didst heal him who was born blind and the leper by My permission; and how thou didst raise the dead by My permission; and how I restrained the Children of Israel from (harming) thee when thou camest unto them with clear proofs, and those of them who disbelieved exclaimed: This is naught else than mere magic; (Surah 5:110)

Again, the Qur'an reaffirms that the miracles Jesus did came by the permission of God.

¹¹⁶And when Allah saith: O Jesus, son of Mary! Didst thou say unto mankind: Take me and my mother for two gods beside Allah? He saith: Be glorified! It was not mine to utter that to which I had no right. If I used to say it, then thou knewest it. Thou knowest what is in my mind, and I know not what is in Thy Mind. Lo! Thou, only Thou, art the Knower of Things Hidden? ¹¹⁷I spake unto them only that which Thou commandest me, (saying): Worship Allah, my Lord and your Lord. I was a witness of them while I dwelt among them, and when Thou tookest me Thou wast the Watcher over them. Thou art Witness over all things. (Surah 5:116–117)

The Qur'an negates that Jesus ever told others to worship him and his mother as gods.

³⁰And the Jews say: Ezra is the son of Allah, and the Christians say the Messiah is the son of Allah. That is their saying with their mouths. They imitate the saying of those who disbelieved

of old. Allah (Himself) fighteth against them. How perverse are they! [31] They have taken as lords beside Allah their rabbis and their monks and the Messiah son of Mary, when they were bidden to worship only One God. There is no God save Him. Be He Glorified from all that they ascribe as partner (unto Him)! (Surah 9:30–31)

The Qur'an restates it is not true what the Christians say about Jesus: that he is the Son of God. God is unique and there is no one else like Him. God has no partners.

And when Jesus son of Mary said: O Children of Israel! Lo! I am the messenger of Allah unto you, confirming that which was (revealed) before me in the Torah, and bringing good tidings of a messenger who cometh after me, whose name is the Praised One. Yet when he hath come unto them with clear proofs, they say: This is mere magic. (Surah 61:6)

Finally, the Qur'an states that Jesus himself predicted a special messenger who would come after him. This prophet would give clear evidence of this, and his name would be "Ahmad (Praised One)."

Jesus in the Bible

There are many similarities in the stories of Jesus that come from both the Qur'an and Bible. These we can celebrate and agree on. As Christians, we can use them to relate better to our Muslim friends. Among the similarities are:

1. Jesus was born of a virgin—Mary.
2. Jesus was sinless.
3. Jesus is highly exalted in this world and in the life to come.
4. Jesus was a teacher. He brought a message from God to mankind.
5. Jesus had disciples/helpers to assist him in his task on earth.

6. Jesus performed miracles. He healed lepers, gave sight to the blind, and brought the dead back to life.

7. At the end of the age Jesus will come back to judge the world.

But there are also significant differences. Because the Bible references to Jesus are so numerous, I only share seven below that are in direct conflict to what appears in the Qur'an.

1. The Qur'an says Jesus was created by God from dust,
just as was Adam.

To the contrary, the Bible declares that Jesus is the creator of everything:

[1]In the beginning was the Word, and the Word was with God, and the Word was God. [2]He was with God in the beginning. [3]Through him all things were made; without him nothing was made that has been made. . . . [14]The Word became flesh and made his dwelling among us. We have seen his glory, the glory of the one and only Son, who came from the Father, full of grace and truth. (John 1:1–3, 14)

In addition, Jesus existed before Abraham:

[56]"Your father Abraham rejoiced at the thought of seeing my day; he saw it and was glad." [57]"You are not yet fifty years old," they said to him, "and you have seen Abraham!" [58]"Very truly I tell you," Jesus answered, "before Abraham was born, I am!" (John 8:56–58)

Finally, Jesus is the creator of everything and He holds everything together:

[16]For in him all things were created: things in heaven and on earth, visible and invisible, whether thrones or powers or rulers

or authorities; all things have been created through him and for him. [17]He is before all things, and in him all things hold together. (Col. 1:16–17)

2. The Qur'an says Jesus predicted the coming of another prophet and messenger after him who would be named "Ahmad" ("Muhammad")

The Bible disagrees. This question was extensively covered in chapters 7 and 8.

3. The Qur'an says Jesus never told others to worship him.

What the Qur'an says about Jesus is partially true—Jesus never told or encouraged others to worship his mother Mary as a god. However, Jesus did accept the worship of Himself as God by others. Three examples are given below.

Others worshiped Him as the Son of God. "Then those who were in the boat worshiped him, saying, 'Truly you are the Son of God.'" (Matt. 14:33)

After his resurrection his followers worshipped Him. "Suddenly Jesus met them. 'Greetings,' he said. They came to him, clasped his feet and worshiped him" (Matt. 28:9); "When they saw him, they worshiped him; but some doubted" (Matt. 28:17).

4. The Qur'an says Jesus is not the Son of God

According to the Bible, at his trial Jesus admitted to being the Messiah, as well as the Son of God:

[63]But Jesus remained silent. The high priest said to him, "I charge you under oath by the living God: Tell us if you are the Messiah, the Son of God." [64]"You have said so," Jesus replied. "But I say to all of you: From now on you will see the Son of

Man sitting at the right hand of the Mighty One and coming on the clouds of heaven." (Matt. 26:63–64)

This topic was also extensively covered at the end of chapter 10.

5. The Qur'an says Jesus is not part of the Trinity

Once again, a few examples are given below.

The apostle Paul wrote that Jesus is the very image of God, as well as the creator of everything:

15The Son is the image of the invisible God, the firstborn over all creation. 16For in him all things were created: things in heaven and on earth, visible and invisible, whether thrones or powers or rulers or authorities; all things have been created through him and for him. 17He is before all things, and in him all things hold together. (Col. 1:15–17)

At his baptism God the Father announced that Jesus was His well-loved Son:

16As soon as Jesus was baptized, he went up out of the water. At that moment heaven was opened, and he saw the Spirit of God descending like a dove and alighting on him. 17And a voice from heaven said, "This is my Son, whom I love; with him I am well pleased." (Matt. 3:16–17)

Upon giving His disciples the Great Commission, Jesus equated the names of God: the Father, Son, and Holy Spirit:

Therefore go and make disciples of all nations, baptizing them in the name of the Father and of the Son and of the Holy Spirit. (Matt. 28:19)

Paul the apostle, as well, equates the Holy Spirit, Lord, and God:

[4]There are different kinds of gifts, but the same Spirit distributes them. [5]There are different kinds of service, but the same Lord. [6]There are different kinds of working, but in all of them and in everyone it is the same God at work. (1 Cor. 12:4–6)

This topic was extensively covered at the end of chapter 5.

6. The Qur'an says that Jesus is not God

The Bible, however, says differently. Jesus said he was God:

[58]"Very truly I tell you," Jesus answered, "before Abraham was born, I am!" [59]At this, they picked up stones to stone him, but Jesus hid himself, slipping away from the temple grounds. (John 8:58–59)

Others said he was God:

[26]A week later his disciples were in the house again, and Thomas was with them. Though the doors were locked, Jesus came and stood among them and said, "Peace be with you!" [27]Then he said to Thomas, "Put your finger here; see my hands. Reach out your hand and put it into my side. Stop doubting and believe." [28]Thomas said to him, "My Lord and my God!" (John 20:26–28)

In addition, Jesus demonstrated he was God by raising people from the dead:

[11]Soon afterward, Jesus went to a town called Nain, and his disciples and a large crowd went along with him. [12]As he approached the town gate, a dead person was being carried

out—the only son of his mother, and she was a widow. And a large crowd from the town was with her. [13]When the Lord saw her, his heart went out to her and he said, "Don't cry." [14]Then he went up and touched the bier they were carrying him on, and the bearers stood still. He said, "Young man I say to you, get up!" [15]The dead man sat up and began to talk, and Jesus gave him back to his mother. [16]They were all filled with awe and praised God. "A great prophet has appeared among us," they said. "God has come to help his people." (Luke 7:11–16)

7. The Qur'an says Jesus was not crucified.

The Bible not only states that Jesus was crucified, but cites eyewitness documentation of the crucifixion:

[31]After they had mocked him, they took off the robe and put his own clothes on him. Then they led him away to crucify him. [32]As they were going out, they met a man from Cyrene, named Simon, and they forced him to carry the cross. [33]They came to a place called Golgotha (which means "the place of the skull"). [34]There they offered Jesus wine to drink, mixed with gall; but after tasting it, he refused to drink it. [35]When they had crucified him, they divided up his clothes by casting lots. (Matt. 27:31–35)

Again, this important topic was covered at the end of chapter 11.

The Shadow When the Qur'an Is Compared to the Bible

All the differences above deal with the person of Jesus. What is notably absent in the Qur'an is Jesus's deity, his crucifixion, and his resurrection—and that's a lot!

We will now examine two of Sayyid Qutb's key nineteen Qur'anic themes that are relevant to the story of Jesus.

Sayyid Qutb Themes

This chapter about Jesus relates most closely to two of our nineteen Qur'anic themes from Sayyid Qutb, 11 and 17, dealing with associating partners with God, as well as using parables to illustrate truth.

11. Danger of "Associating Partners" with God

Sayyid Qutb affirms this to be the most serious mistake any person can make in Islam: believing that any other person is equal to God. To Muslims this is most notably seen when Christians say and believe that Jesus Christ is the Son of God and is truly divine. According to Qutb, associating partners with God is actually a violation of the very fabric of the universe. He states that if anyone ascribes partners to God, they will not be allowed to enter heaven.[2]

> Say: Come, I will recite unto you that which your Lord hath made a sacred duty for you: That ye ascribe no thing as partner unto Him and that ye do good to parents, and that ye slay not your children because of penury—We provide for you and for them—and that ye draw not nigh to lewd things whether open or concealed. And that ye slay not the life which Allah hath made sacred, save in the course of justice. This he hath commanded you, in order that ye may discern. (Surah 6:151)

Qutb reminds us that the foundation on which faith is built is this: *Don't associate partners with God!*[3]

According to Qutb, believing that God has a son is naïve and is based on a wrong concept of God. It fails to see the great gulf between the eternal God and mortal human beings. Also, it fails to see the wisdom that allows humans to procreate in compensation for the shortness of their lives.[4]

> [88]And they say: The Beneficent hath taken unto Himself a son. [89]Assuredly ye utter a disastrous thing [90]whereby almost

the heavens are torn, and the earth is split asunder and the mountains fall in ruins, [91]that ye ascribe unto the Beneficent a son, [92]when it is not meet for (the Majesty of) the Beneficent that He should choose a son. (Surah 19:88–92)

According to Qutb, the entire cosmos is angry at this false assertion about the creator God. All nature is shocked.[5]

17. Use of Parables in the Qur'an—gnat, fly, spider, ashes blown by the wind, growing tree, gardens, etc.

Qutb discusses parables and how they are used in the Qur'an to convey spiritual truth. He reminds us that flies can be very powerful and rob people of that which is most precious—life—through various diseases.[6] He also notes that anyone wanting to be protected by anything other than God is just like a spider in its weak home that is without strength or real support.[7] Qutb further states that ashes blown about on a stormy day illustrate that the works of unbelievers will amount to nothing.[8] Finally, according to Qutb, the two gardens are filled with fruit and laden with date palms. Between the two gardens, a man cultivates a field containing grain and other plants. A river running between the two gardens is inexhaustible and brings in much continuous prosperity.[9] Our next story comes from this same surah (18).

Again, as part of our four-stranded rope model, we look at a unique story from the Qur'an relating to the person of Jesus.

Associated Qur'an Story

The Sleepers in the Cave—from Surah 18 al-Kahf (the Cave)

This surah was revealed in Mecca and has 110 verses. It takes its name from verses 9–10:

[9]Or deemest thou that the People of the Cave and the inscription are a wonder among our portents? [10]When the young men fled

for refuge to the Cave and said: Our Lord! Give us mercy from
Thy presence, and shape for us right conduct in our plight.

This story from the Qur'an is singular because it takes its origin
from Christian rather than Muslim tradition.[10] The Christian version
of the story first appeared in the fifth century AD, through the Syrian
bishop Jacob of Serug. It begins around AD 250 during the harsh
persecution of Christians, under the Roman Emperor Decius. As an
oath of loyalty, the emperor ordered all people to offer sacrifices to the
Roman gods. Seven young Christian men from Ephesus (modern-day
Turkey) refused but were given time to reconsider. They decided not
to offer the required sacrifices. Instead, they donated their worldly
possessions to the poor and retired to a cave outside Ephesus to pray.
The emperor then ordered the mouth of the cave sealed. Decius died
the following year, but it was not until many years later, under the
Emperor Constantine, that Christians ceased being persecuted and
Christianity was announced as the official religion of the Roman
Empire.

According to one version of the story, three hundred years later
a landowner opened the mouth of the cave, intending to use it as a
cattle pen. Inside he found seven youths sleeping. They still appeared
young. When they woke, they believed they had been asleep for no
more than a day. They were hungry and sent one of the seven into the
nearby town to buy food. Arriving in the city, the youth was surprised
to find crosses mounted on the top of buildings. The townspeople were
also surprised by the ancient coins the youth tried to spend, having
been minted hundreds of years earlier during the time of the Emperor
Decius. The bishop was summoned to interview the seven "young"
men. They related their miracle story and died praising God, saying
they had been promised resurrection.

The Muslim version of the story is recounted in verses 9–31 of
Surah 18 al-Kahf, the Cave. That version does not give the exact

number of men, but only that they were three or five or seven and that they were also accompanied by a dog:

> (Some) will say: They were three, their dog the fourth, and (some) say: Five, their dog the sixth, guessing at random; and (some) say: Seven, and their dog the eighth. Say (O Muhammad): My Lord is Best Aware of their number. None knoweth them save a few. So contend not concerning them except with an outward contending, and ask not any of them to pronounce concerning them. (Surah 18:22)

The Muslim version also gives the duration of their sleep as three hundred years, or 309 years in verse 25:

> And (it is said) they tarried in the Cave three hundred years and add nine.

In his commentary on the Qur'an, A. Yusuf Ali adds that the three hundred years were solar years, which was the equivalent of 309 lunar years (as there are 365 days in the solar year and 354 days in the lunar year).[11]

Qutb adds that this story appears in the Qur'an due to difficult questions rabbis in Medina told some Qurayshis to put to Muhammad in Mecca, to find out if he were a genuine prophet of God. The current surah was revealed in response to those questions.[12]

The pattern in each chapter of this book has been to end with a relevant and new perspective on Christianity brought out by an objection Qutb had for Christianity and/or Judaism. This chapter's topic does not arise specifically out of one of Qutb's objections. It is, however, a follow-up on the last chapter's Qur'anic statement that Jesus was not crucified and did not die on the cross. Thus, this chapter closes with what Christians believe happened after Jesus was crucified: His resurrection from the dead three days later.

A New Perspective on Christianity: Jesus's Resurrection from the Dead

I sat with a Muslim acquaintance who was eager to demonstrate the superiority of Islam over Christianity. I made the following comment: "You know, your job is really simple. All of Christianity hangs on the following historical event—the resurrection of Jesus Christ from the dead. If it didn't happen, then nothing else about Christianity matters. If you can disprove the resurrection, you're home free!"

I've related to Muslims for more than forty years. In all that time I've never seen Muslims show much concern about the resurrection of Jesus. My best guess is that it's because the majority of them don't believe Jesus was crucified or died on the cross to begin with. Why then should they be concerned about the resurrection?

Actually, I don't intend to give a full-bodied answer to that issue here, since Qutb never addressed it in his work. However, because it is an essential stone—if not *the* essential stone—in the Christian faith, I wish to briefly mention the four major historical facts supporting this assertion. This topic has been well addressed by others such as Josh McDowell,[13] as well as William Lane Craig and Lee Strobel.[14]

Basically, there are four historically well-documented events supporting the resurrection of Jesus. First was his crucifixion and being placed in a guarded and sealed tomb. Second, three days later the empty tomb of Jesus was discovered and documented by both believers and nonbelievers. Third, there were numerous eyewitness post-resurrection appearances of Jesus in a physical body. These included his appearing to women at the tomb, to the eleven disciples in Jerusalem and at the Sea of Galilee, to two disciples on the road to Emmaus, to upward of five hundred other people (1 Cor. 15:6), Jesus's ascension into heaven, as well as other appearances including to Paul the apostle. Finally, there is the existence of the church itself, resulting from Christ's early disciples and followers who willingly went to their deaths rather than deny Christ. No one willingly goes to their death for a cause they know to be false. Yet many thousands did just that. This continues to be the case today.

This chapter concludes with the following story centering around the person of Christ.

"Do you really believe that Jesus hears your prayers and answers them?"

A Muslim friend of nearly twenty years was also a respected professor born in southern Asia. He kindly arranged for me to interview two other Muslim students for my project. The first was an Egyptian working on his PhD; the second was a postdoctoral fellow from Libya.

We sat in a university building, and my professor friend started by introducing me. "First, I want to tell you about Dr. Hoskins and his family. They were the best neighbors you could imagine. One winter, after a heavy snowfall, the driveway to our house was blocked. When I got up I wondered how I would be able to drive to work that day. I soon discovered that someone had secretly shoveled our driveway. This actually happened twice. The last time I had driven home from work and found it was Mrs. Hoskins doing the shoveling."

After that kind introduction I explained about the project and let them know I was doing this in order to write another book. The purpose of the interview process was to ensure that I would not be misrepresenting Islam or the Qur'an in any way. The second part of the interview was testing one of the many overlapping comparisons I found in both the Qur'an and Bible. Each student chose a specific topic from my list of nineteen major themes I found from Sayyid Qutb.

After reviewing the list of Qutb's nineteen Qur'anic themes, both students affirmed them to be consistent with what they knew about Islam and the Qur'an. The Egyptian graduate student chose theme number 2 (The Nature of God's Revelation and the Miraculous Nature of the Qur'an) for further discussion. The postdoctoral fellow from Libya selected theme number 12 (Relating to People of Earlier Revelations—Jews and Christians).

For the Egyptian student's theme, the point of comparison in the Bible came from Isaiah 33:6: "He will be the sure foundation for your times, a rich store of salvation and wisdom and knowledge; the fear of the Lord is the key to this treasure." He was fascinated to learn that the Old Testament Hebrew word for "salvation" was *yeshua*, the identical word in Hebrew used for Jesus. His topic for Bible comparison had to do with revenge and Jesus's surprising command to his followers to "Love your enemies, and do good to those who hate you" from Luke 6:27–28. With wide-open eyes he said, "We don't have anything like this in Islam!"

This stimulated a flurry of questions from those present. My professor friend asked me to relate my personal faith story, which I was happy to do. The Egyptian student asked, "Since you have extensively studied Islam, how is it possible that you have not become a Muslim?" He also asked, "What did you find about Islam that you didn't like?"

The short answer to both questions I explained as follows. I see the main difference between Islam and Christianity lies in two verbs: "do" vs. "done." In my understanding of Islam it is necessary for someone to "do" something in order to please God. In Christianity Jesus has already "done" everything for us and we must respond back to Him and others through love.

The Egyptian student then asked, "Do you really believe that Jesus hears your prayers and answers them?" I said, "Yes, I've seen it happen many times." He smiled but appeared incredulous, since this meant that Jesus would have to be much more than "just a prophet."

God had opened a friendly but forthright opportunity to discuss the essence of our faiths. May God be honored and glorified!

Summary Questions for Reflection

1. Do you think it is possible to reconcile the differences in the pictures of Jesus that are presented in the Qur'an and the Bible? Whether your answer is yes or no, what are your reasons?

2. Using parables to teach engages the heart as well as the mind. What lessons can we learn from that concept to help Muslims and Christians better listen, understand, and relate to each other?

3. What lessons can be learned from the Qur'an story about The Sleepers in the Cave, and how can they be used in Muslim-Christian relations in today's world?

CHAPTER 13

WHERE DO WE GO FROM HERE?

A seed starts its odyssey of reproduction. It begins like one familiar with the journey and moves step by step. It never makes an error and never wanders from the path. The hand of God guides it.—Sayyid Qutb[1]

Now all has been heard; here is the conclusion of the matter; Fear God and keep His commandments, for this is the whole duty of man. For God will bring every deed into judgment, including every hidden thing, whether it is good or evil. (Eccl. 12:13–14)

"Frankly, Dr. Ed, it's too late!"

In March 2005, I sipped tea with an Iraqi friend. I asked him what our country (America) could do to improve the worsening situation following the second Iraq war. He answered, "Frankly, Dr. Ed, it's too late!" He said that like most Iraqis living here in the United States, he was jubilant over the initial US invasion of his country. "We congratulated each other. We thought, 'In another month we will all be able to go back home.'" A month later Iraqis began asking if they shouldn't be fighting against the American invaders instead of Saddam Hussein's forces. Iraqi moderates mollified them, "Wait for at least a year. Give them time to stabilize the country. If they are not out by then, we will know they are here to stay."

It has been sixteen years since that conversation with my Iraqi friend. The situation in Iraq is not perfect, but I do believe it has improved. Most of the armed conflict has ended and nearly all American troops are gone. Saddam Hussein's tyranny has disappeared. Some suffering continues for the people, but the Iraqis finally control their own destiny. Looking back, I must disagree with my friend's comment, "Dr. Ed, it's too late!" I don't think it's ever too late to grow, learn, or make needed changes. The existence of this book attests to at least one person's ability to grow and learn and change—my own, and hopefully yours too!

More than three years ago, an odyssey was initiated to completely read the monumental eighteen-volume Qur'an commentary by a respected Muslim scholar, Sayyid Qutb. The hope was that this effort might provide Christians a broader, richer, more compassionate, and full-bodied view of Islam and the Qur'an—and in turn, a better understanding of the religious tension found in today's dangerous world. The review itself took almost a year. This final chapter summarizes what was found.

Details of the project, including interview results, are included in Appendix III of the book. Throughout the project were four interwoven threads. The first thread included nineteen major Qutb Qur'anic themes. This "list of nineteen" is a summary of what Muslims believe informationally about Islam and the Qur'an. This "list of nineteen" (found in Appendix I) was also what was used in each mosque interview with Muslims to determine the accuracy of what Qutb wrote about their religion.

In my opinion, the decision to use Qutb's *In the Shade of the Qur'an* to better understand the Qur'an and Islam was a good choice. It was both instructive and profitable, as well as easy-to-read and palatable. Muslims themselves validated by just under 99% that what Qutb wrote in *In the Shade of the Qur'an,* summarized by the "list of nineteen"

Qur'anic themes, accurately reflects both the Qur'an and Islam.[2] Not only that, but as alluded to in this book's introduction, Qutb may well be the link to understanding the modern Islamic Awakening influencing world events today.

Also, by using *In the Shade of the Qur'an* as a guided tour of Islam, a more full-bodied and compassionate view of the Qur'an was obtained, as well as a greater appreciation for both story and historical context. Further, it allows one to see and feel and appreciate more of what our Muslim friends see and feel when they interact with the Qur'an. Yes, it was a risky decision, since Qutb is controversial to both Muslims and Christians. But that does not discount the fact that *In the Shade of the Qur'an* is arguably the most popular modern commentary on the Qur'an used by Muslims today throughout the world. Its use is only rivaled by the modern Qur'an commentaries of Abdullah Yusuf Ali and Sayyid Abdul Ala Maududi.

Twelve Stories of Prophets Found in Both the Qur'an and Bible: What Truths Do the Shadows Reveal?

Earlier in this book I referred to Franco Zeffirelli's 1996 film adaptation of *Jane Eyre*. In the film, Jane instructs her pupil Adele in art. "Remember, the shadows are just as important as the light." Throughout this book each chapter has highlighted one of these stories and shown how the shadow of the prophet of Islam brings out specific truths. The following characters appear: Adam, Cain and Abel, Noah, Abraham (with Lot, Ishmael, and Isaac), Joseph, Moses, Job, Jonah, David and Solomon, Zechariah and his son John the Baptist, Mary, the mother of Jesus, and finally Jesus Himself. These twelve characters illustrate our second, and most essential, strand in our rope of Qur'an understanding: How are the stories similar? How do they differ? Is there a pattern hidden in the shadows?

As brought out in chapters 1–12, in the Qur'an's account, for Adam there is no "original sin." For Cain and Abel, there is no evidence of God pursuing the offender with the goal of redemption.

For Noah, there is no sacrifice presented to God in thanks for Noah's deliverance through the ark and there is no rainbow covenant. For Abraham, other than the Qur'an's promise to make Abraham a "leader for mankind" (2:124), there is no promise from God of descendants beyond number—a multitude of nations who will one day be a blessing to all the families of the earth. Neither is there justification by faith for Abraham that resulted in righteousness. And finally, there is no Melchizedek, king of righteousness, and no paying tribute (tithe) from the lesser to the greater, and thus no prefiguring of Christ.

In Moses's story, there is no Passover, no Ten Commandments, no sacrificial system to pay for sin, no tabernacle, no Holy of Holies, and no "I AM" associated with the creator God. For Joseph's story, there is no promise of a return of the Jews to their promised land of Canaan and no promise of a "multitude of nations" that would come through the line of Manasseh.

Likewise, there is no "sign of Jonah" (see Matt. 12:38-40)—no prefiguring of One who would spend three days and three nights in the grave. In the Qur'an the focus is on Jonah's repentance and not on his understanding of God's compassion for the lost. In Job's story, there is no cosmic conflict between God and Satan. Most notably, there is no focus on the character of God as the cause and solution for Job's problems. And finally, there is no central theme of sacrifice as humankind's remedy for sin.

In the Qur'an's story of David and Solomon, there is no concern and respect for God's "anointed," no building of "Solomon's temple," and no connection with the coming Messiah. For Zechariah and his son John the Baptist, there is no forerunner for the promised Messiah. For Mary, there is no Magnificat and no "sword piercing her own soul" when she watched her own son die. And finally, for Jesus, there is no divinity, no Son of God, no cross, and no savior.

Isolated shadows mean little. However, when they are many and repeated it is difficult, if not impossible, to miss connecting the dots. They form an unavoidable picture that cannot be ignored. I entreat any open-minded person to carefully review this section, since it forms the heart of this book. Indeed, this section may well represent the most important finding of all. These "shadow stories" reveal what our Muslim friends have had excised from their spiritual diets. They are the essential vitamins that are lacking in the Qur'an and desperately needed. As a personal reflection, shouldn't we ask God to deliberately expose our Muslim friends to these topics and pray them into their lives?

Twelve Stories Unique to the Qur'an Highlighting the Early (Meccan) and Later (Medinan) Surahs

The lifeblood of any culture is highlighted in its stories. The same is true for Islam and the Qur'an. This third strand of our four-stranded rope highlighted twelve stories that are near and dear to the hearts of all Muslims. These stories come from early in Islam (before the Muslim community emigrated from Mecca to Medina) and from later after their migration to Medina. These stories help us experience what actually took place in their historical context.

Important lessons are learned from each of the above stories. These include topics such as the unity of God, the importance of taking our values from God and not from humans, listening to all the facts before making final judgments in any matter, being able to perceive spiritual lessons beyond what is normally seen, God's ultimate vindication of truth, and many others. As a final treat, I include one additional story generated from the Qur'an that is not included in the above twelve chapters.

The "Fabricated" Story of the Birds—from Surah 53
(an-Najm—The Star)

"Does it have any sports in it?" the skeptical grandson asks his grandfather, played by Peter Falk in the 1987 cult classic *The Princess Bride*.[3] The grandfather answers, "O my yes! Fencing, fighting, torture, true love, miracles, revenge, and giants." Like *The Princess Bride*, I believe the following story originating from the Qur'an may also have an abundance of adventure and conflict and surprising twists. Want to know more? Read on!

The title includes "fabricated" because that's the description used by Sayyid Qutb. This surah has only sixty-two verses and takes its title from the first verse:

> By the star when it setteth (Surah 53:1)

The controversy emerges from verses 19–20, when three female goddesses are mentioned:

> [19]Have ye thought upon Al-Lat and Al-Uzza, [20]And Manat, the third, the other? (Surah 53:19–20)

These two verses provided an author's idea for an award-winning book published in 1988. A year later, allegations of "blasphemy" resulted in a religious *fatwa* calling for the author's death. Out of respect for my Muslim friends I withhold the name of both the book and its author. The religious *fatwa* resulted in several failed assassination attempts, police protection, and even the death of a Japanese translator of the book.

In addition to much descriptive imagery, the surah's final verse contains the command to Muslims to prostrate in prayer to God (which is what Muslims do five times a day in worship).

> Rather prostrate yourselves before Allah and serve Him. (Surah 53:62)

That injunction is also part of the story, and central to the controversy. So, if this narration produced such a misunderstanding and is most likely only a "fabrication," why do I include it here? The answer is simple—because Sayyid Qutb considered it important enough to write five pages explaining it.[4]

Possibly the most detailed account of this strange occurrence comes from the respected Muslim biographer of the prophet of Islam Ibn Ishaq in his *Sirat Rasool Allah*.[5] I summarize Ibn Ishaq's narration in the following three paragraphs.

Early in Islam there was much opposition to Muhammad's message, even from his own people. He was deeply concerned for the welfare of his Qurayshi people in Mecca and wanted to attract them to Islam. He longed for God to send down a revelation to resolve this resistance. Then God sent down Surah al-Najm (the star). When he came to the part "Have you thought of Lat and Uzza and Manat the third, the others" (v. 20), Satan inserted the following words on his tongue: "These are the exalted *Gharaniq* (high-flying Numidian cranes) whose intercession is approved" (v. 21).

When the polytheistic Qurayshi people heard this, they were delighted, believing that both God and Muhammad approved of their worshipping multiple gods. When Muhammad came to the end of the surah (v. 62) and prostrated in response to God's command, the Qurayshi people also prostrated. News mistakenly went out that the Qurayshi people had accepted Islam. The angel Gabriel came to Muhammad and said, "What have you done, Muhammad? You have read to these people something I did not bring you from God and you have said what He did not say to you." Then God annulled what Satan had put in.

According to our "fabricated story," at that point the Qur'an recitation of verses 19–21 read as follows:

> [19]Have ye thought upon Al-Lat and Al-Uzza, [20]And Manat, the third, the other? [21]These are the exalted Gharaniq whose intercession is approved.

But after God annulled verse 21, the recitation of verses 19–21 was (and is today) as follows:

> [19]Have ye thought upon Al-Lat and Al-Uzza, [20]And Manat, the third, the other? Have you seen Lat, and Uzza, [20]And another,

the third (goddess), Manat? [21] Are yours the males and His the females? (Surah 53:19–21)

The above version is what currently appears in the Qur'an and what most, if not all, Muslims today (including Qutb) believe has always been the correct and only version.

So what are the implications? Is it possible that Satan actually inserted non–Qur'anic verses into Muhammad's recitation? If so, what does that say about God's ability to protect His own word? Also, if it did in fact take place, what does it imply about Muhammad's supposed infallibility? Qutb believed the story was "fabricated" for the following reasons. First, it calls into question the infallibility of Muhammad. And second, it undermines the truth of God's preservation of the Qur'an.[6] Qutb also wrote that another respected Islamic *mufassir* (interpreter of the Qur'an), Ibn Kathir, believed the story had no credible evidence.[7] I checked on this. When I read Ibn Kathir's *tafsir* on Surah al-Najm I found no mention of this story at all. However, other ancient and respected historical documents, Ibn Ishaq (mentioned above), Ibn Sa'd,[8] and Al-Tabari[9] all said the account was genuine. Even Sahih Bukhari gave a partial account of the story. So, what do you think?

Don't imagine that the thirteen stories used in this book are the only ones unique to the Qur'an! I compiled seven others not included due to lack of space. These include fascinating narratives such as the start of the Qur'an, "Read, in the Name of Your Lord" (from Surah 96); victory snatched from defeat, "the Battle of Badr" (from Surah 8); individual combat, "The Battle of the Trench" (from Surah 33); treachery, "Expulsion of the Jewish Tribe of Banu Al-Nadir" (from Surah 59); "My Mother's Back" (from Surah 58); "The Three Fighters Left Behind" (from Surah 9); and finally, the end of the Qur'an, "This Day I Have Perfected Your Religion for You" (from Surah 5). Each story adds context and deeper appreciation of the Qur'an. Each one is precious to our Muslim friends.

Inaccurate Statements Made by Sayyid Qutb about Christianity and Judaism That Beg Clarification

For our fourth and final rope strand, nine major objections by Sayyid Qutb to Christianity and Judaism were found and briefly presented in each book chapter. Complete copies of each of these nine objections are available from the author upon request.

Again, carefully examine this section. Simply ignoring its content by a preexisting dismissal guarantees life foundational cracks that will one day need to be accounted for. They provide a valuable resource for the reader.

What Muslims Want Christians to Know about the Qur'an

These are the answers that came from question number five in the survey I used. Forty-eight people responded to this question. Their answers are revealing and valuable to review and are found in Appendix IV.

Mismatch between Muslims' Basic Knowledge of the Gospel and Jesus's Message of God's Kingdom

This was one of the most personally surprising results of the study. There was near uniform knowledge by Muslims about the basic facts of the Christian gospel from survey question 6a ("original sin" coming through Adam, substitutionary atonement for sins by Christ's death on the cross, obtaining forgiveness and eternal salvation by accepting Christ's atoning work, belief in Jesus as the Son of God and a member of the Trinity). Simply knowing these facts did not mean or imply that Muslims agree with them, but only that they are aware of them. These "facts" are found in Islamic Qur'an commentaries as well as taught in mosques by imams. However, regarding survey question 6b about interpreting what these facts actually mean, I found near-uniform lack of understanding, as measured by Christ's major teaching about the gospel (good news) of the kingdom of God

Jesus went through all the towns and villages, teaching in their synagogues, proclaiming the good news of the kingdom and healing every disease and sickness. (Matt. 9:35)

In fact, during the sum total of my mosque surveys I only encountered one young Muslim, a Pakistani female physician, who I thought was spot-on! Her brief answer was, "Jesus himself is the gospel."

So, according to the Bible, what is the meaning of the phrase "the gospel of the kingdom of God?" Wherever the gospel went, it was associated with teaching, proclamation of the facts of spiritual freedom, and by demonstration of God's power. Jesus's God-given authority was shown by healing diseases and casting out demons. These details come from the Bible.

The "Gospel of the Kingdom" Is Used Four Times in the Bible

The gospel involved verbal proclamation as well as physical healing.

[23]Jesus went throughout Galilee, teaching in their synagogues, proclaiming the good news of the kingdom, and healing every disease and sickness among the people. [24]News about him spread all over Syria, and people brought to him all who were ill with various diseases, those suffering severe pain, the demon-possessed, those having seizures, and the paralyzed; and he healed them. (Matt 4:23–24)

Jesus went through all the towns and villages, teaching in their synagogues, proclaiming the good news of the kingdom and healing every disease and sickness. (Matt. 9:35)

The gospel would be proclaimed on a worldwide basis:

And this gospel of the kingdom will be preached in the whole world as a testimony to all nations, and then the end will come. (Matt. 24:14)

The gospel involves a struggle in order to enter God's kingdom:

The Law and the Prophets were proclaimed until John. Since that time, the good news of the kingdom of God is being preached, and everyone is forcing their way into it. (Luke 16:16)

The Essence of the Gospel is the Glory of Christ

Is there a central common theme to the gospel? Yes—it is the glory and beauty of Christ who is the image of God!

[3]And even if our gospel is veiled, it is veiled to those who are perishing. [4]The god of this age has blinded the minds of unbelievers, so that they cannot see the light of the gospel that displays the glory of Christ, who is the image of God. [5]For what we preach is not ourselves, but Jesus Christ as Lord, and ourselves as your servants for Jesus' sake. [6]For God, who said, "Let light shine out of darkness," made his light shine in our hearts to give us the light of the knowledge of God's glory displayed in the face of Christ. (2 Cor. 4:3–6)

What are the essential "facts" of the Gospel? What events and occurrences must be understood and believed?

The "Facts" of the Gospel

The basic gospel facts are succinctly summarized by the apostle Paul:

[3]For what I received I passed on to you as of first importance: that Christ died for our sins according to the Scriptures, [4]that he was buried, that he was raised on the third day according to the scriptures, [5]and that he appeared to Peter, and then to the

twelve. ⁶After that, he appeared to more than five hundred of the brothers at the same time, most of whom are still living, though some have fallen asleep. (1 Cor. 15:3–6)

The Gospel Is Connected with Salvation and Justification by Faith

¹⁶For I am not ashamed of the gospel, because it is the power of God that brings salvation to everyone who believes: first to the Jew, then to the Gentile. ¹⁷For in the gospel the righteousness of God is revealed—a righteousness that is by faith from first to last, just as it is written: "The righteous will live by faith." (Rom. 1:16–17)

Is there opposition to Jesus's Gospel? Absolutely!

A Cosmic Battle with Evil

¹¹Put on the full armor of God, so that you can take your stand against the devil's schemes. ¹²For our struggle is not against flesh and blood, but against the rulers, against the authorities, against the powers of this dark world and against the spiritual forces of evil in the heavenly realms. (Eph. 6:11–12)

⁴The god of this age has blinded the minds of unbelievers, so that they cannot see the light of the gospel of the glory of Christ, who is the image of God. (2 Cor. 4:4)

John the Baptist Confirmed the "Gospel-bearer"

²When John, who was in prison, heard about the deeds of the Messiah, he sent his disciples ³to ask him, "Are you the one who is to come, or should we expect someone else?" ⁴Jesus replied, "Go back and report to John what you hear and see: ⁵The blind receive sight, the lame walk, those who have leprosy are cleansed, the deaf hear, the dead are raised, and the good news is proclaimed to the poor." (Matt. 11:2–5)

Is Jesus's Gospel Only a "Ticket to Heaven"?

There is a danger here that all Christians should be wary of—
reductionist thinking in regard to the gospel. It's not just a four-point
plan of salvation or a technique for managing our sin problem. Noted
authors and Bible scholars Scot McKnight and N. T. Wright would
second this caution.[10]

From an eternal basis, Jesus's gospel of the kingdom ultimately
involves justification by faith and eternal salvation. But that's not all it
emphasizes. In the Lord's Prayer, Jesus prayed, "Your kingdom come,
your will be done, on earth as it is in heaven" (Matt. 6:10). Everywhere
Jesus and His gospel went God's kingdom was visibly demonstrated
and society was at least partially transformed. This is what naturally
happens when the Holy Spirit of God is set loose in society! This applies
whether it is the abolition of slavery in Britain by William Wilberforce,
the foundation of orphan homes in England by George Muller in
England, the elimination of child temple prostitution in India by Amy
Carmichael, or the building of hospitals and educational facilities
throughout the world, proliferating child vaccines, or even providing
clean water to drink. Jesus and His gospel are transforming forces.

But even at the risk of all the above factors, is it possible to summarize
the gospel? Here is my own four-part attempt.

The Gospel—a Four-Part Summary

1. The Promised Messiah/King Has Come in the Form of Jesus of Nazareth

A voice of one calling: "In the wilderness prepare the way for
the Lord; make straight in the desert a highway for our God."
(Isa. 40:3)

In its most basic form, the gospel of the kingdom of God is the story
of Jesus. And Jesus's story is that of a coming prophesied Messiah/
King who completes the story of the Old Testament—from Genesis to

Malachi—from Adam and Noah and Abraham and Moses and Joseph and Jonah and David and Isaiah and Malachi and John the Baptist, and finally culminating with Jesus of Nazareth.

2. The Messiah / King Came to Proclaim the "Good News" and "to Make Everything New"

[1]The Spirit of the Sovereign Lord is on me, because the Lord has anointed me to proclaim good news to the poor. He has sent me to bind up the brokenhearted, to proclaim freedom for the captives and release from darkness for the prisoners, [2]to proclaim the year of the Lord's favor and the day of vengeance of our God, to comfort all who mourn. (Isa. 61:1–2)

[16]He went to Nazareth, where he had been brought up, and on the Sabbath day he went into the synagogue, as was his custom. He stood up to read, [17]and the scroll of the prophet Isaiah was handed to him. Unrolling it, he found the place where it is written: [18]"The Spirit of the Lord is on me, because he has anointed me to proclaim good news to the poor. He has sent me to proclaim freedom for the prisoners and recovery of sight for the blind, to set the oppressed free, [19]to proclaim the year of the Lord's favor." (Luke 4:16–19)

This "proclamation of freedom for prisoners" and "recovery of sight for the blind" is part and parcel of the transforming power of the gospel. Jesus said, "I am making everything new!" (Rev. 21:5)

3. The Messiah / King Would Be the Promised Suffering Servant

[3]He was despised and rejected by mankind, a man of suffering, and familiar with pain. Like one from whom people hide

their faces he was despised, and we held him in low esteem. ⁴Surely he took up our pain and bore our suffering, yet we considered him punished by God, stricken by him, and afflicted. ⁵But he was pierced for our transgressions, he was crushed for our iniquities; the punishment that brought us peace was on him, and by his wounds we are healed. (Isa. 53:3–5)

He died on the cross and was raised from the dead three days later.

4. Entrance into the Messiah's Kingdom Is by Invitation Only and Requires a Response of Belief, Commitment, Obedience . . . and Yes, Allegiance[11]

The gospel made God's love available to everyone.

For God so loved the world that he gave his one and only Son, that whoever believes in him shall not perish but have eternal life. (John 3:16)

The Gospel made Jesus's death and resurrection available to all:

For Christ also suffered once for sins, the righteous for the unrighteous, to bring you to God. He was put to death in the body but made alive in the Spirit. (1 Pet. 3:18)

The gospel centers around an individual's having or not having the Son of God:

¹¹And this is the testimony: God has given us eternal life, and this life is in his Son. ¹²Whoever has the Son has life; whoever does not have the Son of God does not have life. ¹³I write these things to you who believe in the name of the Son of God so that you may know that you have eternal life. (1 John 5:11–13)

The gospel requires open commitment to Christ:

⁹If you declare with your mouth, "Jesus is Lord," and believe in your heart that God raised him from the dead, you will be saved. ¹⁰For it is with your heart that you believe and are justified, and it is with your mouth that you profess your faith and are saved. (Rom. 10:9–10)

Final Remarks about the Gospel of the Kingdom of God

Even though Jesus began his public teaching by announcing, "the gospel of the kingdom of God," it would be a mistake to believe this to be the sum total of his instruction. Like any good teacher, Jesus started with what people already knew (i.e., from John the Baptist—repentance for sins) and then added to it. It was where Jesus started, but not where he finished. So, what ultimately, was his destination? Everywhere Jesus went, he was doing good (Acts 10:38). But relentlessly, Jesus moved toward the cross!

As the time approached for him to be taken up to heaven, Jesus resolutely set out for Jerusalem. (Luke 9:51)

Jesus was single-minded in heading for Jerusalem, for His destiny with the cross, to accomplish salvation for all mankind. John the Baptist saw this when he initially pointed Jesus out to his own followers.

The next day John saw Jesus coming toward him and said, "Look, the Lamb of God, who takes away the sin of the world!" (John 1:29)

Jesus saw this as he communicated to his disciples his sacrificial journey and looked forward to the end times and His own return to the Father.

⁴⁹"I have come to bring fire on the earth, and how I wish it were already kindled! ⁵⁰But I have a baptism to undergo, and what constraint I am under until it is completed! (Luke 12:49–50)

The apostle John saw this when he penned the final two verses of the Bible.

> [20]He who testifies to these things says, "Yes, I am coming soon." Amen. Come, Lord Jesus. [21]The grace of the Lord Jesus be with God's people. Amen. (Rev. 22:20–21)

So, based on my research findings, there exists a huge gap. My Muslim friends' and acquaintances' knowledge of the Gospel "facts" is extensive—but their practical understanding of how they personally apply this to life is clearly deficient. I end with a brief summary of an idea from pastor John Piper. "It's not the facts of the Gospel that is important, but the beauty of the facts!"[12] In the words of the Bible, it is "the light of the gospel of the glory of Christ, who is the image of God . . . the light of the knowledge of the glory of God in the face of Christ (2 Cor 4:4, 6). Perhaps, more simply, it is what our Pakistani physician said earlier: "Jesus himself is the gospel!"

What is the implication for us as we seek to reach out to our friends with the hope of Christ? If the above is true about the mismatch between our Muslim friends' basic knowledge of the Gospel and its practical outworking, how can we better apply the instruction traditionally? In the words attributed to St. Francis of Assisi, "Preach the Gospel at all times. If necessary, use words!"

Five Recommendations for the Reader

Recommendation #1: Apply the "Shamgar Principle"

I first heard about Shamgar forty-five years ago in a talk given by Dr. John Ridgway in Southern California at a program given by The Navigators. Shamgar was one of the judges in Israel following the death of Joshua. He is only mentioned twice in the Bible, both times in the book of Judges.

After Ehud came Shamgar son of Anath, who struck down six hundred Philistines with an ox-goad. He too saved Israel. (Judg. 3:31)

In the days of Shamgar son of Anath, in the days of Jael, the highways were abandoned; travelers took to winding paths. (Judg. 5:6)

From these two verses Dr. Ridgway made four conclusions about Shamgar's life. First, Shamgar lived in enemy-occupied territory. Israel was controlled by a warring tribe, their perennial enemies known as the Philistines. The usual highways were deserted and travelers had to go by round about secretive ways.

Second, Shamgar started where he was—a farmer in a field. Third, he used what he had (in his hand)—an ox-goad. An ox-goad was a double-ended farming tool. One end of the wooden stick was sharpened and used to direct (prod) oxen along a certain path. On the other non-sharpened end was often a metal scraping tool used to clear a plowshare from clods of dirt.

Fourth and finally, he did what he could. According to Judges 3:31, Shamgar "killed six hundred Philistines with an ox-goad." As a result he "saved Israel." God blessed his actions and the ancient Israelites were no longer in bondage.

A few notes of clarification are in order. First, I doubt Shamgar did all this by himself. More likely, he was the leader of an underground rebellion which succeeded. And second, it's important to note that even though the modern English word "Philistine" currently is translated into Arabic as "Palestinian," from my understanding and investigation there is no connection at all between these two people groups. Thus, there is absolutely no biblical justification for modern-day Israelis to go out and oppress modern-day Palestinians.

To recap, Shamgar started where he was (a farmer in a field), with what he had (an ox-goad), and did what he could—and God blessed his efforts. Since I first heard that talk forty-five years ago, I have tried to emulate that principle in my life and suggest that every individual should apply it. Every person has been given gifts by God. Each one also has certain resources at their disposal. And yes, each individual also has limitations as well as opportunities. The real question then, is this: Are we willing to lay down our gifts, and resources, and limitations, and opportunities at the feet of Jesus and ask Him to use these in any way He deems fit to make "Thy kingdom come, Thy will be done, on earth as it is in heaven"?

After I retired from active medical practice four years ago, this Shamgar Principle was one of the major factors that launched me on my current writing effort. In prayer I asked God how I could possibly serve Him, given my resources. In the medical community I am now officially "geriatric" and classed as "elderly." Physically, I have a bad heart, and daily I experience diminishing health and emotional energy, but I also have more physical time and financial resources. Even with our limitations, God can use us.

One woman in our church suffered from progressively deteriorating ALS (Amyotrophic Lateral Sclerosis—Lou Gehrig's Disease). In her last years she had lost her voice and the entire use of her body except for eye movement. She used that eye movement to activate her computer for communication. But she used it to the glory of God. She was able to maintain an internet site she called Meet My Friend. It was visited by many people from all over the world. I know of at least one person who put their trust in Christ because of those efforts. Recently she went home to be with the Lord. I'm sure one of the very first things she heard on arrival was "'Well done, good and faithful servant!" (Matt. 25:23)

It is important to stress that you don't have to be a Billy Graham, or a pastor, or wealthy, to serve God. Even an educated "geek" can serve the Lord! The only requirements are a commitment to love and serve Him, to yield our lives into His hands, and ask Him to multiply our "five loaves and two fish." It's God's job to do the rest. Our Lord said,

> [28]Come to me, all you who are weary and burdened, and I
> will give you rest. [29]Take my yoke upon you and learn from

me, for I am gentle and humble in heart, and you will find rest for your souls. ³⁰For my yoke is easy and my burden is light. (Matt. 11:28–30)

No matter how little we think we have to offer, our Lord is able and willing to multiply it and use it in His service. As you seek to apply the Shamgar Principle in your own life, may our great and mighty King of the Universe make that idea come true for you!

Recommendation #2: Ask More and Better Questions

Many years ago a dear mentor and friend, Bob Vidano, encouraged me to focus more on being "receiver-oriented" than "sender-oriented." What Bob really meant was that we in the Western world love to "tell" others anything and everything. Basically we are self-centered, not other-centered. We not only love to talk, but we also love to hear ourselves talk. Another friend reminded me years ago that God gave us two eyes, two ears, and one mouth—and that we should use them accordingly. Truth be told, when we hear others talking, most of us spend more time thinking of the next thing we intend to say than listening to what they are telling us. To all the above I plead, at times, "guilty"!

One partial cure for the above malady is to ask more questions. That allows someone else to be the teacher, the disseminator of knowledge. What's more, it takes me off the hot seat. Jesus was the master of that art form of asking questions.

Ten years ago I undertook a simple, relatively unstructured Bible study. Scanning the New Testament, I found every verse where Jesus asked someone a question. I jotted down the context and the result. It only took an afternoon, but I was stunned by what I found. I saw Jesus pry open the hearts and motives of individuals simply by asking questions: "What do you want me to do for you?" "Who do people say that I am?" "Saul, Saul, why do you persecute me?" "Where is your husband?" "Whom do you seek?" "Which one will love him more?" "Which son obeyed his father?" "Boys, have you caught any fish?" Jesus had an uncanny ability to use questions to open hearts and minds. These questions stimulated those asked to generate appropriate responses and actions. Question-asking is now one of my very favorite methods of sharing truth.

Since the time of that Bible study I started collecting questions and trying them out. I am always amazed by the discussions that result, especially from my Muslim friends. My favorites include "Could you tell me about your spiritual journey?" and "If you had a dream tonight and God came to you saying you could ask Him for anything, what would you ask for?" Here's another fun one I have used when discussing the Trinity: "Which one do you think existed first, God, His Spirit, or His Word?" One great resource I recommend comes from Doug Pollock's book *Godspace*.[13] At the back of his book Doug includes a list of ninety-nine possible questions, three questions for each of thirty-three topics. And yes, I have stolen a few of those and adapted them for my own use.

I think asking questions may be so powerful largely because it's truly other-centered (sounds biblical, right?) as well as puts my friend in the driver's seat in the role of teacher. I get the fun of hearing and watching the pins fall and the resulting new conversation paths that evolve. Memorize and use a few stock questions. Keep them for times when you can't think of what to ask. I think you will be pleasantly surprised!

Recommendation #3. Tell More Stories, Your Own and Those of Others—Especially Those That Focus on the Beauty and Glory of Christ!

Equal to question-asking, possibly my favorite form of truth-sharing is telling stories. Everyone loves listening to stories, as long as they are relevant, short, and well prepared. I'm always impressed with Revelation 12:11 (emphasis added): "*They triumphed over him* by the blood of the Lamb *and by the word of their testimony*; they did not love their lives so much as to shrink from death."

Other than being totally conversant with Jesus's story, arguably the most important narrative any believer can share is his or her own faith story. At first blush this seems counterintuitive. When I'm relating my personal journey to faith, isn't this being self-centered rather than other-focused? Actually, it is not! Although my life is the vehicle, the focus is really on the Alpha and Omega, the Morning Star who saved me—Jesus. That's why I believe everyone who wants to share truth with his or her friend needs to have their faith story ready to share. In fact, it's also probably the easiest story to transition into, especially when asked difficult and/or complicated questions we can't seem to handle.

That means we must be prepared. It's definitely not something you want to wing, or do off-the-cuff. Here are a few practical suggestions. First, keep your life story short—no more than three to five minutes. Pick a single significant theme from your own life as the glue for the story. For example, one friend was adopted and this caused him lots of pain as a child. Adoption was the theme he built off. That can be the start of a person's search for meaning or God. In my own case I had rheumatic fever as a child, resulting in a weakened heart. I was afraid of dying. Then include a single verse of Scripture to quote (don't quote the book or numerical reference) and be sure to tell how Jesus became real for you. Try to eliminate the common religious words such as "redemption," "salvation," "baptism," or "atonement." Get someone else to help you practice telling it, then be ready for God to do something special with your story.

There are other great stories to tell besides your faith story. Consider retelling one of Jesus's parables (there are thirty-eight of them—depending on how you count them) and each of them have a spiritual theme or purpose attached. They're easy to introduce simply by starting, "That reminds me of something Jesus the Messiah once said. . . ." Sometimes using precious stories from your friends' culture is appropriate. For example, people who come from Iran are usually enamored by the *Shah-nah-meh* (Book of Kings), an epic poem with the adventures of Rostam and Sohrab.[14] Over dinner once with a group of Iranian friends I said, "I just finished reading the *Shah-nah-meh* and was really impressed by it. Could you tell me a few of the major lessons you can learn from that poem?" You could also use the *Rubayyat* by Omar Khayyam. Both of those examples would mean you need to prepare by reading those works. Those are only examples. Try picking your own, like from *Alf Layla wa Layla* (from Scheherazade and the 1001 Arabian Nights). Every culture has its own precious and valued stories such as *Kalila wa Dimna* (animal wisdom stories) or those of *Juha (Nasr ud-din Hoja)*. You can find them in your local bookstore or even online.

Last but not least are the many stories from the Qur'an I have included in each chapter of this book. The sky's the limit regarding how to use these stories. Have fun!

Recommendation #4: Hand Out God's Word to Your Friends

Once, when Jesus was dealing with some reluctant and discouraged disciples he remarked, "The Spirit gives life; the flesh counts for nothing. The words I have spoken to you—they are full of the Spirit and life" (John 6:63). That's why, over the years, I have come to put less and less reliance on fancy techniques or presentations in sharing truth and more and more trust in simply getting my friends exposed to the actual Word of God.

I also think it's important to read the Bible with your friends, if possible. Most decline the offer, but I still make the attempt. A few have accepted over the years. I read the Bible with a Pakistani friend several times a month for a period of six years. During that time we made it through Matthew, Mark, Luke, Genesis, Exodus, Psalms, Proverbs, Ecclesiastes, and part of John. During each session I would ask a few questions, usually the same ones, "What does this passage tell us about who God is? What does this tell us about who Jesus is? What kind of response does Jesus want us to make?"

More and more I just ask friends, even ones I have just met, if they have ever read the Bible and if they would like to. I either offer one to them or offer to get together with them to read it together. Always be hopeful, but it's God's job to work in hearts. In John 6:44–45 Jesus reminds us:

> [44]No one can come to me unless the Father who sent me draws them, and I will raise them up at the last day. [45]It is written in the Prophets: 'They will all be taught by God.' Everyone who has heard the Father and learned from him comes to me.

Recommendation #5: Be Intentional and Friendly as You Extend Yourself!

My grandfather was one of the last old-time western sheriffs, from Luna County, New Mexico from 1928–1930. This was during "the Great Depression" and the era of "blue-laws" and "prohibition" (of alcohol). He wore a badge on his chest and a .38 Smith & Wesson revolver on his hip. On the few occasions he chased outlaws, he used his Model T Ford, not a horse. Once he solved the murder case of Red Mountain Robinson and was written up in an old Western dime magazine. His passions were deer hunting, fishing, and looking for Indian arrowheads. The following story is illustrative of being intentional.

"If He wants, He can raise up a deer for us out of the rocks in the ground."

Growing up with my brother, our rite of passage was going hunting and getting our first buck. Somehow, that honor always eluded me—at least until I was a grown man with a young son and daughter of my own. Thirty years ago I was on a hunting trip in the Gila Wilderness in southern New Mexico with my father, mother, brother, nephew, and son Matthew. A few days before the official hunt opened, we were scouting our area looking for deer signs. My dad told Matthew, "There are no deer in the area." Discouraged, Matthew brought me the news. I was a follower of Jesus by that time, having come to know Christ personally at age eighteen. I told Matthew, "That doesn't matter to God. If He wants, He can raise up a deer for us out of the rocks in the ground." So, we must be ready and prepared!

We had already spent hours sighting in the rifles a few weeks earlier. For years we had practiced marksmanship. Now we spent the afternoon looking over the mountainside for a good place to come early next morning when the hunt opened. That night I asked God in prayer something I've never prayed before or since: I asked Him to encourage us spiritually by giving us a buck—and I told my son about the prayer.

Early before dawn the next day, Matthew and I were up. We used flashlights to get to our previously chosen hunting spot on the side of a canyon. As the sun rose, Matthew heard some deer below us and there were two bucks. I got one of them. While we were preparing the deer to bring home Matthew looked at me and said, "Dad, God really does answer prayer!" The deer horns hang on our basement wall.

This incident doesn't mean that God is our errand boy or that we can be greedy getting anything we ask Him for. It does mean that even when He doesn't give us what we ask, He is still God. That incident encouraged both of us spiritually then; it still does to this day. God did His part. What was our part? To put ourselves in position for God to run the buck past us. It's still our responsibility today.

So, how do we get next to friends today? I'd like to suggest five possibilities. Most importantly, pray and ask God to lead you to the ones He wants you to share with. "Until now you have not asked for anything in my name. Ask and you will receive, and your joy will be complete" (John 16:24).

Also, ask Him for specific ideas for making natural contacts. Many folks live in university towns, like we do here in West Lafayette, Indiana. Nearly all universities have a high percentage of international students coming from all over the world. Many of these universities also have programs to match international students with local folks to help them with further language study or a place to go to celebrate holidays or for an opportunity to get to know an American family. Many local churches do the same things, or even work sensitively alongside the university programs. It must be stressed here to be sensitive and always follow the individual university rules and regulations. Every time you go shopping you will likely see families or individuals who don't dress or look like you. Walk up and greet them! Tell them you are glad they are part of our community. Then watch what a little friendliness can do.

Next is the absolute importance of closely walking with God. As 2 Timothy 2:20–21 says:

> [20]In a large house there are articles not only of gold and silver, but also of wood and clay; some are for special purposes and some for common use. [21]Those who cleanse themselves from the latter will be instruments for special purposes, made holy, useful to the Master and prepared to do any good work.

If one is thirsty and reaches into the cupboard, which glass is chosen: one that is made of crystal that has a cockroach crawling in it, or the plain peanut butter jar that is clear and sparkling? Remember, God does not use dirty vessels. Make sure to daily spend time alone with God in His Word (quiet time and prayer), and keep going to worship services and spending time with other believers.

Third, partner with others. Ecclesiastes 4:9–12 says:

> [9]Two are better than one, because they have a good return for their labor: [10]If either of them falls down, one can help the other up. But pity anyone who falls and has no one to help them up. [11]Also, if two lie down together, they will keep warm. But how can one keep warm alone? [12]Though one may be overpowered, two can defend themselves. A cord of three strands is not quickly broken.

Jesus sent out the disciples two by two for a reason: we need each other. For that reason, whenever I visit mosques, I always take along another believer.

Additionally, be educated on the basics of the other person's religious standing. Your friend will be flattered to know you care enough about him or her to find out a little bit about what they believe. It will also help keep you from embarrassing situations like serving something which is against their religion, such as accidentally serving pork to Muslims. There are lots of simple, short, and good books on this out. I'd like to suggest a couple here: my own book *A Muslim's Heart*[15]; and *Woman to Woman* by Joy Loewen.[16]

Lastly, be friendly! Proverbs 17:17 says, "A friend loves at all times, and a brother is born for a time of adversity." Learn a few friendly greetings, like the greeting *As-sa-LAA-mu-a-LAY-kum* (Peace be unto you!). This is probably the nicest greeting you can give a Muslim, and the one they give to each other on a daily basis. Even Jesus used this saying:

On the evening of that first day of the week, when the disciples were together, with the doors locked for fear of the Jewish leaders, Jesus came and stood among them and said, "Peace be with you!" (John 20:19)

I know there are some naysayers out there who tell you not to use that greeting since "only Muslims say that to each other." Don't you believe it! I have used this friendly greeting with many, many Muslims over the years all over the world, including those I have only met for the first time, and never once have I seen them offended by my using it.

Being friendly, however, does necessitate moving out of our comfort zones. It's usually OK to go up to an international person you may see for the first time in a store and ask, "Excuse me, but are you from another country? I'd like to greet you and tell you we are glad you are here."You will probably gain a smile and possibly even an invitation to come visit at their house.The only caveat here is to make sure it is a man (if you are a man reading this) or a woman (if you are a woman). Respecting gender difference is really important to most overseas cultures. Incidentally, most international students dream of actually getting to meet and know a real American family. It's also OK to attend their festivals and celebrations (at their invitation). Personally, I enjoy going to mosques for this. *But,* always be respectful. Take off your shoes before entering their prayer area.This is another reason it's helpful to educate yourself first on the subject.

Here a few final notes about being friendly, especially with Muslims. First, Muslims are not our enemies.As Christians, we do have an Enemy, but it is the same enemy that anyone, including Muslims, have: Satan. Also, Muslims, and others who don't believe as we do, are people just like you and me.They want the same things for their families that we want for ours.They love to laugh and have fun.Third, we don't need to be afraid of Muslims.The overwhelming majority are peaceful people who would never think of injuring you or me. Only a tiny minority are the ones that get the media attention.We have folks like that in our own culture, who even call themselves Christians.

Well, that's about it! Let's recap what we can do to better reach out to international neighbors and friends. First, follow the Shamgar Principle. Start where you are, with what you have, and do what you can—then watch God bless it! Also, ask more and better questions.They are really fun and eye-opening. In addition, tell more stories, especially your own story about how you came to know God in Christ better and especially the stories that focus on the beauty and glory of Christ. Fourth, do more distributing of God's Word. And last, be friendly! The overwhelming majority of folks out there are wonderful people.They are worth knowing. Jesus died for them as well as for us and they are precious in His sight!

I leave you with a final concluding remark that is especially applicable to Christians and Muslims: there is hope, even in the face of seemingly insurmountable cultural and religious obstacles! There is hope for Christians. Muslims are not our enemies. They are people just like you and me, with similar hopes and dreams and family goals and aspirations. There is also hope for Muslims. Christians truly want to emulate Jesus's command to "love Thy neighbor" and coexist peacefully with Muslims. So where do the two meet? Where is the common ground?

The answer may surprise you. It is not a question of "which religion is best?" The answer is not a religion, but a Person:

> [13]But now in Christ Jesus you who once were far away have been brought near by the blood of Christ. [14]For he himself is our peace, who has made the two groups one and has destroyed the barrier, the dividing wall of hostility, [15]by setting aside in his flesh the law with its commands and regulations. His purpose was to create in himself one new humanity out of the two, thus making peace, [16]and in one body to reconcile both of them to God through the cross, by which he put to death their hostility. [17]He came and preached peace to you who were far away and peace to those who were near. (Eph. 2:13–17)

Our odyssey concludes with a final story about Jesus—the ultimate sticking point.

"Doctor, you can give me any type of fluid or medicine you want *except* for blood."

More than thirty years ago, I was on duty as an emergency room physician when paramedics brought in a victim with a gunshot wound to the chest. The bullet pierced her heart, but she was still alive. A leak in the heart wall was partially sealed by clotted blood, so her heart kept beating. At most, she had a few minutes to live. I knew if her pressure could be maintained, there might be enough time for the surgeon to arrive, get her to the operating room, open the chest, plug the leak, and keep her from dying. Only one thing could keep her alive until that could happen: administering lots of oxygen-carrying whole blood in a hurry. Still conscious, my patient told me plainly, "Doctor, you can give me any type of fluid or medicine you want *except* for blood." I explained she only had a few minutes to live and that the only thing that could keep her alive was whole blood. She refused, and we couldn't save her.[17]

Every person who has ever lived is dying from a diseased heart. The disease is sin, and it separates us from God. It's a relentless disease that causes vicious hemorrhaging. There is only one treatment—the life-giving blood of Jesus. It would be wonderful if other treatments were enough to save someone—greater compassion, better cultural understanding, or a guaranteed Palestinian land-for-peace proposal. But that would be lying. We need Jesus. Whether we are born Muslim, Christian, Hindu, Jew, or atheist/agnostic, our disease requires the oxygen-rich whole blood of new life in Christ. Nothing else will do.

Summary Questions for Reflection

1. Some stories common to both the Bible and Qur'an deal with farming and seeds growing in soil. Assuming these to illustrate spiritual truths, what do you think determines the different kinds of soil in each person's life?

2. Do you think these different soils are permanent, or can they be transformed? If the latter, how do you think that can be done?

3. Why do some shadows obscure truth, while other shadows make truth more clear?

4. Why do you think both telling stories and asking questions encourage people to think more deeply?

5. Why do you think Jesus's concept of the gospel of the kingdom of God may be difficult for some people to understand?

LIST OF 19 MAJOR THEMES EMPHASIZED BY SAYYID QUTB IN FI ZILAL AL-QUR'AN (IN THE SHADE OF THE QUR'AN)

The following list was used for the project surveys.

1. Nature of God (His attributes—almighty, all-knowing, all-forgiving, accepts repentance, severe in retribution, limitless in bounty, no deity other than Him; to Him is the ultimate return) and the Absolute Importance of God's "Oneness"

2. Nature of God's Revelation, and the Miraculous Nature of the Qur'an (Qur'an—eternal, uncreated, guiding light of Islam everywhere and at all times, code of life for all Muslims, God's light and final message to mankind)—need to interpret the Qur'an based on the historical context and time of revelation

3. Nature of Man (a unique creature created by God, placed in heaven to eat of its fruit—all except the forbidden tree—given a measure of choice by God, man is weak and has two main weaknesses—his love of survival and his desire to possess) and

God's Covenant with Mankind (God allowed man to choose either to obey Him or lean toward Satan [also created by God], mankind's perpetual enemy—God did this to test man in his role to build human life on earth).

4. God's Messengers and a Unified Message for All Mankind—Fear God and worship Him alone, and obey His messengers

5. Nature of Worship and Prayer in Islam—Worship: total submission to God alone. Prayer: celebrates the praise of God, establishes a bond between a believer and his Lord, strengthens a believer's spirit, is one of the best deeds a believer can do and erases sin and error, involves regular and established daily prayer, and includes prostration and standing.

6. Beauty and Wonder of God's Creation

7. Nature of Sin, Repentance, Forgiveness, Testing, and Faith in Islam (see #3 above)—Because of Satan's enmity and man's weakness, man makes mistakes and sins. When he realizes this and repents, asking God for forgiveness, God freely forgives him. God tests the faith of all believers. Faith is the action that demonstrates man's true repentance. Faith is based on God's oneness and is a light that shines in the human heart and illuminates the soul so that it sees the way leading to God.

8. Ever-Present Battle between Satan and Believers, Faith, and Submission (see #3 and #7 above) and the Danger of Jahiliyyah Thinking (anything that is not consistent with Islam)

9. Nature of the Supernatural in Islam (Angels, *Jinn*, Heaven, Hell, and Miracles)

10. Social Systems in Islam: Care for the Poor, Role of Women, Justice, Economics, Marriage, Family, and Divorce (protecting the interests of weaker individuals)

11. Danger of "Associating Partners" with God

12. Relating to People of Earlier Revelations (Jews and Christians)—Islam is tolerant and does not force itself on anyone. Non-Muslims may share their faith, provided that they do not try to win Muslims to their faith and not insult Islam.

13. Nature and Purpose of Jihad and Its Progressive Nature Based on Time of Revelation (Greater and Lesser Jihad—God wants all people to have the opportunity to respond to the message of Islam)

14. Day of Judgment

15. Destiny and God's Ultimate Control over Everyone and Everything

16. Islam—a Complete and Integrated System for Life

17. Use of Parables in the Qur'an—gnat, fly, spider, ashes blown by the wind, growing tree, gardens, etc.

18. Illustrating Qur'anic Truths Using Various Scientific Topics—The Qur'an is mainly concerned with the human soul and the state of the human condition. Even so, scientific truths (meteorology, botany, zoology, physiology, mathematics, astronomy, and others) point to God through the Qur'an.

19. Islamic Views of Poetry and Art—OK when looking at life from an Islamic viewpoint and to achieve an Islamic objective.

APPENDIX II

COPY OF ONE-PAGE SURVEY

Research Project

Date: _____ Location: _____

A Guided Tour of the Qur'an using Sayyid Qutb's
In the Shade of the Qur'an

Dr. Ed Hoskins, MD, PhD

West Lafayette, Indiana

Demographics: Gender, Age, Level of Education,
Native Language, Country of Origin

Questions

1. Major Qur'anic themes overview page (list of 19): In general, is this consistent with what you know about Islam? Comments?

2. Pick one of the 19 Major Qur'anic themes details. Is this consistent with what you know about Islam? Comments?

3. Review the associated Point of Comparison with Bible sheets and answer Questions for Reflection? #____

4. In light of the above, do you have a story that comes to mind or any questions you want to ask me?

5. In light of the above, is there one major topic or truth about the Qur'an you would like for Christians to know or be aware of?

6. Questions about Christianity

   a. Could you tell me three things Christians do or believe as they practice their faith?

   b. The single most important topic that Jesus taught was "the gospel of the kingdom of God." What do you think this phrase means?

RESEARCH PROJECT DESCRIPTION AND RESULTS

I spent nine months reading Sayyid Qutb's monumental work *In the Shade of the Qur'an*, and making notes. These notes were summarized in nineteen major Qur'anic themes (see Appendix I). Although these nineteen themes are not comprehensive, I believe they are representative of what Muslims believe informationally about their religion. This "list of nineteen" is what I used when surveying Muslims regarding how accurately the list represented the basics of Islam and the Qur'an. The purpose of the survey was to make absolutely certain that I was not misrepresenting Islam or the Qur'an in any way by what I had learned from Qutb. A copy of the one-page survey form used is found in Appendix II.

Over the course of the next eighteen months, seventy interviews were conducted. I visited thirty-two mosques throughout the Midwestern United States, driving more than 6,700 miles by car. My original intent was to survey a total of one hundred Muslims. The process was curtailed at seventy in the early spring of 2020, with the worldwide advent of the coronavirus pandemic. Of those interviewed, the majority were male (88.6%). I would like to have had more estrogen in the mix but realize that in the religious cultural milieu men are commonly more visible in Islam than women. They are certainly not more important. I found no qualitative difference in knowledge or results based on gender or country of origin or level of education.

Regionally, those interviewed came from all over the world, representing twenty-seven different countries and twenty native languages. Twenty-two originated from the Middle East, twenty-four from Asia, fourteen from Africa, one from Europe (Bosnia), eight from the United States, and one from Canada. The overwhelming majority were from Sunni Muslim backgrounds (96%). The only major difference I found in Shiite Islam was the objection to #15 in Qutb's list of nineteen (Destiny and God's overall control).

Ninety percent of those interviewed were imams and were, by definition, well educated in their Islamic faith. Two of those interviewed were Shiite clerics, and one of the others had been trained at Al-Azhar University in Cairo, Egypt—arguably the MIT/Cal-Tech of religious instruction throughout the Sunni Muslim world. A third held doctoral degrees (12 MDs and 10 PhDs). All but three had studied on the collegiate and graduate levels. This was a highly educated and highly skilled group of people. In my opinion this difference from the average general population enhanced rather than detracted from my findings. In other words, they are likely to be more aware of and exposed to the history, foundation, and teachings of Islam. Their average age was 48.5 years and ranged from sixteen to eighty-two.

Survey Results

Probably the most important finding of the study was whether or not those interviewed agreed with the nineteen major themes about the Qur'an coming from Qutb's work. Not all those interviewed responded to each survey question. Only question #1 was answered by all seventy. Fifty-nine of the seventy interviewed (84%) agreed that all nineteen themes were consistent with and accurately reflected what they knew about Islam. Of the eleven who did not agree with all nineteen, they collectively only disagreed with a total of fourteen of the nineteen themes: numbers 3 (one), 7 (one), 8 (two), 12 (three), 13 (two), 16 (two), 18 (one), and 19 (two)]. In other words, there was 98.9% agreement (1316/1330—70 interviewees x 19 themes = 1330). No matter how you view it, this was overwhelming support and validation for the list of nineteen Qur'anic themes that came out of my summary of what Qutb wrote about the Qur'an and whether it truly represented the Qur'an and Islam.

Of equal interest were the answers to question #5 (see Appendix IV) about what Muslims want Christians to understand about the Qur'an. The implications of their answers are discussed in Chapter 13, "Where Do We Go from Here?" I encourage all readers to carefully read their responses. Many enumerate the major differences between Islamic and Christian thought. Others clearly come from deeper down in the soul and reflect a heartfelt desire for mutual understanding, tolerance, and respect between Muslims and Christians. I was particularly touched by one Muslim who entreated me, "Please tell them how much we Muslims love Jesus."

Also of great personal interest was the striking difference in the responses to questions 6a and 6b dealing with their basic knowledge about Christians and Christianity. Again, the implications of their answers are discussed in Chapter 13.

WHAT MUSLIMS WANT CHRISTIANS TO KNOW ABOUT THE QUR'AN

Question 5—What would you like Christians to know about the Qur'an?

Only forty-eight of the seventy surveyed answered this question as to what they wanted Christians to know about the Qur'an. The most common responses were as follows:

> Six Muslims wanted Christians to know the importance of the *Tawheed* ("The Oneness of God" i.e., "There is no God but Allah")
>
> Five Muslims wanted Christians to know that the Qur'an consisted of the very words of God.
>
> Four wanted Christians to know that Islam and Christianity came from the same source.
>
> Three urged Christians to read the Qur'an for themselves.
>
> Two emphasized that the Qur'an must be interpreted in light of its historical context.

Two Muslims wanted Christians to know how much they love and revere Jesus.

Other individual comments are below:

The Qur'an is the final book from God. If you believe in the Bible, you must believe in the Qur'an. But the Bible has been changed.

God sent to mankind the prophet Muhammad as a mercy to the world.

Christians need to know that "many Muslims misunderstand and misinterpret the Qur'an a lot" and that "they take it out of context."

The Qur'an is not the words of Muhammad. Rather, it is the words of Allah and is evidenced by the scientific facts it contains.

From The Qur'an: "Lo! Those who believe (in that which is revealed unto thee, Muhammad), and those who are Jews, and Christians, and Sabaeans—whoever believeth in Allah and the Last Day and doeth right—surely their reward is with their Lord, and there shall no fear come upon them neither shall they grieve." (Surah 2:62)

Christians need to know about the differences in the end-times theology of Muslims and Christians.

There is some truth in the Qur'an. Some stories taken from the Bible are not correct.

The main message of the Qur'an and Islam is that everything takes us to the mercy of God—this is connected with our past repentance, and we should never give up.

There are a lot of biblical stories that are also in the Qur'an.

Tell them how much we love Jesus and Mary.

I feel (sorry) for Christianity—tell them to read the Qur'an as a constitutional book for Islamic government.

The Qur'an is a message to humanity, so whether you're a Muslim, Jew, or Christian, or other religion, there will be some verses in the Qur'an that will be talking to you.

Be open-minded, open-hearted, and contemplate the Qur'an.

Christians should not believe in Jesus as divine. Jesus was just like Adam—both were created by Allah. Jesus came from Mary by means of an angel (Gabriel).

The Bible cannot be compared to the Qur'an—it is not on the same level—it is like comparing apples and oranges. The Bible had inspiration of men, but the Qur'an had revelation from God.

The Qur'an teaches us how to live—family and community. There is not a lot different for Christianity.

Islam and Christianity are very similar. The big difference is how we view sin—original sin.

Jihad is much broader than cutting off the hands of a thief.

The Qur'an emphasizes intellect, logic, and reason. There is no gap between reason and faith.

The Qur'an helps Muslims understand their beliefs and to organize their lives.

Muslims believe Jesus was not crucified.

The Qur'an considers Jesus to be a prophet and a messenger from God.

Man was created of seven different colors of clay. Therefore men and women are equal, and we need to have different points of view. Women are not oppressed in Islam. They may look different, but they have equal rights.

There is a continuous story of the Abrahamic message and texts. They are all stepping-stones.

We believe in Jesus and Mary. We believe in Moses and all the prophets starting from Adam.

The miracle of the Prophet is the Qur'an. It is an eternal miracle.

IN THE SHADOW OF THE QUR'AN
BOOK ENDORSEMENTS

I have been reading *In the Shadow of the Qur'an*. The book discusses and gives deep and objective evaluation of the common ground and differences between Islam and Christianity. The book will give Christians deeper and true understanding of Islam and Muslims. This book will also help Muslims know the truth and appreciate the beauty and power of the Christian faith.

God gave Dr. Ed so many years in understanding Islam and Christianity, and the ability to do brilliant comprehensive research which God will use to bless both Muslims and Christians. *In the Shadow of the Qur'an* should be in every bookstore, church, mosque, and public library.

—Samy Tanagho
president and founder of Glad News for Muslims
author of *Glad News! God Loves You My Muslim Friend*

I got to know Dr. Hoskins in the trenches of Beirut, Lebanon, during the Lebanese civil war. We are affectionately known as "Beirut Bomb Buddies." I saw firsthand his love for the Muslim and his intellectual brilliance for truth.

Ever since 9/11, Islamic fundamentalism has been front and center to Americans. But it is confusing to understand what Muslims believe and why they do what they do. In his book, Dr. Hoskins takes us to Sayyid Qutb, the founder of modern-day fundamentalism, to look at his interpretation of the Quran. His approach helps give insight to much of modern-day fundamentalism. Dr. Hoskins confronts Muslim misconceptions with truth and love. It is a compassionate and intellectually stimulating read.

—Bob Vidano
former director of The Navigators of the Middle East (retired)

In an age dominated by rumor, gossip, and fake news, can we agree that it is rare to find someone who actually asks honest questions of others, and then listens to the answer and thinks it through carefully? And if ever there was an age and an issue that needs to have honest questions asked, and understanding reached, it must be our relationship with the many Muslims who have come, for various reasons to live among us in the West. Or perhaps we are the ones living among them?

In the twenty years that we have known Ed and his wife, Ed has been that humble person asking those honest questions, and then sharing the answers he has received. It is not insignificant that he has lived among Muslims, that he speaks Arabic fluently, that he has read the most important books of Islam, and yet remains a joyful Christian and has a genuine and peaceful interest in Muslims and their thoughts about the world and faith.

This is a book written, like others of Ed's, to understand the people of Islam, not on our terms but theirs. Ed always allows people to be who they are. If you can follow his example, using his mindset, you will see the loveliness and neediness of the Muslim heart. This book is invaluable to the person who has faith in Christ and wishes to understand Muslims who do not—and be resolved to do so in a Christlike way.

—Eleanor Grant
artist

When you read Ed Hoskins's book *In the Shadow of the Qur'an*, you see immediately that Ed is a follower of Jesus with a very keen intellect. You can't help but learn from this man who has studied Islam and befriended Muslim people for more than forty years! And while the vast knowledge you will gain by reading this book is certainly *advantageous*, what I appreciate so much more about Ed is that he loves Muslim people and wants to see them with us in the kingdom of God. In Ed's new book, you see a beautiful blend of an amazing knowledge of Islam, and a sincere and tender love for Muslim people. And that is *contagious!*

Ed Hoskins tells us of a man who *changed history* as it relates to Islam, Sayyid Qutb—a man who came to America in 1948 and was so scandalized by American culture and Christianity that he went home to Egypt and subsequently wrote a seminal book, *Milestones*. *Milestones* has been read and used to justify terrorism by jihadists everywhere, including none other than Osama bin Laden. How sad that genuine Christians apparently did not know or obey Leviticus 19:34 and reach out in grace and truth to Sayyid Qutb!

Thank you, Ed, for all your incredible research and writing in order to help all of us grow in "grace and truth" when it comes to reaching out to Muslim people—a people that God loves and that Jesus died for.

—Mark Vanderput
CEO and founder of I Love Muslims

Dr. Ed Hoskins's presentation of the central themes of the Quran in *In the Shadow of the Qur'an* will be helpful for everyone wanting to understand the Quran and wanting to relate to their Muslim friends in a respectful and informed manner. He distilled the central ideas of the Quran from a lengthy commentary by a respected Muslim theologian and then interviewed many Muslim people to discern whether or not the interpretation found in the commentary truly reflected the thinking of mainstream Islam. The book is filled with many interesting stories found in the Koran as well as anecdotes from his interaction with Muslim people while doing his research. Dr. Hoskins gives a straightforward Christian perspective concerning the central themes in the Koran in a respectful manner. I believe his book will help bring mutual respect and understanding to both the Muslim and Christian communities.

—Everett Vanest

This book by Dr. Ed Hoskins, *In the Shadow of the Qur'an*, is the result of hundreds of hours of reading; research; many, many live interviews; and the making of many Muslim friends. These friends of Dr. Ed, as he is affectionately known, can testify to his thorough knowledge of the Quran and his brilliant analysis of Sayyid Qutb's *In the Shade of the Qur'an*. And of course, as a loving Christian believer, he knows, cherishes, and expertly shares the Word of God. This book is an education all on its own. It shines with his comparative study of the Quran and Bible on twelve major biblical characters that are also touched on in the Quran. Add to that the historical background of the secular civilizations that were contemporary with the biblical characters mentioned and you have a delightful, informative read. I highly recommend this gem, the fruit of a lifetime of study in all the fields mentioned above, accompanied by the stories of his loving contacts with Muslims in many lands as well as here in the United States.

—Dr. Don McCurry
president, Ministries to Muslims
author, *Tales That Teach, Healing the Broken Family of Abraham: New Life for Muslims,* and *The Trail of Blood: Sacrifice in the Qur'an and the Bible—From Adam to the Throne*

In Ed Hoskins's book, *In the Shadow of the Qur'an,* the comparison between the biblical figures and the shadow found in the Qur'an is excellent. This is a great comparison pointing out how the Qur'an, in its retelling of the story of biblical characters, has key redemptive elements missing.

—Dr. Roy Oksnevad
founder and former director, COMMA
author, *The Burden of Baggage: First-generation Issues in Coming to Christ*

This fascinating book by Dr. Ed Hoskins immerses the reader into the "shadows" of Islam—how it compares and contrasts with Christianity. Dr. Hoskins's deep love of Muslim people is very evident, which is why this book will be of great interest to thoughtful Muslims who desire to better understand Christianity and the ways it relates to their own holy texts. This unique and valuable book should be on the bookshelf of anyone who wants to understand and relate better to their Muslim friends.

—Harlan R. Day, PhD

Imagine what it would be like to walk into a mosque, receive a warm welcome from the imam, and have an open and respectful conversation—in Arabic—about what lies at the very center of Muslim teaching. Now imagine having that same conversation twenty-eight times over. Think what you would learn!

That is exactly what Ed Hoskins did, and this book is the fruit of those remarkable conversations.

Ed has sought for more than thirty years to understand what lies at the heart of the Muslim faith. In the process, Ed has become a leading expert on the Muslim faith. What makes Ed's knowledge so unique is that it hasn't been acquired primarily through books, though he has studied voraciously. It has come through *relationships*—hundreds of them—with Muslim friends.

Fluent in Arabic, intimately acquainted with the contents of the Quran, and a committed follower of Christ, Ed has devoted the better part of his life to building windows in the wall that divides the worlds of cross and crescent. He wrote both of his previous books, *A Muslim's Heart* and *A Muslim's Mind*, to equip Christians to better understanding the heart of those they are seeking to reach with the gospel.

In *In the Shadow of the Qur'an,* Ed completes his invaluable trilogy. For this book, a Muslim fundamentalist serves as his unlikely guide. Sayyid Qutb, largely unknown to the western world, wrote what many consider the most influential Muslim work outside of the Qur'an. Ed summarizes *In the Shade of the Qur'an,* boiling down eighteen volumes of writings into a simple framework. Then he goes on a road trip and field tests his findings, driving more than 5,000 miles to interview more than two dozen US imams to find out just how influential Qutb's teaching is. Very, it turns out. As a final step, Ed builds points of connection between Qutb's ideas and the Bible, guides us in understanding how those beliefs differ from Scripture, and models gracious and honoring ways to talk about the gospel and share our faith.

Every Christian who is seeking to reach our Muslim friends looks for trustworthy guides. This is a resource you can count on. If you've read *A Muslim's Heart* and *A Muslim's Mind* and you're ready for more, this is your book. You won't want to be without it.

—Dr. David Henderson
senior pastor, Covenant Evangelical Presbyterian Church
author, *Culture Shift* and *Tranquility: Cultivating
a Quiet Soul in a Busy World*

Simple but Circular – I have read, digested, and used Ed Hoskin's two earlier books, ***A Muslim's Heart*** (2003) and ***A Muslim's Mind*** (2011) to help myself and others. I appreciated their clarity and brevity. Ed does not pad his books to impress you with their size. So they are great for helping the average Christian who doesn't have the time for a degree in Islamics but simply wants to relate to Muslims with his faith in Jesus.

With this book, *In the Shadow of the Qur'an*, it was much more challenging to repeat Ed's usual conciseness, as he sought to understand the thought of Sayyid Qutb in his multivolume commentary on the Qur'an. Understanding Sayyid Qutb, possibly the Qur'an's greatest and clearest modern commentator, helps a lot to understand the Muslim mind.

Simulating the circular logic of the Qur'an, Ed structures his thirteen chapters into four strands:

1. A comparison of the Biblical and Quranic accounts of eleven notable personalities in the two holy books.

2. Relating these accounts to nineteen themes from Sayyid Qutb's commentary.

3. Unique Quranic and personal stories that smoothen the jagged edges of discourse.

4. New perspectives on Christianity in the light of Syed Qutb's thoughts.

Being the consummate teacher that he is, Ed continually clarifies what he is saying. He says what he is going to say. Then he says it. Then he says what he has just said. This is very helpful when bridging two logical systems.

The Shadow – Another fascinating piece of pedagogy is the idea of knowing truth by looking at the shadows. Because shadows both enhance the truth as well as hide it. Ed credits this idea to Charlotte Brontë's story *Jane Eyre*. My parallel is from *Silver Blaze*, a story from Sherlock Holmes. An expensive racehorse has disappeared. When asked what he had observed, Holmes referred "to the curious incident of the dog in the night-time." When told that the dog did nothing in the night-time, Holmes said, "That was the curious incident" and concludes that the whole thing was an inside job because the dog didn't bark.

So we can know as much from what we are told, as from what we are not told—a sort of negative epistemology! These shadows lead to gaps in the Quranic, and in Syed Qutb's, understanding of what the Bible teaches.

Speaking the Truth In Love – Ed addresses these gaps by first making the superlative effort to understand the Sayyid's thought through his commentary. He cross-checks his observations with seventy Muslim leaders, mostly imams, who mostly (ninety-nine percent) agree with his analysis of Qutb's main themes. This is an intellectual expression of love.

Most religious and political arguments generate more heat than light because they are dialogues of the deaf. They misrepresent what the other said. Having checked that he actually understood and did not misrepresent what Qutb said, Ed then corrects Sayyid Qutb's, and much of Islam's, misunderstanding of Christian and Jewish truth.

In Ephesians 4:15 the Bible talks about "speaking the truth in love." Speaking the truth, but not in love, leads to vicious judgments that create more misunderstanding. Speaking in love without the truth, leads to superficial engagement that glosses over major differences. Ed strikes what I think is a wonderful balance between love and truth. Christians would wish and pray that a Muslim would also read the Bible in the same way. By reading it assiduously, checking their conclusions with other Christians, and only then sharing their disagreements.

The Paradox of Truth – Sayyid Qutb was imprisoned by the Nasser regime in Egypt for over ten years in the 1950s and early 60s, where he wrote In *The Shade of the Qur'an*. But he also wrote *Milestones*, a manifesto of political Islam. He is studied and respected for the first book but criticized for the second book which is banned in some Muslim countries and seen as the ideological headwater for 9/11 and modern Islamic fundamentalism.

Ed Hoskins sees the thought of Qutb as a Rosetta Stone that explicates Muslim thinking. From the feedback of educated Muslims, Qutb's commentary is in a class by itself for clarity and originality. But Ed also sees it as a Pandora's Box, which when opened gives forth violent ideas that can horrify the world, including Islam. Even a Muslim can be considered unIslamic and subject to harsh judgment. So the good guys quote Qutb, but so do the bad guys. Why this bifurcation of truth?

My thought is that a superior mind produces superior first order ideas, like those of Galileo, Darwin, or Karl Marx. An example from academia was John Nash whose story was popularized in the movie *A Beautiful Mind*. [At] Princeton in 1947 on a mathematics scholarship, Nash waited until the last moment before writing his dissertation because he "didn't want to waste time memorizing the assumptions of lesser minds" but was trying to find a truly original idea. He discovered the mathematical theory of equilibrium that won the Nobel Prize for economics forty-five years later. [Nash's theory] is used a lot in multilateral trade negotiations. But this brilliant mind was also subject to schizophrenia and attacks of delusions.

But superior minds also produce ideas that inspire both the good and the bad, like Galileo, Darwin, or Karl Marx. Friedrich Nietzsche was a German philosopher who is still a stimulus for thinkers, with ideas beyond his time. But he was also accused of saying that God was dead, and his ideas were used to justify Hitler's Nazi regime.

The Bible also has these contradictions of truth. God chooses us, but we choose God. Which is it? Some paradoxes are seemingly contradictory but upon further understanding are seen to be reconciled. But other paradoxes cannot be reconciled. Except perhaps by a higher order of intelligence, which is ultimately God.

"When I was an infant at my mother's breast, I gurgled and cooed like any infant. When I grew up, I left those infant ways for good. We don't yet see things clearly. We're squinting in a fog, peering through a mist. But it won't be long before the weather clears and the sun shines bright! We'll see it all then, see it all as clearly as God sees us, knowing him directly just as he knows us! But for now, until that happens, we have three things to lead us: Trust steadily in God, hope unswervingly, love extravagantly. And the best of the three is love." 1 Corinthians 13:11–13 (Message)

David Bok,
Cross-Cultural Consultant

Two devout communities of faith, both people of their holy books, exist in vast numbers all across the world. They are remarkably similar in that they often know their own writings well, but not those of the other community. How much good will and understanding would flourish if Christians knew Islam better and Muslims knew Christianity better! Dr. Hoskins, an articulate and scholarly Evangelical Christian, is a wonderful guide on just that kind of journey of listening and learning. He is careful and fair, avoiding misconceptions, clarifying mistaken objections, and most importantly laying the stories of the Bible and Qur'an side-by-side for the fair-minded reader.

Along the way, he leads carefully, never demanding, but often provoking thoughts about the similarities and differences. I appreciate both his gentleness and courage to lead along the path of discovery. As both Muslims and Christians believe that one's eternal destiny is determined by their responses to God and his revelation, the journey of faith is the most important one of our lives! I commend this book to you, as one who benefited from it. May the shadows give way to the Light!

Jay Lowder, PhD
Pastor of First Baptist Church of Pinckneyville, Illinois
Founder of Study Practice Teach Ministries

ENDNOTES

Acknowledgments

1. Nabeel Jabbour, *The Rumbling Volcano: Islamic Fundamentalism in Egypt* (Pasadena, CA: Mandate Press, 1993)

2. Sayyid Qutb, *In the Shade of the Qur'an (Fi Zilal al-Qur'an)*, translated and edited by Adil Salahi and Ashur Shamis, 18 vols. (orig. 1965; Leicester: The Islamic Foundation, 2011).

Introduction

1. Qutb, *In the Shade of the Qur'an (Fi Zilal al-Qur'an)*, Volume 5, 17.

2. Ahmed Renima, Habib Tiliouine, and Richard J. Estes, *The State of Social Progress of Islamic Societies* (New York: Springer International Publishers, January 2016), 25–52.

3. Robert W. Hefner, "September 11 and the Struggle for Islam," Social Science Research Council, Brooklyn, NY, Department of Anthropology, Boston University, n.d., essays.ssrc.org/sept11/essays/hefner.htm.

4. Yvonne Yazbeck Haddad, et al., *The Contemporary Islamic Revival: A Critical Survey and Bibliography* (London: Greenwood Press, 1991), 41-42.

5. Sayyid Qutb, *Milestones,* 16th English edition (New Delhi: Islamic Book Service Ltd., 2016), 131.

6. Haddad, et al., 139.

7. Qutb, *Milestones,* 137.

8. Yusuf Al-Qaradawi, *Islamic Awakening between Rejection & Extremism* (London: The International Institute of Islamic Thought, 2006), 8–9.

9. James Toth, *Sayyid Qutb: the Life and Legacy of a Radical Islamic Intellectual* (New York: Oxford University Press, 2013), 12.

10. Toth, 58.

11. Toth, 59.

12. Sayyid Qutb, *Social Justice in Islam,* translated by John B. Hardie; translation revised and introduction by Hamid Algar (Oreonta: Islamic Publications International, 1953).

13. Toth, 65.

14. John Calvert, *Sayyid Qutb and the Origins of Radical Islamism* (London: Oxford University Press, 2013), 18.

15. Calvert, 18, 20, 8 (in order of appearance).

16. Paul Berman, "The Philosopher of Islamic Terror," *The New York Times Magazine,* March 23, 2003.

17. *The 9-11 Commission Report—The Final Report of the National Commission on Terrorist Attacks on the United States* (New York: Cosimo, Inc., 2010).

18. Abu Ammaar Yasir Qadhi, *An Introduction to the Sciences of the Qur'aan* (Birmingham, UK: Al-Hidaayah Publishing and Distribution, 1999).

19. Toth, 81.

20. Dr. Badmas 'Lanre Yusuf, *Sayyid Qutb—A Study of His Tafsir*, (Selangor, Malaysia: Islamic Book Trust, 2009), 96.

21. Yusuf, 96–97.

22. Yusuf, 273.

23. Yusuf, 273.

24. Abu Al-Fida' 'Imad Ad-Din Isma'il bin 'Umar bin Kathir Al-Qurashi Al-Busrawi, *Tafsir Ibn Kathir* (CreateSpace Independent Publishing Platform, 2015).

25. Jalal al-Din al-Mahali and Jalal al-Din al-Suyuti, *Tafsir al-Jalalayn*, translated from Arabic by Feras Hamza (Amman: Royal Aal al-Bayt Institute for Islamic Thought, 2007).

Chapter 1—Adam and the Origin of Sin

1. Qutb, *In the Shade of the Qur'an,* Volume 2, 257.
2. Qutb, *In the Shade of the Qur'an,* Volume 9, 214.
3. Qutb, *In the Shade of the Qur'an,* Volume 11, 323.
4. Qutb, *In the Shade of the Qur'an,* Volume 12, 342.
5. Qutb, *In the Shade of the Qur'an,* Volume 11, 123.
6. Qutb, *In the Shade of the Qur'an,* Volume 2, 102.
7. Qutb, *In the Shade of the Qur'an,* Volume 8, 215.
8. Qutb, *In the Shade of the Qur'an,* Volume 9, 186.
9. Qutb, *In the Shade of the Qur'an,* Volume 9, 186.
10. Qutb, *In the Shade of the Qur'an,* Volume 11, 242.

Chapter 2—Cain and Abel and the Consequences of Sin

1. Qutb, *In the Shade of the Qur'an,* Volume 8, 198.
2. Qutb, *In the Shade of the Qur'an,* Volume 3, 257.
3. Qutb, *In the Shade of the Qur'an,* Volume 6, 50.

4. Qutb, *In the Shade of the Qur'an*, Volume 12, 345.

5. Qutb, *In the Shade of the Qur'an*, Volume 13, 228.

6. Qutb, *In the Shade of the Qur'an*, Volume 13, 230.

7. Qutb, *In the Shade of the Qur'an*, Volume 18, 239.

8. Qutb, *In the Shade of the Qur'an*, Volume 18, 240.

9. Qutb, *In the Shade of the Qur'an*, Volume 16, 451–455.

10. Qutb, *In the Shade of the Qur'an*, Volume 6, 50.

Chapter 3—Noah, Judgment, and the Flood

1. Qutb, *In the Shade of the Qur'an*, Volume 12, 167.

2. Qutb, *In the Shade of the Qur'an*, Volume 1, 187.

3. Qutb, *In the Shade of the Qur'an*, Volume 9, 252.

4. Qutb, *In the Shade of the Qur'an*, Volume 11, 248.

5. Qutb, *In the Shade of the Qur'an*, Volume 11, 249.

6. Qutb, *In the Shade of the Qur'an*, Volume 12, 31.

7. Qutb, *In the Shade of the Qur'an*, Volume 14, 91.

8. Qutb, *In the Shade of the Qur'an*, Volume 16, 237–253.

9. A. Yusuf Ali, trans. and commentary, *The Holy Qur'an: Text,* by A. Yusuf Ali (Brentwood, MD: Amana Corporation, 1983), 360, n. 1043.

Chapter 4—Job, the Wonders of Creation, and God's Divine Justice

1. Qutb, *In the Shade of the Qur'an*, Volume 5, 17.

2. Qutb, *In the Shade of the Qur'an*, Volume 10, 260.

3. Qutb, *In the Shade of the Qur'an*, Volume 13, 129.

4. Qutb, *In the Shade of the Qur'an*, Volume 10, 113.

5. Qutb, *In the Shade of the Qur'an*, Volume 12, 22.

6. Qutb, *In the Shade of the Qur'an*, Volume 14, 214.

7. Qutb, *In the Shade of the Qur'an*, Volume 10, 140.

8. Qutb, *In the Shade of the Qur'an*, Volume 12, 23.

9. Qutb, *In the Shade of the Qur'an*, Volume 14, 213.

10. Qutb, *In the Shade of the Qur'an*, Volume 11, 216-226.

11. Al-Busrawi, *Tafsir Ibn Kathir*, 494–496.

12. Zafar beads: The exact meaning is obscure and unknown. They could simply have been decorative. They could also have been prayer beads (or "worry" beads), since that is what Zafar beads currently represent. They are a string of thirty-three beads (made from wood, plastic, metal, or semi-precious gems like turquoise). The beads are held in the hand, and the person rotates through each bead three times, using the thumb (in remembrance of the ninety-nine names of God).

13. Qutb, *In the Shade of the Qur'an*, Volume 4, 54.

14. Bart D. Ehrman and Zlatko Plese, *The Other Gospels: Accounts of Jesus from outside the New Testament* (London: Oxford University Press, 2014); Ron Cameron, *The Other Gospels: Non-Canonical Gospel Texts* (Philadelphia: The Westminster Press, 1982).

Chapter 5—Abraham and God's Worldwide Covenant with Humankind

1. Qutb, *In the Shade of the Qur'an*, Volume 10, 230.

2. Qutb, *In the Shade of the Qur'an*, Volume 9, 214.

3. Qutb, *In the Shade of the Qur'an*, Volume 11, 323.

4. Qutb, *In the Shade of the Qur'an*, Volume 11, 323.

5. Qutb, *In the Shade of the Qur'an*, Volume 13, 289.

6. Qutb, *In the Shade of the Qur'an*, Volume 1, 137.

7. Qutb, *In the Shade of the Qur'an*, Volume 10, 240.

8. Qutb, *In the Shade of the Qur'an*, Volume 12, 342.

9. Haydn Lea, "The Trinity is like water ... and other bad analogies," *Christian Today,* April 9, 2019, https://christiantoday.com.au/news/the-trinity-is-like-waterand-other-bad-analogies.html.

Chapter 6—Joseph and the Jewish People

1. Qutb, *In the Shade of the Qur'an*, Volume 12, 79.

2. Associated Press, "Israeli Jets Strike Lebanon," *The Guardian,* Feb. 2, 2000, https://www.theguardian.com/world/2000/feb/08/israelandthepalestinians.lebanon.

3. Qutb, *In the Shade of the Qur'an*, Volume 11, 45.

4. Qutb, *In the Shade of the Qur'an*, Volume 14, 54.

5. Qutb, *In the Shade of the Qur'an*, Volume 11, 60.

6. Qutb, *In the Shade of the Qur'an*, Volume 17, 68,

7. Qutb, *In the Shade of the Qur'an*, Volume 3, 281.

8. Qutb, *In the Shade of the Qur'an*, Volume 1, 304.

9. Qutb, *In the Shade of the Qur'an*, Volume 1, 305.

10. Qutb, *In the Shade of the Qur'an*, Volume 1, 382.

11. Qutb, *In the Shade of the Qur'an*, Volume 3, 42.

12. Qutb, *In the Shade of the Qur'an*, Volume 1, 196.

13. Qutb, *In the Shade of the Qur'an*, Volume 2, 20.

14. Qutb, *In the Shade of the Qur'an*, Volume 3, 221.

15. Qutb, *In the Shade of the Qur'an*, Volume 13, 282.

16. Qutb, *In the Shade of the Qur'an*, Volume 5, 31–32.

17. Qutb, *In the Shade of the Qur'an*, Volume 10, 16.

18. Victor Marsden, *The Protocols of the Meetings of the Learned Elders of Zion,* translated by Victor Marsden, Indian reprint of 1923 edition (New Delhi: Kalpaz Publishers, 2018).

Chapter 7—Moses, the Passover, and God's Written Law

1. Qutb, *In the Shade of the Qur'an*, Volume 14, 104.
2. Qutb, *In the Shade of the Qur'an*, Volume 4, 5.
3. Qutb, *In the Shade of the Qur'an*, Volume 14, 29.
4. Qutb, *In the Shade of the Qur'an*, Volume 1, 230.
5. Qutb, *In the Shade of the Qur'an*, Volume 1, 228.
6. Qutb, *In the Shade of the Qur'an*, Volume 1, 230.
7. Qutb, *In the Shade of the Qur'an*, Volume 7, 11.
8. Qutb, *In the Shade of the Qur'an*, Volume 7, 11.
9. Qutb, *In the Shade of the Qur'an*, Volume 7, 150.
10. Qutb, *In the Shade of the Qur'an*, Volume 18, 288.

Chapter 8—David and Solomon and the Unique Worship of God

1. Qutb, *In the Shade of the Qur'an*, Volume 15, 435.
2. Qutb, *In the Shade of the Qur'an*, Volume 2, 187.
3. Qutb, *In the Shade of the Qur'an*, Volume 6, 37.
4. Qutb, *In the Shade of the Qur'an*, Volume 6, 37.
5. Qutb, *In the Shade of the Qur'an*, Volume 14, 155.
6. Qutb, *In the Shade of the Qur'an*, Volume 10, 163.
7. Qutb, *In the Shade of the Qur'an*, Volume 11, 211,
8. Qutb, *In the Shade of the Qur'an*, Volume 13, 5.
9. Qutb, *In the Shade of the Qur'an*, Volume 13, 77.
10. Qutb, *In the Shade of the Qur'an*, Volume 13, 77.
11. Qutb, *In the Shade of the Qur'an*, Volume 13, 80–117.

Chapter 9—Jonah, Judgment, and God's Compassion for the Lost

1. Qutb, *In the Shade of the Qur'an*, Volume 12, 64.
2. Qutb, *In the Shade of the Qur'an*, Volume 7, 8.
3. Qutb, *In the Shade of the Qur'an*, Volume 13, 58.
4. Qutb, *In the Shade of the Qur'an*, Volume 16, 1–17; Al-Busrawi, *Tafsir Ibn Kathir*, 1–14.
5. Qutb, *In the Shade of the Qur'an*, Volume 11, page 274.
6. Dean Dudley, *History of the First Council of Nice: A World's Christian Convention, AD 325; with a Life of Constantine*, originally published by C.W. Calkins & Company, 1880, https://archive.org/details/historyoffirstco00dudl.

Chapter 10—Zechariah and John the Baptist: Preparing for the Coming Messiah

1. Qutb, *In the Shade of the Qur'an*, Volume 17, 372.
2. Qutb, *In the Shade of the Qur'an*, Volume 11, 202.
3. Qutb, *In the Shade of the Qur'an*, Volume 18, 205.
4. Ali, *The Holy Qur'an*, 177.
5. Qutb, *In the Shade of the Qur'an*, Volume 3, 250–253.
6. Ali, *The Holy Qur'an*, note 5383. The Ansar were Muhammad's Medinan "helpers" who had believed his message of Islam and invited him to come from Mecca to Medina.
7. Qutb, *In the Shade of the Qur'an*, Volume 3, 252.
8. Qutb, *In the Shade of the Qur'an*, Volume 4, 247–248.
9. Qutb, *In the Shade of the Qur'an*, Volume 4, 248.

Chapter 11—Mary the Mother of Jesus—Her Prominence and Her Pain

1. Qutb, *In the Shade of the Qur'an*, Volume 1, 401.

2. Qutb, *In the Shade of the Qur'an*, Volume 18, 292.

3. Qutb, *In the Shade of the Qur'an*, Volume 15, 12.

4. Qutb, *In the Shade of the Qur'an*, Volume 3, 342.

5. Qutb, *In the Shade of the Qur'an*, Volume 11, 93–179.

6. James Dunn, *Jesus Remembered—Christianity in the Making* (Grand Rapids: Eerdmans Publishing, 2003).

7. Bart Ehrman, *A Brief Introduction to the New Testament* (Oxford: Oxford University Press, 2008).

8. John Dominic Crossan, *Jesus: A Revolutionary Biography* (New York: Harper One, 1995).

9. William D. Edwards, Wesley J. Gabel, and Floyd E. Hosmer, "On the Physical Death of Jesus Christ," *Journal of the American Medical Association*, March 21, 1986, 255(11):1455–1463.

Chapter 12—Jesus and the Gospel of the Kingdom of God

1. Qutb, *In the Shade of the Qur'an*, Volume 11, 267.

2. Qutb, *In the Shade of the Qur'an*, Volume 4, 159.

3. Qutb, *In the Shade of the Qur'an*, Volume 5, 302.

4. Qutb, *In the Shade of the Qur'an*, Volume 9, 93.

5. Qutb, *In the Shade of the Qur'an*, Volume 2, 299.

6. Qutb, *In the Shade of the Qur'an*, Volume 12, 138.

7. Qutb, *In the Shade of the Qur'an*, Volume 13, 253.

8. Qutb, *In the Shade of the Qur'an*, Volume 10, 210.

9. Qutb, *In the Shade of the Qur'an*, Volume 11, 212.

10. "Seven Sleepers of Ephesus," *The World Book Encyclopedia* (Newington, CT: World Book-Childcraft International, 1979), Volume 17, 252.

11. Ali, *The Holy Qur'an*, Note 2365, 736.

12. Qutb, *In the Shade of the Qur'an*, Volume 11, 241.

13. Josh McDowell, *The New Evidence that Demands a Verdict* (Nashville: Thomas Nelson, 2011).

14. William Lane Craig and Lee Strobel, *On Guard: Defending Your Faith with Reason and Precision* (Colorado Springs: David C. Cook, 2010), 219–264.

Chapter 13—Where Do We Go from Here?

1. Qutb, *In the Shade of the Qur'an*, Volume 15, 329.

2. Out of the seventy interviews conducted Muslims agreed with 1,316 out of 1,330 (98.9%) of the themes (i.e., 70 x 19 = 1330).

3. *The Princess Bride,* directed by Rob Reiner (1987; Act III Communications and 20th Century Fox).

4. Qutb, *In the Shade of the Qur'an*, Volume 16, 207–211.

5. Ibn Ishaq, *Sirat Rasool Allah,* translated by A. Guillaume (Oxford: Oxford University Press, 1955), 165–167.

6. Qutb, *In the Shade of the Qur'an*, Volume 16, 262.

7. Qutb, *In the Shade of the Qur'an*, Volume 16, 300.

8. Ibn Sa'd, *Kitab Al-Tabaqat Al-Kabir*, Volume 1, 237.

9. At-Tabari, *The History of Al-Tabari*. At-Tabari, Volume 6, 111.

10. Scot McKnight, *The King Jesus Gospel—the Original Good News Revisited,* (Grand Rapids, MI: Zondervan, 2011); N. T. Wright, *How God Became King: The Forgotten Story of the Gospels* (New York: Harper One Publishers, 2012).

11. Matthew W. Bates: *Salvation by Allegiance Alone: Rethinking Faith, Works, and the Gospel of Jesus the King* (Grand Rapids, MI: Baker, 2017).

12. John Piper, "The Highest Good of the Gospel," Desiring God, October 17, 2013, https://www.desiringgod.org/messages/the-highest-good-of-the-gospel.

13. Doug Pollock, *Godspace: Where Spiritual Conversations Happen Naturally* (Loveland, CO: Group Publishing, 2009).

14. Abolqasem Ferdowsi: *Shahnameh: The Epic of the Persian Kings*, translated by James Atkinson (1832; London: Penguin Classics, Kindle edition, 2016).

15. Edward J. Hoskins, *A Muslim's Heart: What Every Christian Needs to Know to Share Christ with Muslims* (Colorado Springs: NavPress, 2003).

16. Joy Loewen, *Woman to Woman: Sharing Jesus with a Muslim Friend* (Ada, MI: Chosen Books, 2010).

17. Edward J. Hoskins, *A Muslim's Mind: What Every Christian Needs to Know about the Islamic Traditions* (Colorado Springs: Dawson Media, 2011), 133.

Printed in the United States
by Baker & Taylor Publisher Services